PSP
HACKS™

Other resources from O'Reilly

Related titles   Halo 2 Hacks™   Home Theater Hacks™
Retro Gaming Hacks™   Smart Home Hacks™
Gaming Hacks™

Hacks Series Home   *hacks.oreilly.com* is a community site for developers and power users of all stripes. Readers learn from each other as they share their favorite tips and tools for Mac OS X, Linux, Google, Windows XP, and more.

oreilly.com   *oreilly.com* is more than a complete catalog of O'Reilly books. You'll also find links to news, events, articles, weblogs, sample chapters, and code examples.

oreillynet.com is the essential portal for developers interested in open and emerging technologies, including new platforms, programming languages, and operating systems.

Conferences   O'Reilly brings diverse innovators together to nurture the ideas that spark revolutionary industries. We specialize in documenting the latest tools and systems, translating the innovator's knowledge into useful skills for those in the trenches. Visit *conferences.oreilly.com* for our upcoming events.

Safari Bookshelf (*safari.oreilly.com*) is the premier online reference library for programmers and IT professionals. Conduct searches across more than 1,000 books. Subscribers can zero in on answers to time-critical questions in a matter of seconds. Read the books on your Bookshelf from cover to cover or simply flip to the page you need. Try it today for free.

PSP
HACKS™

C.K. Sample III

O'REILLY®

Beijing · Cambridge · Farnham · Köln · Paris · Sebastopol · Taipei · Tokyo

PSP Hacks™
by C.K. Sample III

794.81576
5192

Published by O'Reilly Media, Inc., 1005 Gravenstein Highway North,
Sebastopol, CA 95472.

O'Reilly books may be purchased for educational, business, or sales promotional use. Online editions are also available for most titles (*safari.oreilly.com*). For more information, contact our corporate/institutional sales department: (800) 998-9938 or *corporate@oreilly.com*.

Editor: Brian Jepson

Production Editor: Reba Libby

Copyeditor: Chris Downey

Proofreader: Reba Libby

Indexer: Ellen Troutman Zaig

Cover Designer: Linda Palo

Interior Designer: David Futato

Illustrators: Robert Romano, Jessamyn Read, and Lesley Borash

Printing History:

January 2006:   First Edition.

ISBN: 0-596-10143-0
[M]

Contents

Foreword

The PlayStation Portable (PSP) is simply stunning when you see it in person—it's like a little glimpse into a sci-fi future where incredibly powerful multimedia uber-devices are all ubiquitously connected and highly portable. When I received my bootleg export from Japan prior to the PSP shipping in the USA, I wanted to lick the screen. The same joy a lot of us had when we got our first PC is now a newfound excitement over having so much richness in such a small form factor.

But! That's the rub—the PSP in all its technological glory is crippled out of the box. The hardware can do more, there are gigabytes of applications the PSP can run, thousands of people making things for the PSP, but only if you know how to use them and how to route around the barriers that come along with every PSP.

Even for the casual gamer, it's not enough that the PSP can display photos, surf the web, and maybe watch a movie or two—oh no, generations of nimble thumbs and eager downloaders have been trained that computing, in all forms, is about doing more, personalizing, and often using technologies in ways it was never intended to be used. It's not about copying games, it's about the expectations of what a computer, even one meant for gaming, could be bent and tweaked for.

We would never be able to use and learn an open source chess game for our PSPs or run Atari 2600 emulators if our only method was to wait for someone, such as Sony (or a third-party game publisher) to release these. Each week, I see more applications come from the homebrew community than all the PSP game publishers combined. These aren't UMD epics, of course—they're PDF readers, emulators, and curiosities that keep me interested in my PSP investment.

Sony, throughout the years, has trained us that it's *all about owning your own*—from the AIBO, to the VCR, to the Walkman. When Sony introduced the VCR over two decades ago, it was met with a lot of resistance: "Recording TV, that's crazy! It's like stealing!" some said. But, Sony and others dragged an entire industry kicking and screaming to new business models, and now, recorded media makes up a significant part of television and movie revenue. Could Sony open up the PSP and let anyone make games and applications? Maybe, but for now that isn't even a rumor.

While hacking, modding, and tweaking is the only way to really get the most out the PSP, one day I suspect that Sony will see how wonderful the community is, how rabid they are about making things, and how they've really made the platform far more interesting. Until then, however, it's a Cold War–era arms race with both sides racing towards different goals—the "makers," as I call them, want their devices to live up to their potential, to do more, to share information with other tinkerers and tweakers; and Sony, well, they want to sell you lots of games and have you repurchase your DVD collection on UMDs.

Read this book, but don't think of it as the best collection of clever hacks and projects for the PSP—think of it as a set of keys that unlocks an almost magical piece of hardware that's normally bound—the more you put into it, the more useful and fun your PSP becomes.

—Phillip Torrone

Credits

About the Author

Originally from Jackson, Mississippi, Clinton Kennedy Sample III (no relation to either president) has been known as "C.K." since he was a child. In fact, none of the men named Clinton Kennedy in his family have used "Clinton" as their name. His father goes by "Ken," from their middle name, and his grandfather used to go by "Sam," from their last name.

C.K. does entirely too much. Besides writing this book, he has contributed in the past to *Mac OS X Panther Hacks* by Rael Dornfest and James Duncan Davidson, and served as technical editor and contributor to *iPod and iTunes Hacks* by Hadley Stern. He is also a sometimes contributor to Hadley's Apple Matters web site (*http://www.applematters.com*). C.K. is an avid blogger and user of Apple computers, and besides writing in his own blog, Sample the Web (*http://www.sampletheweb.com*), he is the lead blogger for The Unofficial Apple Weblog (*http://www.tuaw.com*) and a contributor to TV Squad (*http://www.tvsquad.com*), Cinematical (*http://www.cinematical.com*), and PSP Fanboy (*http://www.pspfanboy.com*).

Besides all these "hobbies," he works full time as an Instructional Technologist, offering professors aid and instruction in the use of technology in the classroom at Fordham University, where he is also working on his dissertation in English.

He currently lives in Bronxville, New York with his lovely wife, Kristin, and his pet Eclectus parrot, Mikhail "Misha" Baryshnikov.

Contributors

- Seth Fogie is the vice president of Airscanner Inc., a security software company that focuses on protecting devices that run the Pocket PC/Windows Mobile platform. Seth has coauthored several security books

(*Maximum Wireless Security*, *Security Warrior*, *Agressive Network Self Defense*, etc.), articles, and technical reviews, and has presented at security conferences such as BlackHat, Defcon, and CSI. In addition, Seth is a security cohost for InformIT.com, where he maintains the Security Reference Guide and writes and reviews articles.

- David P. Julian was born in September 1981, and he works as an aviation communications technician. He currently resides with his wife in Fort Wayne, Indiana. David served in the U.S. Army Special Operations from 1999 to 2005 as a helicopter communication and navigation technician. He constantly maintains a hobby of reverse-engineering consumer electronics to further his understanding of a technologically driven world. NSDQ!

- LiquidIce (*http://psphacks.blogspot.com*).

- Dan Mastin lives to mod. Check out his site, Duey2K (*http://www. duey2k.com*).

- James McMurry (*http://www.jamesmcmurry.com*) is an accomplished technologist with an entrepreneurial mindset, with over 15 years of combined experience in information technology, telecommunications, networking, management, and software development. He is currently working for a start-up he cofounded in Orange County, CA. In his copious amount of free time, he enjoys being with his family.

- Jacob Metcalf is an avid old-school video game hipster nerd. He runs the weblogs 8bit Joystick (*http://www.8bitjoystick.com/*) and Young Democrats of Washington State (*http://www.ydwa.org/*). He lives in Bremerton, Washington and drinks too much coffee.

- Thomas Novotny, born in 1987 in Austria, and currently studying technical computer science at a higher technical school there, is interested in hardware and software development for various platforms and game development.

- Kevin Sample is currently pursuing his Master of Architecture degree at Texas A&M. While not working on projects, he tries to wind down playing his PSP. He does plenty of other things as well, but they aren't really pertinent to this book, and he has never written a biography for himself for a book. However, he is enjoying typing this because he is using a narrator voice as he writes it. It's just good, plain fun.

- Jonathan Terleski is a student at Carnegie Mellon University in Pittsburgh, Pennsylvania. While there, he has focused on combining his skills in philosophy, design, psychology, and computer science to study interaction and user-centered design. Jonathan holds a Bachelor of Science in logic and computation and a Bachelor of Arts in philosophy. Currently, Jonathan is working toward his master's degree in human-computer interaction.

- Phillip Torrone is an author, artist, and engineer, and is Associate Editor of MAKE. He has authored and contributed to numerous books on mobile devices, design, multimedia, and hacks, and regularly writes for *Popular Science*. His projects have appeared in *Wired*, *Popular Science*, *USA Today*, *The Wall Street Journal*, *The New York Times*, G4TechTV, NPR, and elsewhere. Phillip also produces the MAKE audio and video content on the Makezine.com site. Prior to MAKE, Phillip was Director of Product Development for creative firm Fallon Worldwide, best known for their award-winning work on BMW films.

Acknowledgments

Thanks to the O'Reilly team for making this process as pain-free as possible. Special thanks to my editor, Brian Jepson, for being willing to get down and dirty with some code for a few of the hacks.

Thanks to Samuel Cuneo for being the technical editor on this book.

Thanks to my friends, family, and coworkers for supporting this endeavor, especially my sister-in-law, Maggie, for lending her help on a few of these hacks. Thanks to my wife, Kristin, for being very supportive of all the work that went into this book—all the gadgets, games, and bits and pieces of things cluttering our small apartment—and for understanding that all that time with a PSP in my hands was research for the book.

Thanks to God for giving me the strength to stop playing the PSP long enough to write a book about it. I've got several months of game playing to catch up on, once this thing is fully finished!

Also, thanks to the great PSP Internet community and all the contributors who helped make this book what it has become.

Preface

At the end of the first week of North American sales of the PlayStation Portable (PSP), Sony reported that the PSP sold over 500,000 units in the first two days. In the span of this same week, the Internet was abuzz with all sorts of news about the newly released device: reviews, first impressions, how-to articles, and various different ideas for repurposing the device beyond the limited usage that Sony originally intended.

Sony has created a diversely powerful device with the PSP. Not only is the PlayStation Portable a portable game system born from the most popular console gaming system in the world, but it also has a variety of multimedia features, including video (either via UMD disks or MPEG4 video files), music, and digital images. Mix in the USB port, the Memory Stick Duo slot, the IR port, and the 802.11b wireless capabilities of the device, and you have a Swiss Army knife gadget, ostensibly intended primarily for gaming by the manufacturer, and therefore practically taunting and begging the industrious gadgeteers among us to hack and repurpose it. Nothing speaks to this more than the numerous and varied hacks that emerged on the Internet in the time span of a mere week after the North American release of the device: "Read Web Comics on Your PSP" [Hack #28], "Use Your PSP as an E-Book Reader" [Hack #27], "Turn Your PSP into a PDA" [Hack #35], "Read RSS Feeds on Your PSP" [Hack #33]…the list goes on and on.

Why PSP Hacks?

The term *hacking* has a bad reputation in the press. They use it to refer to someone who breaks into systems or wreaks havoc with computers as his or her weapon. Among people who write code, though, the term *hack* refers to a "quick-and-dirty" solution to a problem, or a clever way to get something done. And the term *hacker* is taken very much as a compliment, referring to someone as being *creative*, having the technical chops to get things done.

The Hacks series is an attempt to reclaim the word, document the good ways people are hacking, and pass the hacker ethic of creative participation on to the uninitiated. Seeing how others approach systems and problems is often the quickest way to learn about a new technology.

How This Book Is Organized

You can read this book from cover to cover if you like, but each hack stands on its own, so feel free to browse and jump to the different sections that interest you most. If there's a prerequisite you need to know about, a cross-reference will guide you to the right hack.

Chapter 1, *The Basics*

Consider this the "getting to know your PSP" chapter, as it covers everything from the best practices for saving your games to full disassembly and reassembly instructions.

Chapter 2, *PSP Gear*

This chapter covers peripherals for the PSP, focusing on ones you can hack together yourself, including an external wireless antenna, a case, and an articulating stand for the PSP.

Chapter 3, *Multimedia*

The PSP is a multimedia machine, and this chapter covers all the ins and outs of managing multimedia on your PSP.

Chapter 4, *Games*

The PSP is a also gaming machine, and this chapter focuses on a few game-related hacks, including gems such as playing the PSP over the Internet and running homebrew games on your PSP.

Chapter 5, *Networking and the Web*

Like browsing the Web on your PSP? Didn't know it was possible? This chapter covers all the different online things you can do with your PSP.

Chapter 6, *Eye Candy*

Your PSP is a lovely creature, but this chapter provides a few tweaks you can do to pretty it up.

Conventions

The following is a list of the typographical conventions used in this book:

Italics

Used to indicate URLs, filenames, filename extensions, and directory/folder names. For example, a path in the filesystem will appear as */Developer/Applications*.

`Constant width`

> Used to show code examples, the contents of files, and console output, as well as the names of variables, commands, and other code excerpts.

`Constant width bold`

> Used to highlight portions of code, typically new additions to old code.

`Constant width italic`

> Used in code examples and tables to show sample text to be replaced with your own values.

Gray type

> Used to indicate a cross-reference within the text.

You should pay special attention to notes set apart from the text with the following icons:

> This is a tip, suggestion, or general note. It contains useful supplementary information about the topic at hand.

> This is a warning or note of caution, often indicating that your money or your privacy might be at risk.

The thermometer icons, found next to each hack, indicate the relative complexity of the hack:

 beginner   moderate   expert

Using Code Examples

This book is here to help you get your job done. In general, you may use the code in this book in your programs and documentation. You do not need to contact us for permission unless you're reproducing a significant portion of the code. For example, writing a program that uses several chunks of code from this book does not require permission. Selling or distributing a CD-ROM of examples from O'Reilly books *does* require permission. Answering a question by citing this book and quoting example code does not require permission. Incorporating a significant amount of example code from this book into your product's documentation *does* require permission.

We appreciate, but do not require, attribution. An attribution usually includes the title, author, publisher, and ISBN. For example: "*PSP Hacks* by C.K. Sample III. Copyright 2006 O'Reilly Media, Inc., 0-596-10143-0."

If you feel your use of code examples falls outside fair use or the permission given above, feel free to contact us at *permissions@oreilly.com.*

Safari® Enabled

 When you see a Safari® Enabled icon on the cover of your favorite technology book, that means the book is available online through the O'Reilly Network Safari Bookshelf.

Safari offers a solution that's better than e-books. It's a virtual library that lets you easily search thousands of top tech books, cut and paste code samples, download chapters, and find quick answers when you need the most accurate, current information. Try it for free at *http://safari.oreilly.com.*

How to Contact Us

We have tested and verified the information in this book to the best of our ability, but you may find that features have changed (or even that we have made mistakes!). As a reader of this book, you can help us to improve future editions by sending us your feedback. Please let us know about any errors, inaccuracies, bugs, misleading or confusing statements, and typos that you find anywhere in this book.

Please also let us know what we can do to make this book more useful to you. We take your comments seriously and will try to incorporate reasonable suggestions into future editions. You can write to us at:

O'Reilly Media, Inc.
1005 Gravenstein Highway North
Sebastopol, CA 95472
(800) 998-9938 (in the U.S. or Canada)
(707) 829-0515 (international/local)
(707) 829-0104 (fax)

To ask technical questions or to comment on the book, send email to:

bookquestions@oreilly.com

The web site for *PSP Hacks* lists examples, errata, and plans for future editions. You can find this page at:

http://www.oreilly.com/catalog/psphks

For more information about this book and others, see the O'Reilly web site:

http://www.oreilly.com

Got a Hack?

To explore Hacks books online or to contribute a hack for future titles, visit:

http://hacks.oreilly.com

The Basics

Hacks 1–11

You've probably played a few games on your PSP, placed a few music files or pictures on it, and perhaps even gone so far as to watch a movie. Basically, you've taken advantage of the information provided in the manual. If you happened to throw your copy out, grab a new PDF version online for reference (*http://www.us.playstation.com/psp/Manuals.aspx*). You may even want to convert that PDF to JPEGs for viewing on your PSP [Hack #29]. Now, however, it's time to think outside the basic uses for which the PSP was originally intended.

The hacks in this chapter will cover some of the basics about the PSP, while taking them a step further: giving you a breakdown of the different technologies involved. Along the way, we'll give you a few useful tips and tricks and try to cover some topics and ideas you might not have thought of when using your PSP.

Did you know that there are multiple ways to back up your saved game data? Did you ever think of using your PSP as another place to back up important files? We did, and you can.

HACK #1 Quit a Game Quickly

You're in-between projects, waiting for a response from one of your coworkers, so you pull out your PSP and start up a quick race in *Wipeout Pure*. Knock-knock. The boss walks in. Here's how to quickly get out of game play, saving both your game and your job.

In designing a portable PlayStation platform, fortunately, Sony did a good job of accounting for the on-the-go nature of PSP game play. The power button on the right bottom corner of your PSP can be pushed up quickly to power down the PSP without harming the game you are currently playing. A quick movement of the power button up and then back down to the locked position should become rather habitual when the phone rings, it's time to switch buses, your favorite TV show comes on, or the boss walks in.

The only thing you need to make sure of is that the PSP is not writing to the Memory Stick Duo Card when you need to quickly power down. Check for a flashing orange light on the bottom-left corner of the device. If there's no light, then you're in the clear to simply power down. That's it. Simple.

Now, to quickly hide the PSP from your boss, I recommend keeping a bottom drawer of your desk open and one of its hanging folders filled with cotton. When the boss walks in, quickly (but calmly) put the PSP into power-save mode, drop it in the drawer (see Figure 1-1), close the drawer, and say, "Hi, boss. Just filing away a report. What can I do for you?"

Remember: practice makes perfect. Try several dry runs, so you'll be ready for the real deal.

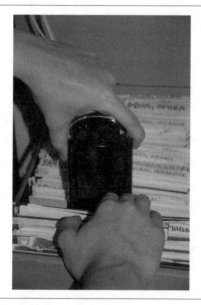

Figure 1-1. PlayStation Portable being filed away

Manage Your Saved Games

Save your game progress on the PSP, move these saved games to a computer, and share saved games with others.

Games: you love them. You like to have multiple concurrent sessions of the same game, as if each slightly different character or choice were but one manifestation of you in the multiverse.

Most hard-core game players know that having multiple file saves can be the key to progressing effectively through a game. We've all experienced that sinking feeling when you discover in level four that you cannot defeat the boss without the magic cap that you didn't find in level three, and it is much less frustrating to start over from level three than it would be to start over from the beginning or spend a lot of time backtracking.

If you haven't been able to track down that 1GB Memory Stick Duo card that you've been looking for, the 32MB stick included with your PSP is probably feeling a little cramped. This hack will discuss various options for managing your saved game files and moving them between your PSP and your computer.

Saving Game Progress

You know how to quit a game quickly [Hack #1], but if you actually want to save your game progress, either to switch to another game, watch a movie, or listen to some tunes, all you have to do is press the Start button. A menu will pop up, providing you with a variety of options, including Save Game (Figure 1-2).

Figure 1-2. The Start button brings this menu up on Untold Legends: Brotherhood of the Blade

Not all games will allow you to save your progress in the middle of game play. Several games require you to save at special places along the way called *save points*, so make sure to glance at the manual that came with each game to find out which saving mechanism the game uses.

For example, *Wipeout Pure* will only let you save your progress in between races and via a save dialog provided within the game. *Metal Gear Ac!d* saves to two different types of save game files: one that you create by saving in Intermission mode between boards and another for saving progress in the middle of a board.

Of course, if you are playing wirelessly along with friends [Hack #38] or with strangers over the Internet [Hack #37], you cannot save game progress, since stopping play disconnects you from the shared game.

Once you have saved your game file, hit the Home button. A dialog will pop up asking, "Do you want to quit the game?" Select Yes and hit the X button to choose to quit the game, and the O button (or select No and hit X) to choose not to.

Now that you have successfully saved your game progress and exited out of the game, I'll explain what else you can do to manage your game files via the PSP itself.

Copy and Delete Files

Under the Game menu on the PlayStation Portable, just below Game Sharing and just above UMD/Memory Stick (depending on whether you have a UMD disk inserted or not), you'll find the Saved Data Utility (Figure 1-3). Highlight it and hit the X button.

You will be presented with a list of all the saved game files on your PSP. When you highlight each saved game, you will see a screenshot or animation from the game, usually along with music from the game, and a good amount of metadata associated with the game; this usually includes the date and time the file was saved and the size of the file alongside game-specific data that varies from game to game. Some games include information about the board you were on when you saved, the level of difficulty of game play, the type of game-save data, and possibly the name of the player and the total time spent playing the game.

Now, if you hit the Triangle button, you will be given another menu with options for Copy, Delete, and Information (Figure 1-4). If you select Copy and hit X, a dialog will appear noting: "You will be asked to change the

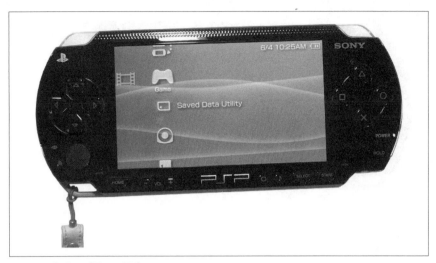

Figure 1-3. Saved Data Utility

Memory Stick 3 times. Press the X button to begin." Hit X to begin the copy process or O to go back to the previous menu (Figure 1-5).

Figure 1-4. Hitting Triangle gives you the option to copy, delete, or get more information on the file

The Copy Data Utility allows you to copy your games to another Memory Stick in case you want to give a copy of a game-save file to your friend, or if you just want to keep a backup Memory Stick and game data without bothering to use a separate computer to host your game files.

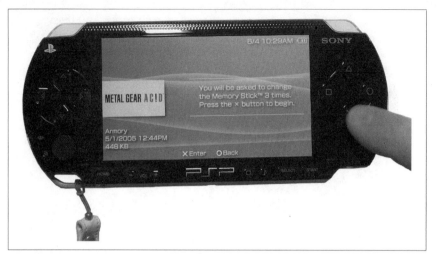

Figure 1-5. Copy Data Utility

Even if you save up and grab a 1GB or even 2GB Memory Stick Duo, I recommend keeping on hand the measly 32MB stick that was included with your PSP. It can come in handy as a game-only backup space.

The PSP will copy the game data into its memory, then prompt you to remove your Memory Stick and insert the Memory Stick on which you want to copy the data. As you can see in Figure 1-6, the PSP tells you that the whole process will require switching out the Memory Stick three times, but what it doesn't tell you is that each of these three times actually entails switching out the Memory Stick twice. Be prepared to spend a few minutes swapping out the two cards a total of six times. When it is finished, you will be prompted to switch back to the original Memory Stick.

If you instead choose Delete from the Saved Data Utility menu, the PSP will ask whether you are sure you want to delete the game data file. Make sure you are sure before choosing to delete, as there is no recovering the data (unless you have previously backed up the information).

And, finally, if you select Information from the Saved Data Utility menu, you are presented with a slightly more detailed view of the metadata associated with the file (see Figure 1-7).

Manually Copy Game Data to Your Computer

To really keep a nice backup of your saved game files, you're going to want to move them onto your computer. There are a few programs that will do

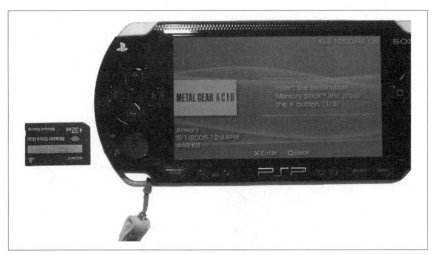

Figure 1-6. Copy step one

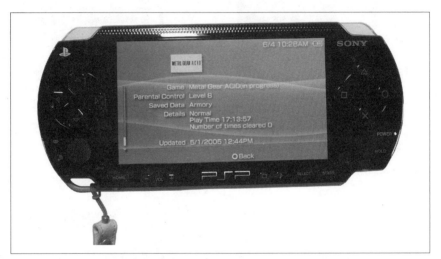

Figure 1-7. Save Data Utility info

this automatically for you, but first let us discuss how to do it manually. There are two ways to make your saved game data accessible to your computer: either by hooking your PSP up to your computer via a USB mini to USB cable, or by removing your Memory Stick from the PSP and placing it in a Memory Stick–capable card reader attached to your computer.

Connecting your PSP to your computer via USB. You need a USB mini to USB cable. Plug the USB mini end of the cable into your PSP and the regular USB end of the cable into your computer (Figure 1-8 shows a hybrid data/USB power cable). Now turn on your PSP and navigate over to the Settings menu. Scroll over to USB Connection and hit the X button. If you are on Windows, the Memory Stick Duo will show up in your drives list under My Computer. If you are on Mac OS X, the Memory Stick Duo will show up on your desktop as a new drive. If you're on Linux, see "Exchange Files with Any Computer" [Hack #3].

Figure 1-8. A PSP connected to a PowerBook G4 with a USB to USB mini/Power Adapter by Innovation

If you're going to keep your PSP connected to your computer via USB for a while, you will want to make sure that it is not set to go to sleep before connecting. If you unplug or disconnect the PSP before dismounting the Memory Stick properly, you could damage the data on the stick. If the PSP goes to sleep while connected to your computer, it can have the same negative results.

To avoid this, under Settings on your PSP, select Power Settings, and then select Auto Sleep and change the setting to Off. To conserve power, you can still change the Backlight Auto-Off setting, also under Power Settings, to two minutes (its lowest setting).

Alternately, you could invest in a USB cord that also supplies power to the PSP.

Open the Memory Stick by double-clicking on it. Inside you will see a folder called PSP. Inside that folder, you will see a SAVEDATA folder. Inside the SAVEDATA folder, you will find all of your saved games. Simply copy the entire SAVEDATA folder over to your computer.

After you have finished copying the files, you must dismount the Memory Stick before severing the connection. To do this, eject the Memory Stick by dragging it to the Trash in Mac OS X or choose "Safely Remove Hardware" from the Windows toolbar. After you have dismounted your PSP, hit the O button on your PSP to disconnect it fully from your computer. Now remove the USB cable.

Connecting your Memory Stick to your computer via a card reader. If you have a Memory Stick Duo capable card reader, there is no need to connect your PSP via USB to transfer files to your computer. Instead, simply power down your PSP, then open up the Memory Stick Duo panel on the bottom-left side of your PSP. Press in lightly on the Memory Stick to eject it from the port. Once it is sticking out of the PSP, grab onto it and pull it free.

Now, simply attach your card reader to your computer and insert the Memory Stick into the card reader. If you have a card reader that is only capable of reading regular Memory Stick cards, you will need a Memory Stick to Memory Stick Duo adapter. Your memory stick will appear as a disk drive on your operating system, and you can follow the instructions in the preceding section to work with files on it.

If you don't like the GUI interface of your OS, you can avoid all this clicking by using the command line.

The Mac OS X Terminal. Launch the Terminal (found in *Applications/Utilities/*), and at the command line, you can type:

```
open /Volumes/<NAMEOFYOURMEMORYSTICK>/PSP/SAVEDATA/
```

Here you would replace *<NAMEOFYOURMEMORYSTICK>* with the actual name of the device as it appears mounted on the desktop. By default, this will be "Untitled." If the name has been changed to something like "My PSP," then you will need to add an \ before the space in the name. For example, if your Memory Stick were named "My PSP," you would type the following:

```
open /Volumes/My\ PSP/PSP/SAVEDATA/
```

Then hit Return. This will open the folder in the Finder, so that you can drag all the files to wherever you like on your Mac.

If you would rather keep the process GUI-free, simply type the commands:

```
cd /Volumes/Untitled/PSP/SAVEDATA/
cp -R * ~/Desktop/PSP/
```

Hit Return after each line. The first cd command will change the directory on your mounted Memory Stick (named Untitled) to the SAVEDATA folder. The cp -R command will then copy all the files and folders within this folder into a folder called PSP on your desktop.

> You need to already have the *PSP* folder created on your desktop for this to work.

The Windows Command Prompt. In Windows, you can simply go to Start → Run and type **E:\PSP\SAVEDATA** to open the appropriate folder, assuming that the PSP mounts as drive E:. (If you already have a drive E:, then the PSP will be drive F:. If you already have a drive F:, the PSP will be drive G:, and so on through the alphabet.)

This will open the folder in a window from which you can copy all the files.

If you would rather copy them from the command prompt, launch the Command Prompt, found under Start → All Programs → Accessories. Once the command prompt comes up, type the following:

```
cd e:\PSP\SAVEDATA\
xcopy e: c:\gamesaves\ /S
```

Hit Return between each line. Substitute whatever drive letter your Memory Stick mounted on for e: in the above example. The first command will switch to the SAVEDATA directory on the Memory Stick. The second command will copy all the directories and subdirectories within the SAVEDATA folder into a new folder called "gamesaves" at the root level of your C: drive.

> Keep in mind that you can substitute any path you like for *c:\ gamesaves*, but make sure to keep the */S* flag at the end, as this ensures that xcopy copies all the directories and subdirectories within the SAVEDATA folder.

Automatically Copy Game Data to Your Computer

Sony should come out with their own software to automatically copy game data to your computer, but they haven't as of yet. In the meantime, there are several alternatives for a variety of platforms.

iPSP. iPSP from RnSKSoftronics (*http://ipsp.kaisakura.com/*) runs on Windows ME, 2000, XP, or on Mac OS X. The program is described as a full multimedia manager for your PSP; in addition to backing up your saved games each time you connect your PSP or your Memory Stick Duo to your computer, iPSP syncs music, photos, and videos to your PSP, converts video to the proper format, and can convert PDF files into JPEGs for mobile viewing on your PSP. iPSP costs $19.99 USD.

Upon launching, iPSP automatically begins saving your game data to your computer (see Figure 1-9). Once it finishes copying the games to your computer, you can then select the Gamesaves button at the top of the main iPSP window. This will bring up a browser of all the locally saved games (see Figure 1-10).

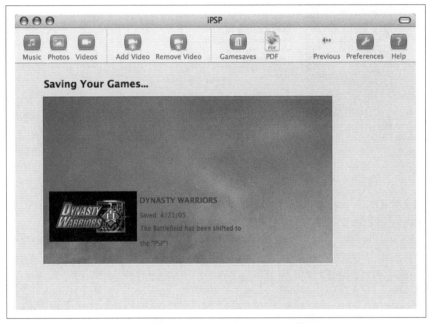

Figure 1-9. The Mac OS X version of iPSP transferring game files

The sidebar will list all the individual game files saved to your computer. When you highlight a game in the sidebar, a history of all the different versions of the game that have been saved to your computer via iPSP in the past will be displayed by date in the first panel to the right of the sidebar. Selecting the date will list all the different times during that day that the game was backed up to your computer. If you select one of the times, you will see any metadata associated with the file in the far right panel, and you can choose either "Erase from Drive" or "Restore to PSP."

PSPWare. If you are using OS X and you like the GUI goodness of iSync and the iLife suite, before going for iPSP, you'll probably want to try the demo of PSPWare for Mac OS X (*http://www.nullriver.com/index/products/pspware*;

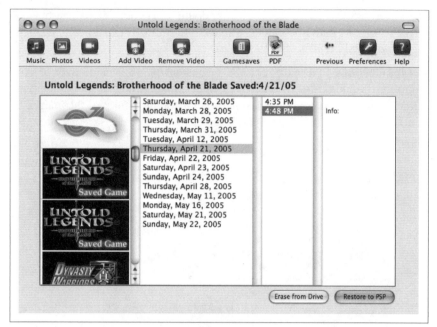

Figure 1-10. Browsing saved games with iPSP

$15 USD). If you are on Windows, NullRiver has recently released a Windows version (*http://www.nullriver.com/index/products/pspware.win*). If you click on the Backup button (see Figure 1-11) in PSPWare, you can choose to automatically sync games to your computer each time you sync PSPWare. There's an Options button where you can select to keep the last 10, 25, 50, or all of your past backups. There's another Restore button via which you can restore your old backups to your PSP. An added benefit of PSPWare is that you can set up sync profiles for managing multiple Memory Sticks (and multiple games).

Hacking the Hack

If you're a scripter and neither iPSP nor PSPWare fits your bill, consider using the command line instructions discussed in this hack as the basis for a script of your own for backing up your games.

For example, using AppleScript in Mac OS X, you could build a simple two-line script, like this:

```
do shell script "cd /Volumes/Untitled/PSP/SAVEDATA/"
do shell script "cp -R * ~/Desktop/PSP/"
```

Figure 1-11. The Backup pane of PSPWare ·

If your Memory Stick Duo card is named something other than Untitled, you will need to change the first line of the script to account for the card's name. If there are any special characters or spaces in the card's name, you will have to escape them by putting a \ before the space or character. Save this file as an application to simplify backing up your game saves to your computer.

Now that you have managed to successfully save files to your computer, the possibilities are endless. You can email the saved files to friends as attachments. Offer a saved file on your web site as backup or as bragging proof of the speed with which you won *Metal Gear Ac!d*. With Version 2.0 of the firmware, you can navigate to the page and download the file directly to your PSP (see "Find Yourself a PSP Web Browser" [Hack #41]). If your friend has unlocked all of the levels on *Tony Hawk Underground 2: Remix*, why not grab a copy of his file so that you don't have to go through all the trouble of actually unlocking all the levels before you play them? Think about it. People are willing to pay money for virtual items these days. If you're a gaming pro, you could develop a lucrative career selling your tricked-out characters from forthcoming PSP RPG titles via eBay (*http://www.ebay.com*).

Exchange Files with Any Computer

HACK
#3

You know that you can put music, pictures, videos, and saved games on your PSP's Memory Stick Duo. Did you ever think you could also use the PSP as a makeshift USB drive for backup and easy portable storage?

While you are carrying that little gaming wonder around in your bag, why not keep some of your important documents saved on the Memory Stick Duo card for easy access via any computer with a USB connector?

While working on this book, I kept backup copies of all the documents involved on an encrypted, password-protected disk image, zipped and sitting on my 1GB Memory Stick. Easy and secure access.

Things You'll Need

- A PSP
- A USB mini to USB cable (preferably one with a built-in charger for the PSP)
- A Memory Stick Duo card with some free space (for files)
- Some files to store
- A computer with an available USB port

The Basics

In "Manage Your Saved Games" [Hack #2], you learned the basics of connecting your PSP to your Mac/PC via USB to copy game files to your computer. This essentially works the same way. Simply plug a USB mini to USB cable into your PSP and the computer you will be using. Navigate to Settings (see Figure 1-12), USB Connection, and hit the X button.

If you are connected to a machine running Windows XP, the PSP's Memory Stick will show up as a removable USB drive under My Computer, and it will be assigned an available letter in the alphabet (most likely E:, F:, or G:, depending upon how many drives you have connected to your computer). When you first plug it in, a little notice will pop up in the System Tray saying that a new USB device has been detected.

On Mac OS X, the Memory Stick will mount on the desktop and will most likely be named Untitled, unless you have changed its name at some previous point in time.

On Linux, the Memory Stick should be available as any other USB mass storage device. Examine the kernel messages with *dmesg* to see what device the PSP was recognized as:

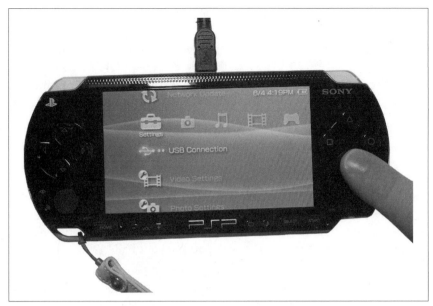

Figure 1-12. USB Connection can be found under the PSP's general settings

```
$ dmesg
Linux version 2.6.8.1-5-686 (buildd@vernadsky) (gcc version 3.3.4 (Debian 1:
3.3.4-9ubuntu5)) #1 Wed Aug 17 23:34:53 UTC 2005
BIOS-provided physical RAM map:

[...] lots of output deleted [...]

scsi0 : SCSI emulation for USB Mass Storage devices
  Vendor: Sony       Model: PSP               Rev: 1.00
  Type:   Direct-Access                       ANSI SCSI revision: 02
USB Mass Storage device found at 2
usbcore: registered new driver usb-storage
USB Mass Storage support registered.
SCSI device sda: 487936 512-byte hdwr sectors (250 MB)
sda: Write Protect is off
sda: Mode Sense: 00 6a 20 00
sda: assuming drive cache: write through
 /dev/scsi/host0/bus0/target0/lun0: p1
```

If it's not automatically detected, run the command modprobe usb-storage as
the root user and examine the output of *dmesg* again. Once you've identified the device, you can mount it (if it was identified as *sda*, you want *sda1*,
the first partition):

```
$ sudo mount /dev/sda1 /mnt -o uid=$USER
$ ls -l /mnt/
total 128
-rwxr--r--   1 me   root        5125 2005-09-04 12:35 index.html
```

```
-rwxr--r--   1 me   root       4060 2005-09-04 12:34 make_index.pl
-r-xr--r--   1 me   root          0 2005-01-30 22:28 memstick.ind
drwxr--r--   4 me   root      32768 2005-09-02 22:50 mp_root
-r-xr--r--   1 me   root          0 1979-12-31 23:00 mstk_pro.ind
drwxr--r--   9 me   root      32768 2005-04-08 23:55 psp
```

The *sudo* command lets you run *mount* as root, and the -o uid $USER mounts it so that the currently logged-in user is the owner of the files on the stick.

You can now treat the Memory Stick just like any other drive on your computer. Drag files over to the Memory Stick or write a document in Microsoft Word, and choose Save As and select the Memory Stick as the location to save the file.

You can also open any file you have previously stored on the Memory Stick by simply double-clicking the file. Double-click on an Excel spreadsheet to input some information, choose Save, and then quit Excel. Everything will be updated nicely and ready to go with you and your PSP.

When you are done copying files to and from the Memory Stick, you have to dismount the Memory Stick before unplugging the USB cord from your computer. Otherwise, you could risk harming the data (including all those saved games) contained on your Memory Stick.

To do this in Windows XP, click on the little USB device icon in the System Tray, and select "Safely remove USB Mass Storage Device" from the menu that pops up (see Figure 1-13—if you have more than one USB device connected, there may be multiple entries in this list). It should immediately tell you that the device is now safe to remove.

Figure 1-13. Select this menu from the System Tray to safely remove your Memory Stick

 If Windows or Mac OS X complains that the drive *couldn't* be removed, make sure you've closed all the files on the drive, including any open command prompts or terminal windows. Then try to remove it again.

In Mac OS X, drag the Memory Stick to the Trash/Eject icon, or click the Eject icon next to its name in a Finder window.

After you have successfully dismounted your Memory Stick from your computer, hit the O button on your PSP to turn off the USB connection. Now unplug the USB cable and be on your merry way.

Keep Things Organized

The PSP keeps a rudimentary file structure on the Memory Stick that you shouldn't tamper with too much. There are two locked files at the root level of the Memory Stick, *MEMSTICK.IND* and *MSTK_PRO.IND,* that you should leave alone. I'd avoid putting any of your files inside the PSP folder, which the PSP uses to organize your game saves, photos, and music. Nor would I place these files inside an MP_ROOT folder that you may have created for videos. These files would show up as corrupted data files on the PSP. Scrolling through corrupted data files while trying to pick a song to listen to isn't really as fun as it sounds.

Instead, create a new folder at the root level of the Memory Stick. Perhaps make it a Documents folder for holding all these files that you will be using on various machines. If the files are HTML or plain text files and you have Version 2.0 of the firmware on your PSP, you can view these files using the PSP's Browser (see "Find Yourself a PSP Web Browser" **[Hack #41]** and "Turn Your PSP into a PDA" **[Hack #35]**).

Think Security

This is a good tip for regular files you may be working on, but you should consider the security issues involved in carrying any type of sensitive data around with you, especially if these files are crammed on an object as desirable of thievery as the PSP.

Since I am working almost exclusively on an OS X system, I've created a password-protected and encrypted disk image of my files using Disk Utility (located in */Applications/Utilities/*).

There are many ways to encrypt and lock up your data on Windows, Mac OS X, and Linux. For Windows and Linux, you can use the open source software TrueCrypt (*http://www.truecrypt.org*). For more information on Linux disk encryption, see *http://www.tldp.org/HOWTO/Disk-Encryption-HOWTO/*.

Also, consider practicing a little social hacking. Keep all your backed-up files inside a folder named Virus Quarantine Folder to persuade anyone who might come across the information to throw it away immediately rather than rummaging through your top secret files.

Change the Background Color on Your PSP

#4

Do you hate green, but love blue? Find out you how to keep your PSP's background set to your favorite color.

This is a simple trick to keep the background color in your PSP's main interface set to whatever color you like best. If you are running Version 2.0 of the firmware, you can set your background color by navigating to Settings → Theme Settings, hit the X button, select Theme, hit the X button again, and select a color from the menu that appears on the right. The colors will change as you scroll through the list. If you choose Original, then the color will change each month. Hit the X button to make your selection and you are done.

If you are running an earlier version of the firmware [Hack #11], you lack this function, and the background color is solely determined by month. You just have to have a correct charting of the different colors according to month, and then reset the PSP's date to the corresponding month for the color you'd like. Sure, you have to remember to update it once a month, but this shouldn't adversely affect your PSP in any way (although your saved games will all be dated incorrectly to whichever month you choose).

Charting the Color Calendar

If you want to discover things on your own, it's a rather simple process:

1. In the PSP's main menu, simply navigate to Settings → Date & Time Settings → Date and Time.
2. Hit the X button and move the date ahead one month.
3. Hit the X button again, and you will see the color change to whatever color goes with the next month.
4. Repeat steps 2 and 3 until you've charted the full year.

To make things easy for you, you can look the colors up in Table 1-1.

Table 1-1. PSP background color by month

Month	PSP background color
1. January	White/grey/silver
2. February	Light yellow/gold
3. March	Light green
4. April	Pink
5. May	Dark green
6. June	Blue/purple

Table 1-1. PSP background color by month (continued)

Month	PSP background color
7. July	Ocean blue/teal
8. August	Dark blue to light blue
9. September	Purple
10. October	Dark yellow/gold
11. November	Sepia/brown
12. December	Red

Get Your Wireless Network On

Set up a wireless network at home so that you can connect your PSP to the
Internet for upgrades, faster infrastructure, LAN parties with more players,
and even browsing the Internet.

If you want to connect your PSP to the Internet to download a few new racetracks for *Wipeout Pure*, to browse the Web [Hack #41], or to play with other
PSP owners over the Internet [Hack #37]—in short, if you want to use the wireless capabilities of your PSP to do anything other than simply play games in
ad hoc wireless mode with your local friends—then you are going to need to
set up a wireless network environment that works well with the PSP.

The Basics

If you don't already have a wireless network set up, you'll need to get your
hands on some equipment.

Even if you are still working off of a dial-up connection,
you can find wireless routers that plug into your phone
line. For example, Apple's AirPort Extreme Base Station
(with Modem and Antenna Port) has a 56k modem built in,
and will still connect to a DSL or cable modem if you decide
to upgrade in the future.

Wireless routers are relatively cheap these days, especially if you are going
for the slightly slower 802.11b variant, which will play very nicely with the
PSP (see the next section). As an Apple user, I'm a big fan of AirPort, Air-
Port Extreme, and AirPort Express. The latter of these solutions is a nice,
portable wireless access point that simply needs an Ethernet connection to
your DSL/cable modem and an open electrical plug. However, all these
Apple-branded solutions are rather expensive, as they all run in the over-$75
range.

If you have a desktop computer that is plugged directly via Ethernet cable into your broadband modem, and no other computers are in need of a wireless solution, your best bet may be to get an internal wireless card for your computer, and set your computer up as a wireless access point via which you can connect your PSP.

Otherwise, shop around online and in your local electronics stores for the best deals. Linksys, D-Link, and Belkin are just a few of the manufacturers of 802.11 wireless products, and you can usually find nice deals online and some good-quality store-rebated items, so you shouldn't have to spend over $35–45 for an effective 802.11b router. Once you purchase your router, follow the instructions included with the device for setting it up.

802.11b

One of the slight disappointments (for me, anyway) when I first got my hands on my PSP was discovering that the wireless capabilities of the device were 802.11b and not 802.11g.

My network at home is all 802.11g; I have an AirPort Extreme Base Station acting as an access point, an AirPort Express acting as a wireless bBridge for my ReplayTV, and two Apple PowerBooks with AirPort Extreme inside. This meant that I could only set the AirPort Base Station to be 802.11g, thereby ensuring the fastest connection speeds possible.

Now, fortunately, 802.11g is backward compatible with the slower 802.11b wireless protocol used by the PSP. However, in order for my 802.11g network to be compatible with the PSP's 802.11b, I had to enable connectivity between 802.11b devices as well. Why is this bad news? Well, anytime an 802.11b device hooks into the network, it slows down the connectivity of all those 802.11g devices. All of this is relative, of course, as both 802.11b and 802.11g speeds plugged into a cable modem blow dial-up out of the water.

Security

Another issue with the PSP is security. If you have a PSP with Version 1.0–1.52 of the firmware, the only wireless security option available to you is WEP, which is the most easily cracked wireless encryption protocol out there. WPA is more secure, so both the PSP and, more importantly, your network, will be more vulnerable while using WEP.

WEP is better than nothing, however, so if you're using older firmware, configure your network for a WEP password, and navigate to your network settings on your PSP (Settings → Network Settings, hit the X button and choose Infrastructure Mode, and hit the X button again). Choose the connection that you want to edit and scroll forward until you reach the WLAN Settings pane.

Make sure that your wireless network's name appears under SSID. If it doesn't, scroll down to Scan, hit the X button, select your wireless network from the list that appears on the next page, and hit the X button again. This will take you back to the WLAN Settings page.

Now scroll down to where it reads None under Encryption and hit the X button. Use the up or down arrow on the keypad to toggle None to WEP and hit the X button. Now hit the right arrow on the keypad to bring up a screen asking you to enter your WEP key. Hit the X button, and the PSP's text entry screen will come up. When you are done entering your password, scroll up to the Enter button on the text entry screen and hit the X button again.

If you already have WPA set up in your current network, you're going to have to disable it for your Version 1.0–1.52 firmware PSP to be able to access your network. If you have a PSP with Version 2.0 of the firmware, however, you can set the WPA settings on your PSP to work with your WPA-enabled network. This will be nearly identical to the procedure for enabling WEP encryption, except you will toggle down to WPA-PSK under the WLAN Security Setting and enter your WPA password.

Now, your PSP should connect with your WEP-/WPA-encrypted network; however, I have found that I get a better connection with the PSP when I disable the encryption, so I usually do when I am going to be using the PSP wirelessly with my home network. Part of this is a luxury of location. I'm in an old, thick-walled apartment on the top floor of my apartment building that blocks 802.11 like you wouldn't believe, so very little, if any, of my wireless broadcast is extending outside of my apartment. If you are living in a paper-thin-walled building, you might not want to disengage your encryption with such frivolity.

Conclusions

When connecting your PSP to a wireless network, all you really need to do is make sure that you have an 802.11b-compatible wireless network running and that you've flipped the WLAN switch on the bottom-left corner of your PSP into the on position. All the other options discussed in this group of tips are merely to help improve upon the wireless connectivity of the PSP. I always disable security and switch my network to Channel 1 when I'm about to use my PSP for online fun, but it doesn't mean that this is something you must do. If you are having trouble connecting to your network, however, try giving these measures a shot.

Channel 1

For whatever reason, the PSP seems to handle Channel 1 more easily than any other channel for 802.11 broadcasting. In ad hoc mode, the PSP offers Automatic, Channel 1, Channel 6, and Channel 11. When you are connecting to your home network, or to any network in infrastructure mode, the PSP should be automatically scanning to find whatever channel your network is broadcasting on. However, I've found that whenever I am having any trouble connecting, switching the access point to Channel 1 makes for the best connection with the PSP, and when you decide to try playing games over the Internet [Hack #37], you'll find that Channel 1 is a necessity for trouble-free gaming.

Hacking the Hack

If you really want to trick out your wireless network connectivity, make sure you check out all the other wireless related hacks in this book, especially "Add an External Wireless Antenna" [Hack #17].

HACK #6 Troubleshoot Your PSP

What to do when the PSP freezes, a game consistently skips, a game won't load, or if a memory stick isn't showing up.

You're stuck. Your PSP isn't acting the way it once did, and you're not sure why. Here are some common problems you may encounter, along with a few ideas for troubleshooting those problems.

UMD Game/Movie Won't Load

This is one of the most common problems you will run into with your PSP. You've just placed your favorite UMD game in, but the PSP doesn't seem to recognize that it is there. Here are some things to do.

Check for a clean disk. First, simply remove the disk and put it back in. Maybe it wasn't firmly seated the first time you tried. If that does nothing, remove the disk again and make sure that it is clean. If you've been out in the summer heat and have come indoors to some cool air-conditioning, check for condensation. If that's the problem, play another game while you wait for the moisture on the disk to dissipate.

If there are any particles or dust on the disk, try blowing these particles off. Consider using a compressed air can to blow particles from the inside of the disk; you can find these cans in any computer or electronics store.

If you have smudged the disk via the little open window compartment on the UMD disk, then you are going to need to wipe that smudge off. Try to rotate the disk by pushing in the middle with your index finger and turning your finger, as shown in Figure 1-14. Do this until the smudged part of the disk is lined up with the open portion. Now, clean the smudge just like you would clean a CD/DVD or a camera lens. Breathe lightly on the disk to get a slight fog on it and then use a soft non-abrasive cloth (see Figure 1-15) to gently wipe from the inner ring of the disk outward. If the smudge extends to other parts of the disk, continue to rotate the disk, working section by section until it is fully clean.

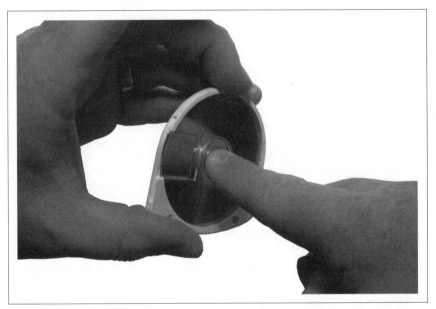

Figure 1-14. Push your index finger into the spindle of the disk and turn gently to rotate the disk for cleaning

Figure 1-15. Using a soft cloth, gently clean the disk by going from the middle to the outer edge

> If you aren't having any luck cleaning your UMD disks using these methods, there are several commercially available UMD disk-cleaning solutions available that you may want to try. The DragonPlus PSP UMD Disk Cleaning System includes a high-quality shammy cloth and nontoxic cleaning solution.
>
> Pelican also makes a UMD disk cleaner that comes with one of their PSP kits and operates like many of the CD/DVD cleaning solutions with which you are most likely familiar. Stick the UMD disk in, turn the crank a few times, and it spins the disk around, cleaning it nicely.

Check the clear plastic cover on the disk. Another thing that can happen with a UMD disk that has been squished inside a bag is that the clear plastic disk cover on the top of the game can snap loose from the white plastic frame of the disk (see Figure 1-16). The clear cover then exerts pressure on the back of the disk, preventing it from spinning up when the UMD is put inside the PSP. If this happens, simply hold the UMD disk on either side of the white plastic casing, and then take your index finger and push gently up against the middle of the disk until you hear a slight clicking noise (see Figure 1-17). If all went well, you have successfully popped the clear plastic cover back into place and the disk will spin up properly the next time you insert it in the PSP.

Figure 1-16. Check to make sure that the plastic cover on your UMD is lined up perfectly with the white plastic casing

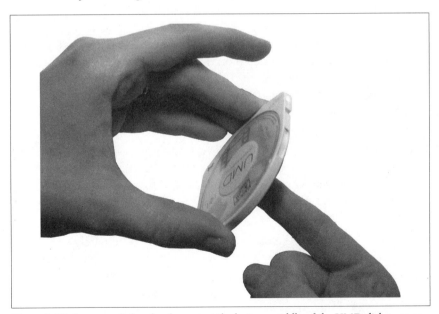

Figure 1-17. Press gently but firmly against the bottom middle of the UMD disk to pop the clear cover back into place

Is it a bad disk? If none of these solutions work, try putting another UMD disk in your PSP to see whether it works. If it does, the good news is that your PSP works fine. The bad news is that game or movie is dead. Time to go buy a replacement.

Check your PSP. If none of your UMD disks are working, things are looking a little more grim, but there is no reason to totally panic.

Eject your UMD disk and leave the tray door open. Look inside and make sure there is nothing in there. If your UMD disks were dirty, chances are that some of that dirt could have been freed on the inside of your PSP. If any dirt or grime somehow got inside your PSP, it could be blocking some of the inner workings of the device. Turn the PSP around the other way with the tray open and try to shake out any bits that may be in there. Insert a UMD disk and see if it works.

> If you find yourself with dirty UMD disks and a dirty PSP as a result, and actually having to employ these troubleshooting tips, how about a little preventive medicine? Get a case for your PSP and your UMD disks. See "Make Your Own PSP Case" [Hack #12] and "Repurpose Everyday Objects as UMD Cases" [Hack #13] for more information.

If you are still having no luck, try using a compressed air can to blow free any dirt or grime that has collected on the inside of your PSP. After blowing air over the inside of the tray, turn the PSP upside down again and try to gently shake any remaining particles free. In the very middle of Figure 1-18, you can see the lens that reads your UMD disks. If it isn't clean, you won't be playing any games any time soon.

If, after testing again, your UMD disks are still not loading, you could try putting a small bit of the solution from a DVD/CD cleaning kit on the end of a Q-Tip and reaching carefully inside the PSP to try to clean off the lens that reads the UMD disk, but I'd wait for a UMD disk-based PSP cleaning kit before trying this one.

Still no luck? Time to take your PSP in for repair. Alternately, if it is no longer under warranty, or if you did something that voids the warranty, you pesky hacker you, then you should check out "Repurpose a Dead PSP" [Hack #10]. If it looks like the lens inside the PSP is damaged, and you are out of warranty, you could try repairing it yourself—I recently noticed a lens replacement kit for sale online.

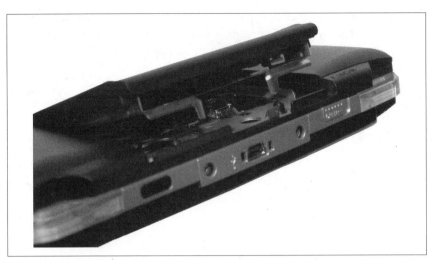

Figure 1-18. Peering into the UMD tray of your PSP, you can look for any debris on the lens that reads UMD disks

Can't Read the Memory Stick

If your PSP isn't recognizing your Memory Stick Duo card, first try removing the card and then replacing it, just to make sure it is firmly seated and properly inserted into the PSP.

Check the physical parts. If it still isn't registering, remove the card again and take a look at the contacts of the card (see Figure 1-19). Some slight abrasion is to be expected, but if there is any dirt here, clean it off.

Figure 1-19. The little metal contacts on the Memory Stick

If the contacts look smudged or there is any sort of dirt on them, take a soft cloth and clean them off. Also, in Figure 1-19, you will notice that there are some slight abrasions on the card. This is to be expected. However, if there is major scarring, your card might be beyond hope. To prevent major scarring of the card, keep it in some sort of case when it is not in use and try not to swap it in and out too often. Over time, these contacts will eventually fail, so make sure you back up your data often [Hack #2].

If the card was dirty, but you've cleaned its contacts and it still isn't reading properly, check inside the card slot.

Make sure that there is nothing sticking in the slot that shouldn't be there, and if the area around the slot looks dirty, hold the cover open as in Figure 1-20, turn the PSP on its other end, and shake gently to try to free any debris. Remember: a can of compressed air is your friend. Blow a gust of air down the slot to try to free up anything that your card might have smashed in there, and then turn the PSP on its end and shake again.

Figure 1-20. Taking a peek in the Memory Stick card slot

Check the data. If you have a Memory Stick Duo compatible card reader, try hooking the Memory Stick up to your computer. If it doesn't show up at all on your computer either, then it looks like the card is probably dead. Time to buy a new one.

If it does show up, check to see whether the data looks right. Make a backup of the data (separate from any previous backups you may have on file) and reformat the card. Now put the card back into the PSP and see whether it shows up.

If the Memory Stick shows up but doesn't seem to be behaving properly, or if it still isn't showing up, navigate to Settings → System Settings and hit the X button. Select Format Memory Stick (see Figure 1-21) from the list of settings and hit the X button. The PSP will ask you twice whether you are sure you want to format the Memory Stick. Select Yes and hit X, then select Yes again and hit X again. This will erase all of the data on the Memory Stick.

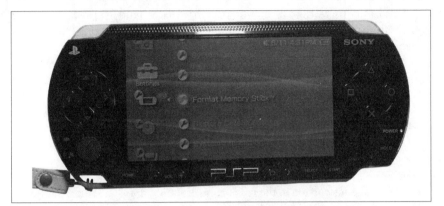

Figure 1-21. If all else fails, try selecting Format Memory Stick from the System Settings

If it still fails to show up, or if the PSP gives you an error saying there is no Memory Stick to format, then either your card is dead or your PSP's Memory Stick slot is damaged. Try another card (borrow one from a friend if you don't have one on hand) in the slot. If this second card shows up, then your card is dead—go buy a new one. If it doesn't show up, it's time to get your PSP repaired.

PSP Won't Turn On

If your PSP won't turn on, then of course you are going to want to check the power. Maybe your battery has been fully depleted. Plug in the AC adapter and watch to see whether the power indicator light has turned orange to indicate charging. If yes, check to see whether the PSP will now turn on. If so, then your battery was simply discharged.

If the power indicator light did not turn on and turn orange when you plugged in the PSP, then see whether you can turn the PSP on. If so, look on the upper-right corner of the screen. Is the battery indicator showing up? If so, perhaps your battery was simply discharged and is now charging, but for some reason the charging indicator light didn't turn on. Unplug the unit and see whether it stays powered.

If it shuts down, then there is most likely something wrong with the unit or your battery. Likewise, if the PSP still isn't turning on, then there is quite possibly something wrong with the unit or the internal battery.

Open up the battery compartment on the back of your unit. Remove the battery and check the contacts to make sure they are clean, as shown in Figure 1-22. Reinsert the battery and try repeating the above steps. If everything still fails to work, ask one of your friends to lend you her battery so you can test to see whether it is the battery or your PSP. If your PSP powers up with your friend's battery, there is something wrong with your battery and you should get a replacement. If your PSP does not power up on your friend's battery, there is something wrong with your PSP and you need to have it serviced.

Don't Try This at Home!

I inadvertently fried my own PSP while researching for this hack. Sony offers a rather mild instruction in the PSP's manual stating that you should put the battery in before attaching the AC adapter for charging. What they should include is a large warning saying: *Don't try removing the battery and running the PSP without the battery inserted!*

I tried this in the middle of my tinkering and found that nothing happened. However, when I put the battery back in, nothing continued to happen. I thought the entire PSP was dead; a quick trip to Best Buy later, I had a brand new PSP in hand, as well as an extra battery pack that I purchased on a hunch. When I put the new battery pack in my seemingly busted PSP, I discovered that it did turn on and functioned normally.

I then tried to plug it into the AC adapter, thinking that my original battery had somehow failed. No orange light. No charging. Evidently, my earlier tinkering had fried the connection where the AC adapter plugs into the PSP to the battery, or perhaps it just failed on its own and this was simply a hardware failure specific to my unit.

This could have been a total fluke—I'm not really interested in risking another PSP to find out—but consider yourself warned: the PSP is designed to run with the battery in place. You could possibly fry your PSP by trying to run it without the battery.

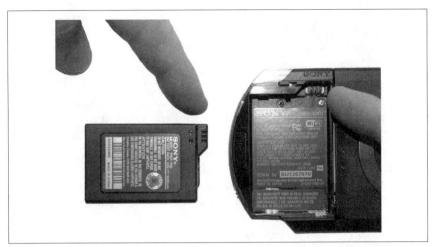

Figure 1-22. Open up the battery compartment and make sure that the contacts on both the battery and the PSP are clean

Miscellaneous Problems

Here's a short list of other problems and their possible solutions:

All of the buttons on the PSP suddenly stopped working.
> Make sure that you didn't accidentally slide the power button into the Hold position.

My PSP suddenly went to sleep during a game/movie/etc.
> Make sure that you didn't accidentally slide the power button up into the Sleep position.

There's no sound/I can barely hear the sound.
> Make sure that you have the volume turned up, that you didn't accidentally hit the music note button (which mutes the console), and that you do/don't have the headphones plugged in (depending upon whether you are wearing headphones or not).

The picture on the screen is too dim/too bright.
> Try hitting the little square button underneath the screen. This toggles through different screen brightness settings.

I cannot seem to connect to my wireless network.

Make sure that you have turned on the WLAN switch on the bottom-left corner of your PSP. Check out "Get Your Wireless Network On" [Hack #5] for a few pointers.

My PSP's screen has a dead pixel.

If it is an actual *dead* pixel, then it isn't fixable. Learn to live with it, or try to sell it online and buy a new PSP. However, you may just have a *stuck* pixel. This may be fixable. There's an MPEG4 video available from various online PSP-associated sites, such as PSP Hacker (*http:// www.psphacker.com*), called Dead Pixel Cleaner by Placasoft. This two-minute video will need to be loaded onto your Memory Stick. It flashes through red, blue, and green repeatedly and rapidly, filling your PSP's screen. The rapid instructions to change between these three key RGB colors can sometimes stimulate a frozen/stuck pixel, knocking it back to full functionality. So, if you have what looks to be a dead pixel, give this video a try. I've read several recommendations online that say you should leave it running in a loop for a good couple of hours, checking intermittently to see whether it has had any effect. You might learn that your dead pixel is just a stuck pixel when you find it quickly unstuck.

If all seems lost, and you cannot seem to solve whatever problem has befallen your PSP, don't despair. Check out "Repurpose a Dead PSP" [Hack #10] for some pointers on trying to recoup some of the money from your PSP toward a purchase of a replacement PSP.

Hacking the Hack

Of course, if you run through all these troubleshooting tips and things still aren't working, you—as a would-be hacker—are left with an entirely new set of choices:

1. Do you try to return the unit to the store where you bought it for a replacement?

2. Do you send it off to Sony for repair?

3. Do you crack the sucker open and try to fix it yourself?

If you chose #3, then you are definitely reading the right book. Head on over to "Take Your PSP Apart" [Hack #8] for some help in finding your way through the maze of your PSP's electronic innards. If your hacking and attempted repair job doesn't work, you can always try some of the options discussed in "Repurpose a Dead PSP" [Hack #10].

Keep Your PSP Clean

Tired of seeing smudges, dust, dirt, and grime on that gorgeous PSP screen?
Here are some tips to alleviate the dirt and the glare.

In both "Watch UMD Movies" [Hack #21] and "Troubleshoot Your PSP" [Hack #6], I touch upon how the PSP, as a portable gaming console, would seem to be some sort of magical dirt and smudge magnet. This brief hack will cover some basic ways you can help cut down on the filth and get rid of any built-up grime.

Prevention

When dealing with dirt, the best offense is a good defense. As clichéd as this bit of advice sounds, it's the most overlooked bit of common sense. If you don't want your PSP to get dirty, keep it in a dirt-free environment. Don't leave it lying around your home. Whenever you aren't using the PSP, either put it away in a case [Hack #12] or in the sleeve that came with your PSP. If you want to keep the PSP itself clean, make sure that you keep all of the PSP peripherals clean as well. Keep your UMD disks in cases [Hack #13] and only use clean USB cables to connect your PSP to your computer. If you find an old USB cable sitting in the corner of a drawer that, for some unknown reason, had cookie crumbs all over the bottom, take the time to make sure any dust or bits of cookie that were in the drawer are carefully cleaned from the connectors before shoving it into your PSP.

In addition to keeping the PSP and all of the PSP's peripherals clean, make sure you keep yourself clean. If you find yourself regularly complaining about greasy smudges all over your PSP's screen and controls, you have to look no further than your own greasy hands for the culprit. Wash your hands. Make sure they are clean, dry, and grease-free when you want to play. If you don't want smudges on the screen, don't touch the screen.

Cleaning

Use the soft cloth that came with your PSP to wipe off the screen whenever it becomes smudged. If you ever get more than basic smudging on your PSP, unplug the PSP and turn it off. Use a damp cloth to clean off the casing. Do not use any cleaning products, since they could harm the PSP.

If anything sticky gets on the PSP, try putting a small amount of cooking oil on a soft cloth and use this to rub it free. To remove the oil, use a damp cloth with a light amount of soap.

If anything gets in the different ports of the PSP, such as the headphone jack, the USB jack, or the power jack, try gently rubbing the open ports with a soft dry cloth. If anything gets in the Memory Stick compartment or the UMD compartment, you can try using a compressed air can to clean out these areas. If the lens inside the PSP that reads the UMD disks appears to be dirty, you can try putting a small bit of the solution from a DVD/CD cleaning kit on the end of a Q-Tip and reaching carefully inside the PSP to clean off the lens, but I'd wait for someone to offer a UMD disk-based PSP cleaning kit before trying this one.

Keep the Screen Smudge-Free

The simplest way to keep the screen on the PSP smudge-free is to avoid touching it with your fingers, keep your hands as clean and grease-free as possible, and keep a soft cloth handy to wipe smudges away. However, if these methods aren't working for you, there are some alternatives.

One option is a commercially available plastic screen overlay from JAV-Oedge (*http://www.javoedge.com/simtrix/productMtce/jsp/productListScreen_PSP.jsp*; $12.95 USD). The PSP JAVOScreen comes in both an anti-glare and an ultra-clear version. The anti-glare version works very well, as I have one that I've used, but I usually end up using it only while playing video games. The matte finish tends to make the picture quality of movies look a bit fuzzy. I haven't yet tried the ultra-clear version, as it has just recently been announced.

The JAVOScreen is just a thin piece of plastic, and $12.95 is a little expensive for such a thing. You can find inexpensive cellophane at your local craft store that will most likely work just as well.

Overall, remember that the best way to keep your PSP clean is to prevent it from getting dirty in the first place.

HACK #8   Take Your PSP Apart

This hack is a step-by-step guide on how to take your PSP apart, from top to bottom, from case to wireless network card.

There may come a point in time where you will need to take apart your PSP. For example, your keypad may stop working, or perhaps you will need to remove a stuck Memory Stick. Regardless of the reason, this hack will provide you with the blueprints needed to successfully take your PSP apart. And yes, before we go any further, my PSP still worked even after it was spread out, exposed, and naked before me on my work desk.

I realize many of the readers will want to jump right in and start dismantling their device, but please heed the words of warning spread throughout this hack. Too much enthusiasm is not a good thing when dealing with electronics. A steady hand and some patience can go a long way when dealing with tiny and fragile components. That said: please do not feel threatened. Even the most inexperienced "hacker" can accomplish this hack. Just follow the instructions, and all should go right! For your convenience, the disassembly process has been broken down into several different sections.

The Tools of the Trade

In order to take your PSP apart, I recommend that you have the following supplies on hand. You do not have to use them all, but things can go much more smoothly with these items available and a few minutes of preparation:

- Paper for screw placement notes
- Pen/pencil
- Small flat head screwdriver
- Small Phillips head screwdriver
- Needle nose pliers (handy for picking up dropped screws)
- Flat and clean white surface (easier to see parts)
- Digital camera for snapping photos along the way (use these photos to help you remember how it goes back together and to post cool photos on your weblog)

Critical Suggestions

In addition, you should also keep these suggestions in mind:

- Remove the battery when instructed and leave it out when taking apart the PSP. In addition, do not attempt to plug in any power source to the PSP until it is fully reassembled. You can easily kill off large parts of the PSP [Hack #6] by not following this advice.
- Use extreme care when releasing circuit strip/ribbon catches, since they can easily break.
- Do not drink or eat around the open PSP.
- Do not take your PSP apart in a high traffic area. There is nothing like a hyper kid, slobbering pet, or three-foot drop to turn your PSP into a $250 paperweight.
- Be careful how much dust is in the air. Since your PSP will be apart, it is easy for that dust to cause problems at a later date if it takes up residence inside the device.

Taking the Top Off

Prior to beginning, place your PSP and all tools on a clean and clear surface. I recommend you have some sort of mat to provide some comfort for your PSP while its internals are removed. Next, create a few sketches of your PSP on the piece of paper, in order to track where the screws go when trying to put the PSP back together again. Figure 1-23 provides you with an illustration of the first screws that need to be removed.

Figure 1-23. Layout of PSP case screws

Here's how to take the top off:

1. Remove the battery cover and remove the battery.
2. Take out the Memory Stick.
3. Remove the black screw (1) from the upper-right quadrant, shown in Figure 1-23.
4. Remove the black screw (2) from the lower-right quadrant.
5. Remove the warranty seal from inside the battery cavity (yup, you've just voided the warranty).
6. Remove the black screw (3) from the upper-left quadrant (battery cavity).
7. Remove the black screw (4) from the lower-left quadrant (battery cavity).
8. Remove the silver screw (5) from the battery cavity.
9. Remove the silver screw (6) from the battery cavity.
10. Remove the silver screw (7) from bottom side of PSP.
11. Turn the PSP over and slowly lift the top shell off.

Removing the LCD

The next step is to remove the LCD from the PSP. Be careful, as this is arguably the key component to your device and almost certainly the most expensive to replace. A scratch or too much pressure could cause serious problems. Figures 1-24 and 1-25 provide you with illustrations for the following steps:

1. Carefully pry the catch off the left side of the lower button circuit strip with a small flat head screwdriver.

2. Lift the button bar assembly off the PSP.

3. Carefully release the catch to the circuit strip that connects the bar to the PSP. This is accomplished by using a small flat head screw driver to lift the brown catch up, which allows the circuit strip to slide free of the catch.

4. The LCD is held in place by four bevel catches to keep the LCD screen in a metal LCD tray. *Carefully* slide a flat head screwdriver between the LCD screen and the tray at the top-left corner and lift the LCD screen out of the tray. Once it has freed the catch, do the same on the lower-left side of the LCD tray. Once this side is free, slowly lift the LCD screen up a few millimeters out of the tray and then lift only the top of the LCD screen. There are two circuit strips behind the LCD that need to be removed before taking out the LCD.

5. Lift the left (smaller) catch from the top to release the circuit strip.

6. Lift the right (larger) catch from the bottom to release the larger strip.

Getting a feel for releasing the catches takes a little practice. You do not want to break off the plastic catches or break a circuit in the connector.

Removing the LCD Tray

The most important part of this stage is that you carefully record where each screw goes. Since most of the screws are different sizes, it would be easy to mix them up. Figure 1-26 illustrates where each of the screws is located.

Be careful not to strip the screws. It is better to apply pressure to ensure the screwdriver head does not slip than it is to strip the screw.

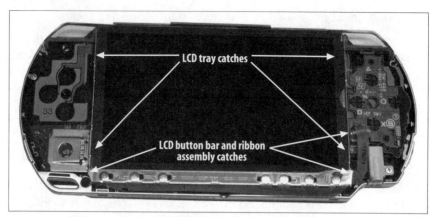

Figure 1-24. Removing the LCD from tray

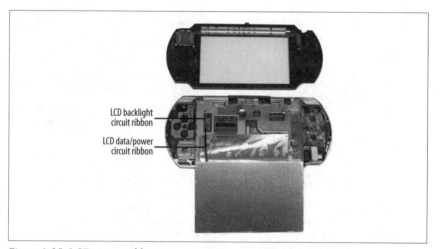

Figure 1-25. LCD circuit ribbon connections

Here's how to remove the LCD tray:

1. Remove the silver screw (8) from top right of tray.

2. Remove the two silver screws (9 & 10) from the top left of the tray.

3. Remove the two silver screws (11 & 13) and one black screw (12) from the lower left of the tray.

4. Eject the UMD disk tray.

5. Lift the tray from the bottom of the PSP and slowly wiggle it loose from the UMD catch at the top of the PSP.

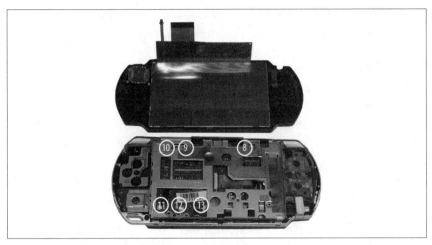

Figure 1-26. LCD tray screw positions

Removing the Main Circuit Board

This part of the disassembly process is the most difficult. The main board is connected via screws, a USB connector, and a circuit connector hidden under the board. In addition, there are wires at the lower end of the board that connect to the speakers and components under the board. You do not have to remove these to get under the board if you simply flip the circuit board over onto its top when it is removed. Figure 1-27 highlights the various points you need to pay attention to when removing this circuit board.

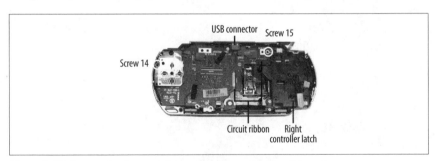

Figure 1-27. Screws, latches, catches, and more on the circuit board

To remove the main circuit board:

1. Unlatch the right controller circuit strip and the UMD drive circuit strip.

2. The controller lifts from the bottom, and the UMD catch requires slight pressure from the left against the black plastic arms.

3. Remove screw 14 from the top right of the circuit board.

4. Remove screw 15 from the left side of the left controller.

5. On the top right of the main circuit board, carefully remove the power connector (white with black wires). This will require you lift the board first before disconnecting the white plastic socket.

6. On the lower side of the left controller, pry up the circuit board over the catch and lift the controller over the top of the PSP.

7. Peel back the tape holding the black power wire and lift the antenna off the main circuit strip, disentangling it from the tape and the right controller.

8. Slowly lift the circuit board up off the PSP by slipping out the USB connector from the top plastic shell, then raising the top of the board and flipping it over the bottom of the PSP. You will need to apply pressure and pry the board off a hidden connector that keeps the board connected to components deeper inside the PSP.

Figure 1-28 highlights the various chips found on the main circuit board. The following list names them and shows the identifying information you'll find on each chip:

Chip 1
> CXD2962GG
>
> ©2004SCEI
>
> 507D10E
>
> 641711

Chip 2
> CSD1876
>
> ©2004SCEI-102GG
>
> 504A99E
>
> 278491

Chip 3
> SAMSUNG 501
>
> K5E565H8CM-D060

Chip 4
> SC901583EP
>
> MXAEA0423

Chip 5
> MB44C001
>
> 0505 M51

Figure 1-28. PSP chips on the main circuit board

Removing the Wireless Network Card

The following requires you to remove several components before you actually get the network card board (SWU-BXJ154N). This part of the removal is layered, so be sure to follow the instructions. Figure 1-29 highlights the significant pieces and Figure 1-30 provides a shot of the network card with antenna and wire.

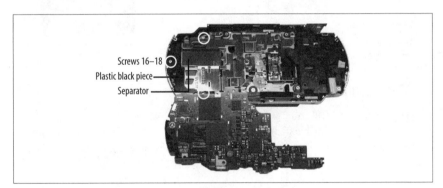

Figure 1-29. Pieces and parts of the lower PSP

To remove the network card:

1. Remove the silver screw (16) from the top left of the PSP, holding the silver tray onto the device.

2. Remove the silver screw (17) from the bottom left of the PSP, holding a black plastic supporter.

3. Remove the silver screw (18) from the left of the PSP, holding the black plastic supporter.

4. Lift the black plastic piece out and then remove the silver grounding tray.

5. Lift the network/Memory Stick combo circuit board out of the PSP shell.

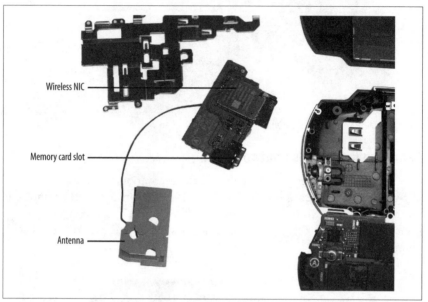

Wireless NIC

Memory card slot

Antenna

Figure 1-30. Shot of the network card and antenna

The End Result

Figure 1-31 shows the final results of disassembling the PSP. All of the major pieces are out of or at least disconnected from the body. Nothing appears to be broken, which means it is time to put it back together! However, that particular chore is left for "Reassemble Your PSP" [Hack #9].

Hacking the Hack

Now that you know how to take apart the PSP with some semblance of safety and order, you can take your knowledge and put it to use as you find ways to modify the PSP. External antennas, FM receivers, bling-bling, or even just a simple case mod are now easily within your grasp!

—*Seth Fogie*

Figure 1-31. The completely disassembled PSP

Reassemble Your PSP

HACK #9

If your PSP is in pieces, you'll no doubt want to know how to put it back together again.

Taking apart your PSP [Hack #8] is really only half of the puzzle. In fact, many have said that taking something apart is easy; putting it back together again is what really separates the wheat from the chaff. So, in this hack, I am going to provide you with the necessary instructions to get that torn-apart PSP back together again. Assuming you have not caused any permanent damage from spilt soda, four-foot drops, or a frustrated fist, when reassembled, your PSP should turn on and work as originally designed.

The Large Print, etc.

At this point, you know your warranty is worthless and all bets are off as to what will happen when you finally put the battery pack back into the PSP and turn it on. However, that doesn't change the fact that you need to be cautious and use a delicate hand. Before continuing, please review "The Tools of the Trade" and "Critical Suggestions" sections in "Take Your PSP Apart" [Hack #8].

Installing the Network Card

This step is fairly simple, with the only tricky part being the correct insertion of the WNIC (wireless network interface card)/Memory Stick circuit board. Be sure to take advantage of the many guide pins included in the PSP to ensure that you insert this component, and others, correctly. Figures 1-32 and 1-33 provide illustrations of the following steps.

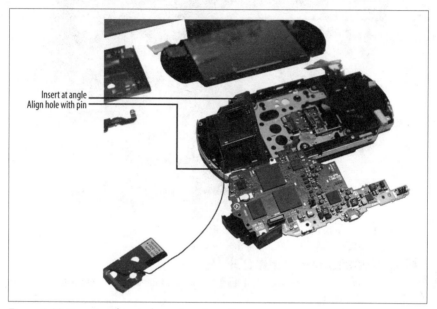

Figure 1-32. Inserting the wireless network card

To install the network card:

1. Insert the small circuit board, wireless network card side down, into the PSP by placing the bottom of the circuit board in first at an angle. Be sure that the wireless antenna is wrapped around the side of the board.

2. Lay the metal grounding separator in, with the long end at the top. Align the guidance pins and the circuit socket to be sure the separator is in the correct location.

3. Place the black plastic supporting piece on top of the WNIC, ensuring that both the top and bottom guide pins slip through their respective holes. Be careful to not break the wireless on/off switch as you insert the black plastic piece. You will probably have to move the switch into the On position for easiest installation.

4. Insert screws 16, 17, and 18.

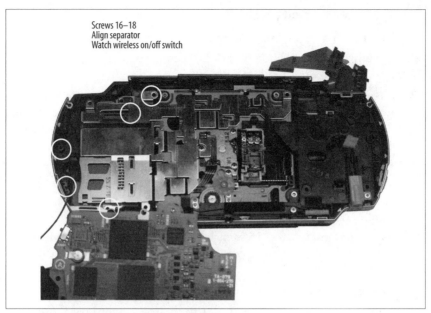

Figure 1-33. Screw positions, WiFi switch, and separator alignment

Installing the Main Circuit Board

This section is the hardest part of reassembling the PSP. It can be a bit tedious to ensure that you have the board seated correctly, but patience is necessary. Pay attention to the critical areas highlighted in Figure 1-34.

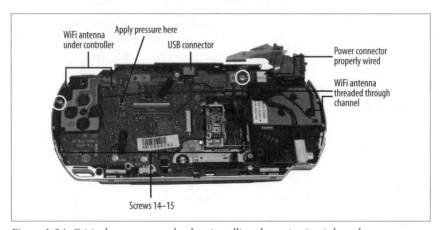

Figure 1-34. Critical areas to watch when installing the main circuit board

To install the main circuit board:

1. Place the main circuit board in roughly the correct location.

2. Carefully bend out the top of the PSP plastic case and slip the USB connector into its corresponding hole.

3. Line up the screw holes and apply a slight but firm pressure about one inch in from the left side of the circuit board. This is to seat the connector on the other side of the board into the smaller circuit board that holds the WNIC and Memory Stick components.

4. Run the antenna wire across the circuit board and install the wireless antenna. Once the antenna is properly seated, install the antenna wire correctly, ensuring it is held in place by the black fuzzy tape, and that it is threaded through the channel on the right side of the PSP.

5. Line up and insert screw 15 to install the left controller. If you removed the left controller completely from the PSP, be sure to connect the circuit ribbon.

6. Insert screw 14 in top-right hole of the main circuit board.

7. Connect the white power connector to the PSP circuit board, using the fuzzy tape to hold the wires onto the board.

8. Lay the right controller on top of the antenna and snap it into place, paying attention to the catch on the lower side of the controller circuit.

9. Connect the right controller strip by sliding the ribbon into the catch. It will slip under the tiny silver guides on each side of the catch. Finally, flip the brown movable part of the catch down into place.

10. Slip the UMD drive circuit ribbon into its catch. Be sure that the black part of the catch is in its Out position. Otherwise the ribbon will not insert into the catch. Once it is lined up in the catch, apply pressure to *both* sides of the black catch to seal the connection.

Installing the LCD

You are nearly there. The trickiest part of this step is to be sure that the LCD backlight power strip (the small one) is properly seated. You will note two small extensions on the sides of the strip near the end. These will come in handy when you attempt to seat the connecter. Figures 1-35 and 1-36 highlight the areas you will be working with when reinstalling the LCD.

To reinstall the LCD:

1. Lay the LCD tray into place. Do this slowly and carefully, since the wrong position can cause problems. The top of the tray should slip behind the USB connector. The bottom of the tray has a screw mount

that slides under/behind the black PSP shell. Finally, the left side of the tray merges with the left controller. Once it is in place, shut the UMD tray. If it clicks smoothly shut, the tray is probably installed correctly.

2. Insert and tighten screws 8, 9, 10, 11, 12, and 13.

3. Flip the LCD over on its back, slide the large and small circuit ribbons into their respective slots, and close the catch. Start with the large ribbon first, and then do the small ribbon. Use the little wings on the small ribbon to guide it into the catch.

4. Flip the LCD over and carefully insert it into the tray. Start with the right side, and then apply light but firm pressure on the left side to click the LCD into place.

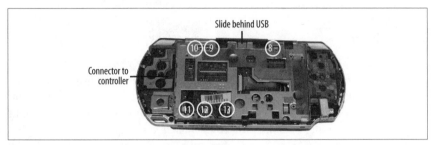

Figure 1-35. Installing the LCD tray

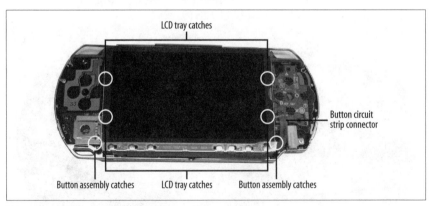

Figure 1-36. Installing the LCD

Putting the Buttons and Shell into Place

You're almost there! Try not to jump ahead and insert the battery just yet. Honestly, it is all downhill from here. Figure 1-23 earlier in the chapter provides you with an illustration of where to insert the final screws.

Here's how to wrap things up:

1. If you took the left and right trigger buttons out, now is the time to put them back in.
2. Insert the circuit ribbon connected to the LCD buttons into its slot on the right side of the PSP.
3. Lay the button strip onto the LCD and click it into place.
4. Carefully clean off any smudges on the LCD using a soft cloth.
5. Lay the PSP top onto the device and apply pressure to snap it into place. Be sure that the bottom button strip lines up.
6. Flip the PSP over onto its back and insert screws 1, 2, 3, 4, 5, 6, and 7.
7. Finally, insert the Memory Stick and battery/cover back into the PSP.

Turning It On!

It is now time to see whether you are the owner of a working PSP or a $250 paperweight. As you can see from Figure 1-37, my attempt was successful. However, I will admit that the first time I tried this, the PSP's backlight did not turn back on. I was still able to see the screen, but only in the right light and at the right angle. I suspect it was because I was testing various components out with the board exposed. I probably shorted out a circuit and fried some capacitor or diode. I learned my lesson, though, and have now successfully taken apart and reassembled a PSP.

Figure 1-37. Turning it on!

Hacking the Hack

Now that you know how to take apart and reassemble your PSP, make sure to check out all the hardware-related hacks in this book. Have fun voiding your warranty!

—Seth Fogie

Repurpose a Dead PSP

You were trying to play *Tony Hawk's Underground 2 Remix* on the PSP, while actually skating, and now you're left with a broken PSP. This hack will walk you through what can be done with your shattered PSP, as well as how to recoup as much of the original cost of the PSP as possible.

You're past the denial stage where you sat rocking back and forth in the corner of your room, cold and alone for hours, clutching it close to your chest, repeatedly switching it on and off, removing the battery, replacing the battery, plugging it in, hoping that suddenly your PSP would turn back on. You've followed all the recommendations in "Troubleshoot Your PSP" [Hack #6]. You took it to a friend skilled in the art of soldering. He opened up your PSP, gently reconnecting all the aged connections, perhaps even replacing the USB port. You tried new batteries and even an odd voodoo ritual that you discovered online. Nothing has worked. You've finally come to grips with the dreadful reality of it all: your PSP is dead.

Although everything has seemed hopeless during your futile attempts to resurrect your PSP, don't throw that PSP away in frustration. There are several different things you can do with it, and this hack will discuss some of the possibilities.

Use Your Dead PSP to Get a New PSP

You're already in serious withdrawal from the games, the videos, the pictures, and the music you were used to enjoying via your little digital friend. You need to replace your PSP. Here are three ideas for ways to recuperate some of the money you invested in your dead PSP, either to help in the purchase of your next PSP or to simply pad the wallet:

- Repeat after me: eBay (*http://www.ebay.com*) is the seller's friend. If you have a broken PSP, chances are that there is some cocky technician obsessed with buying things on eBay who will be willing to spend some money on your PSP just to see whether he can resurrect it. A quick search on eBay for "broken PSP" will turn up lots of people just like this. If you filter your search results to include completed auctions, you can see what people were willing to pay for these.

- Mantra #2: people pay more for parts than they do for an entire PSP. If you as an individual decided to build your own PSP from scratch, you would quickly discover that all the necessary parts would cost you more than buying it from Sony. Why? Because Sony is a big corporation with the resources to buy in serious bulk, which helps drive the prices down on the materials. You are just you with a dead PSP. However, there are probably lots of other people in similar situations to yours who still think they can fix their broken PSP with that magic part. Pop open your PSP [Hack #8] and carefully remove any parts that aren't broken. Sell the screen. Sell the control pad. Sell the earphones. Sell every bit you can. Make sure you say that you cannot guarantee that any of these items will actually work. It won't matter. Someone will buy them.

- When you're auctioning off all these items, make sure that you offer to sell and ship them internationally. PSPs may be more expensive outside your home country (and sometimes harder to come by), so if you are selling parts that may help repair some poor Brit's ailing PSP that she imported from Japan before the European release of the PSP, she will be likely to pay more than possible U.S. customers. Make sure you point out to them that the same high taxes for importing a fully functional PSP won't apply to the parts you are selling. Make sure your auction states that the buyer pays for the actual shipping cost.

If you don't want to pay eBay's fees, you could try to barter or sell your dead PSP or its parts on Craigslist.org (*http://www.craigslist.org/*). If, on the other hand, you are a wealthy person who has five or more PSPs lying about and you don't want to soil yourself by using eBay or Craigslist, there are other things you can do with your dead PSP.

Uses for Your Dead PSP

Here's a short, no-frills list:

- Use your dead PSP as a stylish paperweight.
- Or a stylish doorstop.
- Gut the PSP, seal the case with a watertight adhesive like the silicone used in fish tanks, fill it with water, and add Sea Monkeys. Watch 'em grow!

- Gut it and seal the case with a watertight adhesive. Cut the screen section out of the faceplate and leave the space where the screen was out and open. Drill small holes in the back of the PSP for drainage. Fill your deceased PSP with soil and the seeds of your favorite small flower or grass. Water and watch 'em grow! Voilà! Your own stylish Manhattan apartment–sized garden!

- Three words: PSP hockey puck.

- Use the dead PSP to test the moral fiber of your friends, neighbors, and coworkers. Leave it lying around and watch to see whether anyone nicks it!

- People repellant: sure, it may be broken, but nobody else has to know. Put those earphones in and walk around town ignoring people as you please, pretending that you are in your own little portable music world, impervious to their intrusive "Can I interest you in taking a brief survey?" types of questions. This is also a good way to listen in on unsuspecting suspects when you start up your own private detective agency.

- Find a really small, portable color TV. Remove all of its insides. Gut the PSP. Squeeze the TV's innards into the gutted PSP's case. Cause a media storm with your announcement that you hacked the first TV tuner for the PSP!

Think of your dead PSP as a craft project waiting to happen. Be creative and have fun! The important thing is to make sure that you aren't focusing on your recent loss. Life goes on.

HACK #11 Downgrade Your Firmware

If you have purchased a PSP running Version 2.0 of the firmware, complete with browser, you can downgrade to Version 1.5 with a few easy, albeit somewhat risky, steps. When you are done, the entire world of homebrew will be open to you.

Fortunately, some industrious hackers discovered a buffer overflow error that occurs when loading an appropriately created image file through the PSP's Photo menu. Then, someone realized that the buffer overflow allowed for a modicum of code to be run. Finally, the pieces fell in place when someone thought to overwrite the PSP's System Information during this error, so that a PSP running Version 2.0 of the firmware would be fooled into thinking that it was running Version 1.0. A simple substitution of a 1 for a 2, and suddenly you are able to run the 1.5 Software Update to replace the Version 2.0 firmware, effectively downgrading your system to a more hacker- and homebrew-friendly version of the firmware.

Keep in mind that working with firmware is always risky. Having the power supply cut in the middle of a regular Sony-authorized firmware upgrade could very quickly turn your $250 PSP into a $250 doorstop. Such an error in a normal firmware upgrade, though, would be covered under Sony's warranty. Anything that goes wrong with this hacked downgrade won't be covered, so make sure you follow these steps carefully, and consider yourself warned. Proceed at your own risk. Also, be careful where you grab your copy of the downgrader and the 1.5 updater used in this hack; there have been reports of malicious packages posing as these two items that can actually destroy your PSP.

Everything in the Right Place

Download the MPHDowngrader from either *http://www.chez.com/mph/*, *http://www.psp-hacks.com/downloads/MPHDowngrader.zip*, or *http://www.alden0186.freeserve.co.uk/MPHDowngrader.zip*. You will also need a copy of the original 1.5 firmware update. I found my copy via Shockzone (*http://shockzone.free.fr/PSP/Tool/EBOOT_1.50.zip*). Once you have downloaded the necessary files, unzip them. You will find a Read Me file included with the MPH downgrader that you can follow if you don't want to read through this entire hack; however, the Read Me is a little confusing. So unless you are fluent in "I'm a hacker too busy coding to write a Read Me" shorthand, I suggest you read on.

EBOOT.PBP. Connect your PSP to your computer via USB. On your Memory Stick, create a folder called UPDATE inside */PSP/GAME/* and place the *EBOOT.PBP* file from the 1.5 update inside this UPDATE folder.

MPHDowngrader pieces. Drop the *overflow.tif* file that was included in the MPHDowngrader folder into your */PSP/PHOTO/* folder, as you would with any image that you wanted to view on your PSP.

Put both *h.bin* and *index.dat* in the root directory of your Memory Stick (in other words, just drop them straight into the Memory Stick without placing them inside any folders).

Trigger the Overflow

After you have all the files in the right places, disconnect your PSP from your computer and plug it into the AC adapter. Make sure that there is no UMD in your PSP and that you have wallpaper turned off before you begin.

On your PSP, navigate to Photo → Memory Stick and hit the X button to start scrolling down through your photos (see Figure 1-38) until you reach the *overflow.tif* picture. You'll know you've hit it when everything freezes and you get a black screen with a bunch of white text output. This may happen before you even see the *overflow.tif* file name, but if not, simply select the image and hit the X button. The black screen with white text should appear. If your PSP freezes without going to this black text screen, hold the power button up for about 10 seconds until the PSP shuts down, then hit the power button again to start it back up. Repeat this step until you get that black screen.

Figure 1-38. Begin scrolling through the images

 If the black screen with white text doesn't appear to be showing up for you, try connecting your PSP to your computer again and check at the root level of your Memory Stick for a new file there called *index.dat.bak*. If that file is there, then the overflow worked, but you just didn't get the lovely black and white screen. Go ahead to the next step.

Don't panic. The frozen black screen with white text is what was supposed to happen. Hold the power button for about 10 seconds until the PSP powers off. Hit the power button again. Your PSP will start up, and if you navigate to your System Information (Settings → System Settings, hit the X button, then scroll down to System Information and hit the X button again), you'll discover that your PSP thinks it is running Version 1.0 of the firmware. It isn't, and you cannot run homebrew (yet). The important thing is that the PSP *thinks* it is running 1.0, which means that it will allow you to run the 1.5 Firmware Update over your 2.0 firmware.

Run the 1.5 Updater

Navigate to Game → Memory Stick, hit the X button, and navigate to the 1.5 Updater. Make sure that you have your PSP plugged in, or the upgrade won't work. Hit the X button and update as you normally would. At the end of the upgrade, the update will freeze at 99% completion, and you will receive an error saying that the upgrade failed and to contact Sony. Don't panic, and don't contact Sony. Ignore this warning and again force your PSP to power off and reboot.

After the PSP reboots, you will receive an error screen that is scary and confusing because it is in multiple languages (see Figure 1-39). Don't panic. Find the language you can understand and read the corresponding line. It notes that your preferences are fragged and that you need only hit the O button to restore some default-ish settings. Hit the O button.

Figure 1-39. Multiple languages appear on the error screen after conducting the 1.5 update—don't panic

Some hackers have claimed that unplugging the AC adapter and pulling the battery when this warning appeared resulted in them having a PSP running 1.5 firmware capable of running homebrew, but retaining the 2.0 browser. However, you should never leave the PSP plugged in when you remove the battery (I fried one PSP this way), and a few people have reported that following those directions turned their PSPs swiftly into nonfunctional bricks.

Set up Your PSP

The PSP will start back up and you will go through the initial setup like the day you first bought your PSP. Do so, and then go to the system info pane again, where you will see that you are rocking Version 1.5 of the firmware (Settings → System Settings, hit the X button, then scroll down to System Information and hit the X button again). Run homebrew at will [Hack #40].

Hacking the Hack

If you really love your PSP's browser and don't really want to give it up, don't worry. Simply back up all the browser-related files from your Memory Stick before downgrading. I ran through this entire procedure, downloaded the 2.0 update and installed that again, and then went through the entire procedure again. It worked like a charm. It's a little time-consuming, but you can have the best of both worlds. Have fun! Just make sure that you don't install any firmware past 2.0, as I am sure Sony intends to plug this hole again as soon as possible. Even if they do, though, I'm confident that the PSP hackers out there will find a way around it.

PSP Gear
Hacks 12–20

This chapter covers different peripherals available for the PSP, alongside homebrew projects for making your own peripherals. It also covers manipulating the PSP's interface and ways of repurposing the PSP for other uses.

HACK #12 Make Your Own PSP Case

There are plenty of third-party cases available for the PSP, but why not make your own?

You've eyed them in stores and online. Yet none of the commercially available PSP cases that you have seen manage to blend individuality with the coolness of the raw PSP in the necessary ratio to warrant their purchase. You want something to protect your PSP, but you also want something that maintains the coolness factor and makes your PSP definitively *yours*. The only option left within easy reach is to design and make your own PSP case. This hack will walk you through the necessary steps to make your own PSP case out of cardboard.

Why Cardboard?

The short answer: why not cardboard?

The longer reply is that cardboard is a good choice for a do-it-yourself PSP case because of many of the same reasons why it is one of the most common forms of packaging. It's cheap, strong, impact-resistant, easily replaceable, bendable, and although it can be rigid, it still has some give. And, perhaps most importantly, you can probably find a suitable piece of cardboard for this project lying around your house or place of work.

If you are a recycling maniac and just sent the cardboard out yesterday, nicely stacked in the little blue bin that will transport it to cardboard heaven, never fear: there are many places where you can find free cardboard in good shape. Try your local bookstore or liquor store. They are very familiar with people asking for boxes when moving, so your request for a box won't be met with any looks of surprise or disgust. If you just bought your PSP, consider that you *could* use the cardboard in which the PSP was packaged. The only downside to this is that the PSP box is made of a very rigid and thin cardboard, so it won't provide as much cushion when you inevitably drop your PSP. Ideally, I recommend snatching the top of a case of paper from work (make sure that your boss knows you are only taking the cardboard top, and not the entire case of paper). For this hack, I am using the box that my copy of Mac OS X Tiger came in. This cardboard isn't quite as thick as I'd like to use, but it's thicker than the PSP box's cardboard, and it's what I have on hand.

Cardboard is a very forgiving medium to test run your first PSP case. If you screw up, it won't cost anything to start over. After you've gone through these instructions with cardboard, you can try designing your own case out of other materials.

You may be thinking, "Try better, more stylish materials." If you're a cardboard hater, I just want to point out that designers such as Frank Gehry actually build furniture out of cardboard. If you Google "cardboard chair," you'll find some of Gehry's designs alongside design school assignments that require students to design chairs out of cardboard. As the price tags associated with Gehry's designs will testify, cardboard may be inexpensive, but— when nicely styled—*it ain't cheap!*

Things You'll Need

Besides time, patience, and a steady hand, here's a short list of things you will need or that you might find useful in designing your PSP case:

A PSP
> For testing the case and listening to music while you work on the case. Can also be used for measuring if you want to wing the measurements (not recommended).

Corrugated cardboard
> I recommend 1/8-inch thick, but I'm using 1/16-inch thick.

A very sharp knife
> Scissors won't cut it; they'll squeeze and bend the cardboard, marring the surface. I am using an Xacto knife, although box cutters or any other suitable tool for making precision cuts in cardboard will work.

A pencil
> Use this for taking notes and marking the cardboard for cutting.

Some sort of straightedge with ruler

A T square would be ideal, but two good quality rulers with nicely flat ends can be used together as a makeshift T square. The straightedge will be used both for drawing lines and for directing your cuts.

Paper clips

You need these to hold things together.

Glue (quasi-optional)

I recommend Elmer's Wood Glue for this project, although any glue capable of holding cardboard together is workable. If you want to avoid using glue, you can always include tabs and inserts in your design to make your PSP case a glue-free, foldable masterpiece.

Tape (optional)

Here's an alternative to glue, which can have the added effect of making your cardboard water-resistant if placed all over the case.

Sandpaper (optional)

Use this for smoothing any rough cuts in the cardboard. Can be useful for cleaning out the small circles cut for the PSP's controls.

A compass (optional)

You can use this for drawing the circles for the PSP's controls. You can simply draw boxes around these areas, using the boxes as guidelines for drawing the circles freehand. Either way, when it comes time to cutting the circles, you will be working more or less freehand.

Also, if you have a computer and a printer handy, you could easily design the layout for your cardboard PSP case in a program such as Quark, Illustrator, Photoshop, or any other program with a ruler that is capable of accurately drawing measured lines. Then you could print this template out on a regular piece of paper, glue that paper to your cardboard, and start cutting away. Figure 2-1 shows everything you need to get started.

Designing the Case

In the interest of speed and clarity, I'm keeping the design to a bare bones minimum, focusing on the fundamentals that any cardboard PSP case will need (this will also allow for quite a bit of improvement, customization, elaboration, and reconfiguring on your part when you go to make your PSP case).

The first thing you need to do is take the PSP's measurements. The PSP is roughly 74 mm (or just under 3 inches) tall, 170 mm (or 6 3/4 inches) long, and 23 mm thick, which is just about an inch. While the manual that came with your PSP will tell you that the screen is 4.3 inches, that measurement is

Figure 2-1. What you'll need to make a PSP case

from corner to corner. The screen area is roughly 3 3/4 inches (or 96 mm) wide by 2 1/8 inches (or 54 mm) tall.

You first need to design the case in the rough without opening up a space for the screen or the controls. The base design for the case will be a solid cardboard shell that you can wrap around the PSP. Take the dimensions from the previous paragraph and imagine that the PSP is a box that you need to unfold. There will be front and back panels of cardboard, each measuring 3 inches × 6 3/4 inches. There will also be a pair of thin rectangles for the top and bottom of the PSP. Each of these will measure 1 inch × 6 3/4 inches. The two sides will be two other rectangles measuring 3 inches × 1 inch.

Now all you have to do is stack the front, back, top, and bottom rectangles on top of one another and leave a little wiggle room at each intersection of these rectangles to account for the width of your cardboard. The result is a rectangle a little over 8 inches tall (depending on the thickness of your cardboard) by 6 3/4 inches wide. Measure and draw out this rectangle on your cardboard. Make sure you use a T square or two straightedges to draw the corners at 90 degrees. After drawing the rectangle, feel free to cut off the excess cardboard, but leave about half an inch on the top and the bottom and an inch on each side. See Figure 2-2.

Figure 2-2. The rough rectangle on the cardboard

After you have this rough triangle together, mark the 3-inch front of the case, the 1-inch bottom, the 3-inch back, and the 1-inch top, leaving a little give in your measurements to account for the thickness of the cardboard and the places where you want to make your bends in the cardboard.

Cutting, Folding, and Fitting

After marking up your cardboard satisfactorily for the basic fit, it is time to start bending, cutting, and piecing together your PSP case.

You could use something blunt such as the back part of the blade on a pair of scissors or a flat edge of your straightedge to flatten the corrugated cardboard along the seam where you want to fold it, in effect crimping the cardboard at the folds. This method will make your case a bit more durable.

I chose a different method. Corrugated cardboard is made of two thin pieces of paper attached to another piece that runs in waves. Very carefully making sure to only cut through the outermost layer of paper, I cut on either side of each line where the cardboard needed to bend around the PSP. After cutting the top layer, I gently and carefully pulled it free, revealing the ribbed effect of the cardboard. Then I carefully folded along the different seams, using my straightedge to help bend along the lines and shaping the piece around my PSP.

If you do not like either of these methods, consider using some thread and a needle to sew along the seams, pulling the thread tight to collapse the cardboard into a crimped seam.

After you have all the proper parts bent, you will need to cut free the tabs that would meet on the corners of the PSP, as shown in Figure 2-3. Next, fold the cardboard around the PSP, as shown in Figure 2-4.

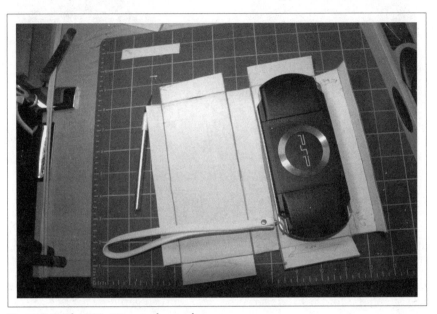

Figure 2-3. The PSP sitting on the rough case

Make sure that you are cutting on a surface that you don't mind marking up. I use a self-healing cutting mat designed especially for cutting stuff up with very sharp knives. I highly recommend the purchase. You can find them in most general office supply and art stores.

If nothing else, just put the cardboard that you are cutting on top of other cardboard.

Building the Box

For now, you're going to ignore the open holes that you will later need to cut for the PSP's screen and controls, since you need to first properly build the box for the case. If you had cut the hole for the screen before bending the overall structure of the case, the cardboard most likely would have bent in places that would ruin the strength and design of the case.

Figure 2-4. Folding the cardboard around the PSP

You need to figure out how to take advantage of the trim your cardboard left around the original rectangle. The best way to do this is to build a few tabs that will hold the case together.

The remaining side tabs aren't large enough to make insertion tabs, so those will simply be folded over each other and glued together. The PSP will be inserted and removed from the case via the top, where you will build a tab.

Since the top and bottom parts of our original rectangle become the top of the case, you're going to need to trim them in order to make space for the L and R triggers, and to prepare for the design of the tab, as shown in Figure 2-5. Place the PSP face down on the top part of the cardboard. This will become the front of the case. You can simply center the PSP and use it to mark the amount you will need to trim off to leave a port open for the L and R triggers. It's about 1 1/4 inch on either side. Remember that you need to take this off from both the very bottom and top of the rectangle, since these two parts, folded together, make the top of the case.

Make a tab by measuring in an inch on either side of the top bit of cardboard and cutting these little flaps away. Then on the bottom section of cardboard, measure in an inch on either side flush with the crease and cut a slot of roughly the same height as your cardboard's thickness (see Figure 2-6).

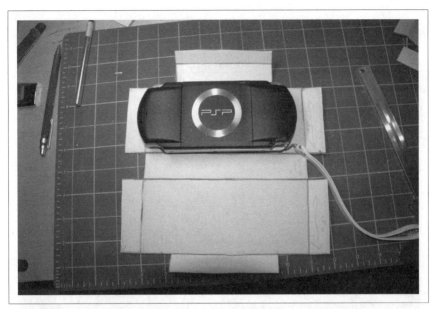

Figure 2-5. After you make space for the L and R triggers on the PSP

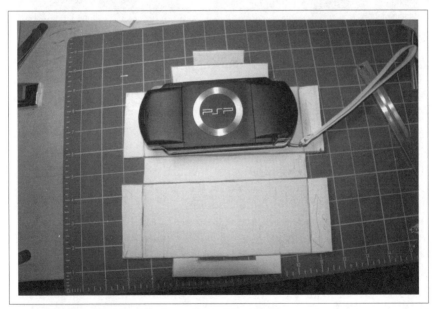

Figure 2-6. The tab and slot for the top part of the case

Now fold the case back around your PSP and test to make sure that the tab fits snugly into the slot you have created, as in Figure 2-7. When I folded this together, I discovered I needed to cut in a slight bit on the bottom panel of the case to make space for the strap that comes with the PSP and to allow access for the power switch and the WLAN switch. I only removed about a quarter inch from either side of the bottom panel, and I winged it without any formal measurements.

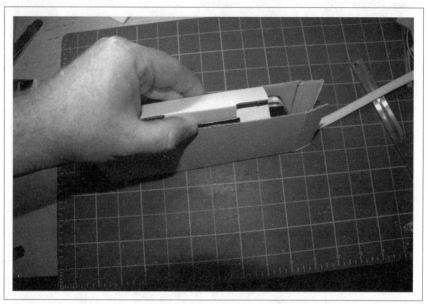

Figure 2-7. Testing the tab and slot

After this step, the basic box is completed, but don't glue those sides together yet. It's time to make space for the controls and the screen.

Screen and Controls

If you measure in an inch and a half from either side of the front of the case, then measure down a quarter inch from the top of the front of the case, and up three-eighths of an inch from the bottom, you will have the exact dimensions of the screen marked off. At the bottom section of the screen, mark out a quarter inch (even with the sides of the top panel) to make space for the controls along the bottom of the PSP.

Place the PSP upside down (see Figure 2-8) on top of the front part of the case and trace around its perimeter to help guide your placement of the four buttons, the analog stick, and the control pad. Both the four buttons and the control pad are centered just slightly north of the center of the screen. I didn't actually measure this part with a ruler, but instead estimated by sketching lines across based on the screen, and drawing rough circles, which I then carved into pizza slice-like sections for better mapping of the circles.

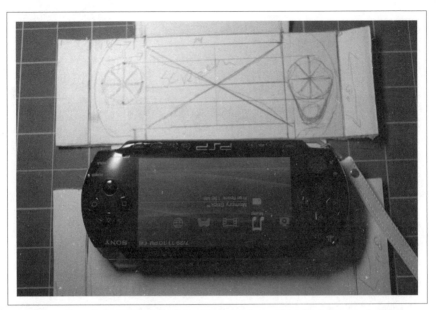

Figure 2-8. Placing the PSP upside down beneath what will be the front panel of the case

After you have everything drawn, cut out both the small control area along the bottom and the screen as one piece. Cut slowly and with enough force to ensure that you get through all three levels of the cardboard and prevent pulling the paper on the other side. Then, very carefully, begin trimming away at the circles needed for the controls. On the side with the analog stick, I extended the circle down like a cone. Cut less than you think you need to at first. Then put the case together and hold the PSP in place to see whether you need to trim away some more. Remember, you can always take more away, but you can't put back what you've cut off. Figure 2-9 shows that I need to take more away from the bottom of the buttons on the right and a slight bit more from the right side of the cone I've made, to accommodate the analog stick.

Finish the Case

After making all the necessary cuts, it's finally time to glue the side panels. Place the wood glue on the flap coming from the back of the case, and fold the flap coming from the front of the case on top of it. Don't make the mistake of squeezing the front and back of the case too close together during this step. Try to get the front and back to stand parallel to one another. Once you have them lined up correctly, slip some paper clips in from the top and bottom to hold them together as shown in Figure 2-10.

Figure 2-9. After the initial cut

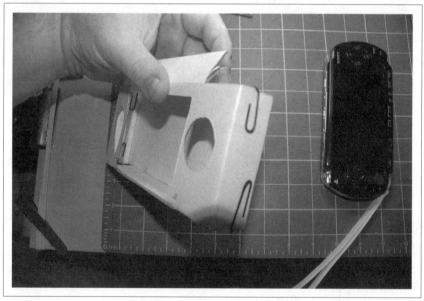

Figure 2-10. The freshly glued and paper-clipped sides of the case

If you want, you can leave the paper clips as a permanent part of the case, but if you let the wood glue dry for several hours, you should be able to safely remove them without any risk of the case falling apart.

Make sure to wipe away any excess glue and let the glue dry to the touch before putting the PSP inside. To insert the PSP, if you have the strap attached, first string it through the proper corner of the case and then carefully lower the PSP into the case through the top panel (see Figure 2-11).

Figure 2-11. Sliding the PSP in through the top of the finished case

Close the top flaps and slide the tab into the slot. You'll find you can reach in the bottom-right side of the case to turn your PSP on, and that the PSP functions normally inside your brand new cardboard case, as shown in Figure 2-12.

Hacking the Hack

Admittedly, this is a horribly ugly hack with plenty of room for improvement. If I'd been less lazy, I would have taken a transparency meant for use with an overhead projector and trimmed it to just slightly wider than the

Figure 2-12. Playing Lumines on my stylin' cardboard PSP

size of the screen and glued it carefully to the inside of the case to protect the screen from scratches. As is, if I drop the PSP flat on its face, the thickness of the cardboard protects the screen from hitting a flat surface. Nevertheless, the front is rather unprotected.

An additional piece of cardboard could be glued to the back of this case and folded nicely over the screen to protect it while on the go, and to function as a glare shield when playing games. Flip this flap around the other way and use it to prop the PSP up while watching a movie.

These suggestions are sticking with the cardboard motif, which does have its advantages. As you can see, I went for a sort of rough and cheap look to keep the New York muggers from considering stealing my PSP. However, your case doesn't have to be as rough around the edges as mine. There are a nearly infinite number of ways you could hack this hack. The most important things you need to keep in mind when designing a PSP case are measurements and materials. Think about which materials could work, in what ways they will work best, and consider how difficult working with those materials can be.

I chose cardboard because it is freely available and because if I drop my PSP when it is in my cardboard case, the cardboard will offer protection from scratching and some absorption of the impact with a bit of pushback bounce, unlike materials such as metal or a hard wood, which lack the sponginess of cardboard. If you are a wood shop hobbyist and would like to go the wood route, consider using a soft wood like balsa that you whittle to the right shape and size, and then cover with a thin veneer of some harder wood to protect against scratches. If you stick with the cardboard design, consider ways that you could make the case water-resistant with different paints or sprays. If you get your cardboard from a liquor store, consider designing your case so that the logo of your favorite drink adorns the back of the PSP. I'm considering taking some soda cans and trying to glue some flattened aluminum to my cardboard case to make it match my aluminum PowerBook. If cardboard, box cutters, and glue aren't your cup of tea, but fabric and sewing machines are, consider using these measurements to design yourself a quilted and padded PSP case out of your favorite fabric. Whatever you choose to do, have fun, post pictures of your results online, and send me the link!

Repurpose Everyday Objects as UMD Cases

Although there are some commercially available sleeves and cases for your UMD discs, there are some homebrew options you should consider as well.

You've probably noticed the gaping hole in the back of the UMD disks. Why Sony didn't make a little cover over that spot is anyone's guess. You need some sort of case for your UMDs to cover that hole, and you don't want to carry around the cases your games originally came in because they are nearly the same size as the PSP itself. In this hack, I'll cover four ideas for some handy and inexpensive cases for your UMD disks.

Altoids Circular Tins

Shortly after the release of the PSP, several people realized that the small, round metal tins in which Altoids Curiously Strong mints and sours are sold make a curiously effective case for holding a nice little stack of UMDs. The metal makes it a tough case that will protect the disks from basic impact damage. The tins are designed for being carried easily, so the case is small enough that you can carry it around in your pocket. They are also sturdy enough that they won't collapse upon the UMD disks, whether in your pocket or in your backpack, scrunched under your laptop and a stack of papers.

Since the tins are metal, simply dump out the contents and remove the little paper discus in the bottom of the case. Then rinse it all in water to remove the Altoids dust (wouldn't want to get that in your UMD disks!) and dry thoroughly with a clean towel. Stick up to three UMD disks in the tin and check out the fit (see Figure 2-13). The first two fit nicely, while the third fits in, but skewed diagonally.

Figure 2-13. Three UMD disks per Altoids case

Pringles Short Stack

Now, if you have a large collection of UMDs that you'd like to take with you, you could simply purchase multiple Altoids tins and divide them in threes. This option would ensure that your UMDs remain in good condition, even if you have them crammed in your pockets. If you have a messenger bag or backpack to work with, however, you might find that a short stack can of Pringles works better.

These little cans of Pringles aren't metal like the Altoids tins, so they aren't quite as sturdy. They are made of a pretty firm cardboard with a metal bottom and a metal ring at the top to keep the cardboard in shape. My guess is that you could fit about 15–20 UMDs in there comfortably. I only had 11 when I was testing it out, and they fit with plenty of room to spare. See how 11 UMDs stack up to the Pringles short stack can in Figure 2-14.

To make your Pringles short stack can into a UMD holder, you first have to get rid of all the little Pringles bits and the potato chip greasiness. Follow these easy steps:

1. Remove the plastic top.
2. Peel back the little paper lid. Discard.
3. Eat all the Pringles in the can (or put them someplace safe for later munching).
4. Squirt a little soft soap inside.
5. Put some water in.
6. Quickly close lid, shake violently, and dump out the suds.
7. Rinse quickly with water.

Figure 2-14. How do they stack up?

8. Dry carefully with a paper towel.

9. Fill with UMD disks.

I'm sure you could do the same thing with a full-sized can of Pringles, but that sort of defeats the portability of the case. Not to mention that if someone sees you with a full stack of UMDs in a full-sized Pringles' can, your chances of getting either beaten up or mugged will increase dramatically for every half-inch of UMDs.

Intec Game Cases

One of the commercially available options, the Intec Game Case (*http://www.inteclink.com/inteclink/products/psp/psp.asp*) comes in a pack of two for about $5 USD in most places. Each case holds three UMDs snugly (see Figure 2-15).

These cases are made out of a rigid, black, formfitting plastic and hold your UMDs firmly in place, albeit at a slightly higher price tag than two tins of Altoids.

Pelican Disc Jackets

The Pelican Disc Jackets are clear plastic sleeves for the UMD disks, and I have only seen them offered as a package with four jackets alongside a face armor attachment for the PSP (*http://www.pelicanperformance.com/psp/psp_spec_sheet/6019.htm*).

Figure 2-15. Each Intec case holds three UMD disks

As you can see in Figure 2-16, the Pelican Disk Jackets work with a single UMD disk and only cover the one side where Sony left the gaping hole. The disks slide into them, and a slight rim over the front and top part of the disks hold them firmly in place.

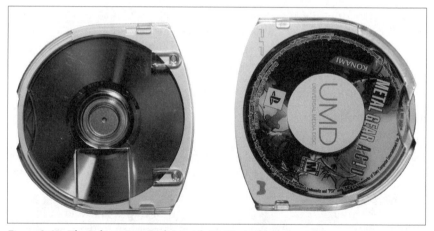

Figure 2-16. The Pelican Disc Jackets with UMDs in them

Unfortunately, since there is no top cover, the UMD disks are still vulnerable to pressure on the top of the disk, which can cause the clear plastic faceplate to push in to the disk [Hack #6] and prevent it from spinning properly in the PSP.

Which Case Is Best?

While I would recommend avoiding the Pelican Disc Jackets, which leave the UMD disks somewhat vulnerable, any of the other three solutions offered in this hack will keep your disks safe. The Pringles can, being made of cardboard, is somewhat less secure and protective than the Altoids or Intec solutions, but you do have the advantage of being able to carry many more UMDs at once.

If quantity isn't your thing, but having a small and sturdy case is, then it really is a toss-up between the Altoids tin and the Intec cases. The Intec cases are pricey in comparison to the Altoids (and sans the Altoid goodness inside), but they are still only $5 USD. They are the most compact solution and tend to be the cases I use most often.

Nevertheless, the Altoids tin is definitely the most retro-styling cool of these four solutions.

Hacking the Hack

There are tons of prepackaged products, such as the Pringles short stack and the Altoids tin, which can be easily cleaned and repurposed as UMD disk holders. Look around your house and see whether you can find a few. There are also many more commercially available options than the two covered here.

Also, if you prefer the strength of the Altoids tins, but you wish they held more than three UMDs, why not bolt two of them together, as I have done in Figure 2-17? All you need is a short bolt, a nut, and a drill, and you are in business: six UMDs in a nice, strong tin.

However, if you are really feeling professional, why not design your own case for the UMDs? I think a nice one could be made out of cardboard [Hack #12].

Make an Articulating PSP Stand

Take an old desk lamp and turn it into an adjustable stand, complete with PSP charging capabilities.

When you're watching a UMD movie on your PSP, don't you just hate having to carefully balance your PSP in your hands without accidentally hitting either the L or R trigger? Me too. So I decided to design and build a PSP stand to hold my PSP in place while I sit comfortably at my desk. If you like the sound of this, but you want something a little more portable, check out "PSP Hands Free" [Hack #18].

Figure 2-17. Two Altoids tins bolted together

Things You'll Need

Several of the items on this list can easily be replaced with something else. This is the list of things I used:

- A PSP and an AC adapter for the PSP that you don't mind tearing apart and putting back together.
- An inexpensive desk lamp with an adjustable arm. You could try to build your own version of this from scratch, but I had an old desk lamp from Ikea lying around that fit the bill perfectly. The Ikea lamp I am using is the Tertial ($6.99 USD from *http://www.ikea.com/*).
- A sharp-pointed knife or wire strippers.
- A small Phillips head screwdriver.
- Scissors.
- Duct tape.
- Electrical tape.

If you opt for the cardboard mount design:

- A small, rectangular piece of some stiff and strong cardboard
- Some large rubber bands

If you opt for the metal mount design:

- Pack of 4 3/4-inch screw bumpers
- Two 2-inch flat metal brackets

- Four 2-inch corner brackets
- Six 1-inch #8 bolts (you could actually use much shorter bolts if you wanted, but 1-inch bolts are easier to find), #8 washers, and #8 nuts

Disassemble the Lamp

After you have all the essentials together, it's time to start taking apart the lamp. Make sure the lamp is unplugged before you go any further.

The head of the lamp (see Figure 2-18) is attached to the lamp's arm by two screws and two nuts. With the bulb removed, simply place your finger on top of one of the nuts and begin unscrewing the corresponding screw with your Phillips head screwdriver. These aren't on too tight, so the pressure from your finger should be enough to hold the nut in place as you unscrew the screw. Remove both screws. Once you do, put the screws, nuts, and washers to the side, because you'll need them later.

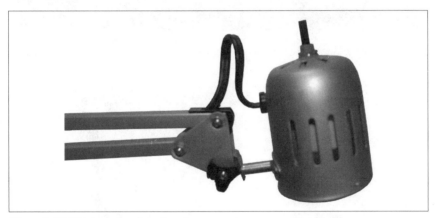

Figure 2-18. The lamp head needs to be removed

The only thing still holding the lamp head to the arm of the lamp is the electrical cord. Make sure the lamp is unplugged, then take your sharp knife or a pair of sharp scissors and cut this wire. For both the unscrewing and the cutting, I used my Swiss Army knife (see Figure 2-19).

Once I cut the cord, I tossed the lamp head aside, and I was able to rather easily pull the cord free from the top part of the lamp arm. Unfortunately, the cord wasn't pulling free from the bottom part of the arm, so I had to remove this section, starting with the connection at the middle joint (see Figure 2-20).

This section, just like the lamp head, is attached by a long screw and a nut. Apply pressure to the nut with a finger and remove the screw. A slight tug

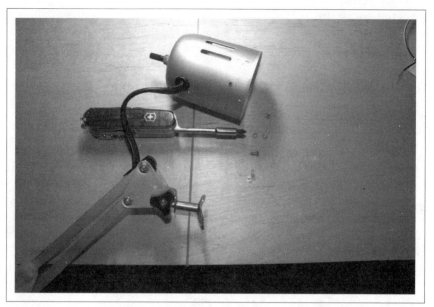

Figure 2-19. Now that the lamp head has been unscrewed, I just need to cut the lamp's cord

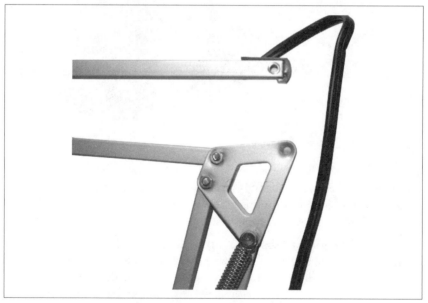

Figure 2-20. Disconnecting this section makes the plastic plug removable

will pull this outer rung of the arm loose from the middle joint. Once it is free, you can pull loose the black plastic plug that was holding the power cord firmly in place. Detach the lower part of this outer rung from the base of the lamp in the same fashion, and remove its black plastic plug as well.

If the black plugs aren't coming free easily, use something such as a flat head screwdriver to apply steady pressure from beneath the plug (see Figure 2-21).

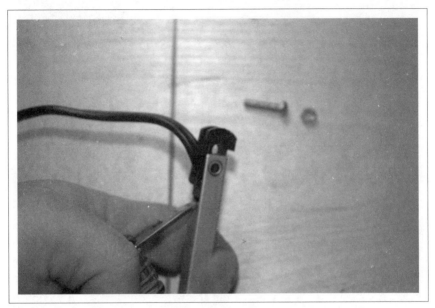

Figure 2-21. Applying slow and steady pressure upward should free the plug

Once you have removed the plug from both ends of this piece, the cord should pull free easily. Once it is free, it is time to run the PSP's AC adapter cord up this same tube.

Add the PSP Adapter to the Stand

Compared to the power cord that was running through the arm piece, there is ample room in the tube for the PSP adapter cord to fit. The L-shaped plug at the end of the cord won't fit (see Figure 2-22), so you're going to have to cut it off several inches from the plug, run the cord through the entire length of the adjustable arm, and then re-splice the plug onto the cord. Make sure you give at least a good three inches from the plug, verify that it's not plugged into the wall, and cut straight through the cord.

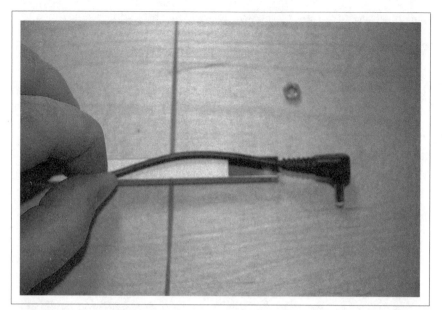

Figure 2-22. The PSP adapter plug won't fit in the shaft

I threaded the cord through the black plastic plug, then through the bottom part of the arm piece that I had removed (see Figure 2-23), pulling it through the top of the arm piece and threading it through the second black plastic plug. I then slid the plugs back into place and reattached the arm piece to the rest of the arm.

Once I reattached the arm piece, I ran the wire through the top section of the arm piece. It should go rather smoothly up the entire length of the shaft and then catch on the lip of the plastic plug at the far end. No need to disassemble this joint this time, as you can easily stick the pointed, sharp end of your knife in the hole and lift the cord slightly up as you push the cord from the other end of the shaft. This should make the cord tip pop through on the top. Pull the cord all the way through, but leave a little bit of give around the middle joint. Use duct tape to tape the power brick to the outside of the base of the arm to hold it securely in place (see Figures 2-24 and 2-25).

After threading the cord through the entire length of the arm and securing the power brick to the base of the arm with duct tape, it is time to reattach the power plug to the other end of the cord. To do this, take the plug and a sharp knife and carefully cut a slit down 1 inch from the place where the cord was severed. After making this incision, pull back the cord's plastic sheath (see Figure 2-26).

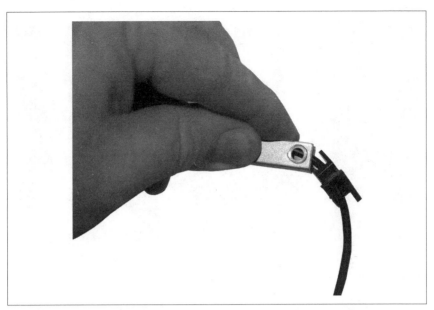

Figure 2-23. Threading the PSP adapter cord through the plastic plug and then through the arm piece

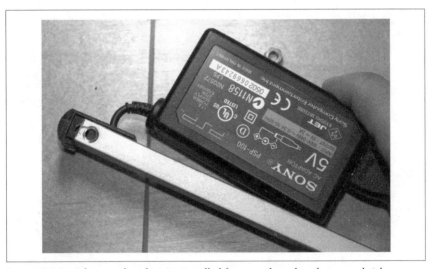

Figure 2-24. Make sure that the wire is pulled far enough so that the power brick rests close to flush with the bottom

Once you pull back the black plastic, you will find a bundle of copper wires wrapped around another white wire. I didn't use wire strippers here, because I wanted to make sure I didn't lose any of the copper wrapped

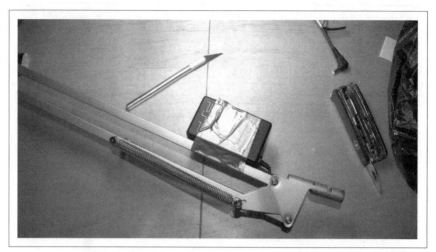

Figure 2-25. After reassembling the arm, I duct taped the power brick to the outside shaft of the base

Figure 2-26. The PSP adapter's coaxial cord

around the inner wire. Unwrap this copper from around the inner wire and twist it together into one wire shooting off in the same direction as the black sheath you pulled back. If you don't think you have quite enough wire to make a good splice with the cord, pull back some more of the black sheath, pull down more wire, and twist it together.

Take the knife and carefully make a similar incision on the white inner wire, but make sure to leave distance between this incision and the bundled copper wire that was wrapped around the white wire. You don't want these two groupings of copper touching, since it would cause a short circuit. At the six volts coming down this part of the wire, it wouldn't be too dangerous, but better safe than sorry. Peel back the white plastic and twist the copper wires inside this white sheath together (see Figure 2-27).

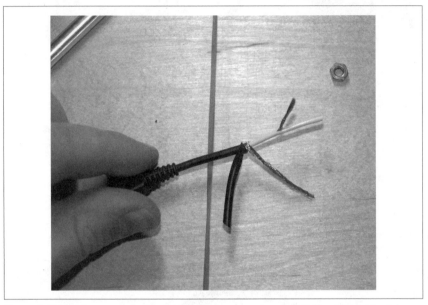

Figure 2-27. Both groups of wires with enough separation where there is no risk of them touching

Duplicate these steps with the end of the cord that is coming out of the arm piece of the former lamp. Once both the cord and the plug are properly prepared, twist the copper wires from the outer section of each together, and the copper wires from the inner white wires of each together, as in Figure 2-28.

Everything should work fine at this point, but those two differently charged bits of copper are still exposed and could hit each other and cause some sparks, so you need to grab some electrical tape and seal everything up nicely before proceeding to test your handiwork. Because the two pieces of black sheath that are jutting out from the line originally held both the white and the black sections of wire, they are loose enough to wrap around one of the wire bundles. I wrapped them around and then wrapped electrical tape around this section (Figure 2-29).

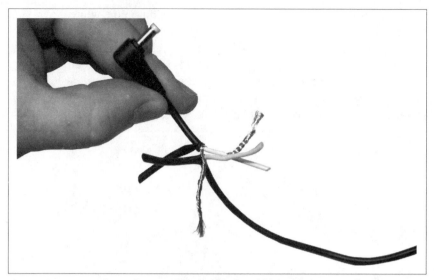

Figure 2-28. Reattaching white to white and black to black

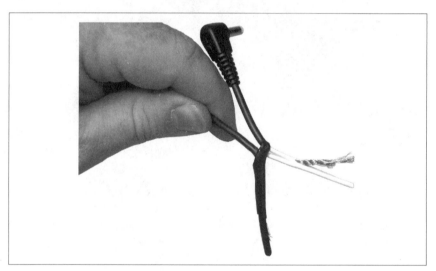

Figure 2-29. One bundle of wires taped; one to go

The white plastic won't wrap as nicely around the remaining bundle as the black plastic did around the other, but try to get them to and then tape these wires together (Figure 2-30).

Everything is taped off nicely, but the plug is pointing in the wrong direction and there's still a little bit of the outer copper exposed right in the middle intersection of our splice job. To make this look more like a regular cord,

Figure 2-30. Both bundles of wires taped separately

I taped the long part that had been the bundle of outer wires to the cord side of the splice, and the shorter part that had been the bundle of inner wires to the plug side of the splice. I then wrapped a fresh layer of electrical tape down the entire length of the splice for good measure (see Figures 2-31 and 2-32).

Figure 2-31. Taping the outer wire bundle down toward the cord end of the splice

After the splice is completed, it's time to test the line. I plugged the PSP adapter into the outlet and the PSP and was met with the kind orange light of a successful charge. Now, to finish the stand.

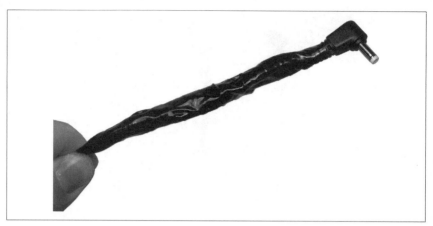

Figure 2-32. The completed splice

Mount the PSP

After completing the combination of the arm and the PSP power adapter, it's time to build a mount to hold the PSP on the end of the arm. I went through two iterations of this: first, the cardboard version, or, as I like to call it, the "Lazy Mount Deluxe," and second, the metal version, or, as I like to call it, "What I Should Have Done in the First Place." I'll take you through both.

Mount Version 1.0: cardboard. For Version 1.0 of the stand, I chose to go a little bit low-tech. Since I'd already built a cardboard case for my PSP [Hack #12], I decided to devise some simple way to attach this case to the end of the arm. I still had some rather rigid pieces of cardboard lying around from that hack, so I took one thin strip of rigid cardboard and attached it to the end of the arm using the screws and nuts that originally held the head of the lamp in place (Figure 2-33).

After attaching this rigid piece of cardboard to the end of the arm, all I had to do was place the PSP inside the cardboard case between the arm and this piece of cardboard, then carefully wrap the large rubber bands around either side of the case and this piece of cardboard.

If you go this route, simply plug the PSP power cord into the bottom-right corner of the case, adjust the arm for optimum viewing, and sit back and enjoy a UMD movie of your choosing (Figures 2-34 and 2-35).

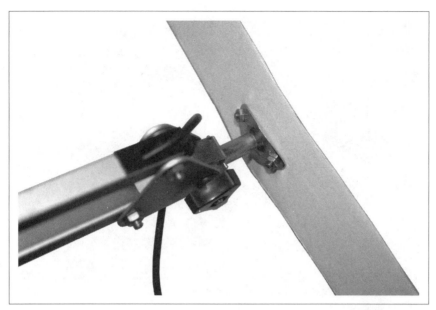

Figure 2-33. Back view

Figure 2-34. Plugging in the power cord

Figure 2-35. Arm extended

If I were simply improving upon the current design, I would build an entirely new cardboard case for the PSP, designed specifically to be permanently attached to the end of this stand with a slot at the top for removing and replacing the PSP. Ideally, there would be some sort of shade or tent to block reflections from ambient light and to give it more of a theater feeling.

However, both the existing cardboard mount and the imagined one struck me as unsatisfactory, so I went back to the drawing board and came up with a much more functional and stylish mount for the PSP.

Mount Version 2.0: metal. After ripping off the cardboard mount, I took the same bolts and nuts that originally held the head of the lamp in place and attached one 2-inch bracket to each bolt (Figure 2-36).

After you have attached these two brackets, you will create a metal "claw" of sorts, by using two of the #8 bolts, nuts, and washers to attach two of the 2-inch corner brackets to either end of these two flat brackets (so, a total of four 2-inch corner brackets attached). Then, on the outermost holes of the claw, attach the rubber screw bumpers with the remaining bolts and nuts. The finished product should look like Figure 2-37. The PSP slides in through the side and is held nicely in place by the grey bumpers (see Figure 2-38).

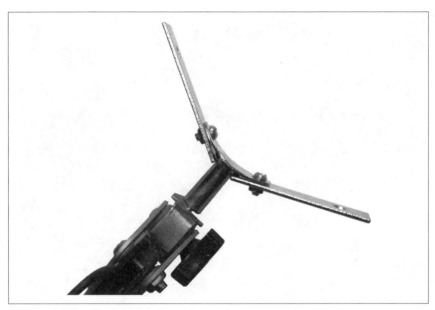

Figure 2-36. Attaching the 2-inch brackets to the arm

Figure 2-37. The finished "claw"mount

Figure 2-38. PSP in the stand; even facing down, the PSP is held securely in place by the bumpers

Hacking the Hack

The actual mount for the PSP in this PSP stand is the weak point in my design and the area that could see the most improvement.

Ideally, I'd like to have a mount that didn't actually surround the PSP. This would bring to the forefront the beauty of the PSP. The stand would make the PSP appear as if it were magically floating in the air. Unfortunately, such a design would entail actual modifications to the PSP. If I didn't mind screwing some holes in the back of my PSP, I would have removed the plastic casing over the UMD tray (using as much information as I could glean from "Take Your PSP Apart" **[Hack #8]**). I then would have attached some sort of hook or latch to this piece with a combination of some drilling, screws, and some strong adhesive. Then I would have attached a metal plate to the end of the arm and the corresponding male attachment piece to the female slots on the back of the modified PSP.

I'd also run more wires through the former lamp arm. I'd have a USB cable coming up for syncing with my computer, and an audio line coming down so I could plug the PSP into some external speakers. If I decide to add this later, I can simply run the wires along the outside of the outer arm piece with ties holding the wires in place along the length of the arm. However you decide to make your stand, have fun.

Make a Battery Pack for Your PSP
#15
This hack will build an external battery pack for the PSP to extend the internal battery pack's life from the just-a-bit-too-short three to six hours.

Sure, you could plop down a load of cash for some company's prepackaged external battery for your PSP if you need to extend the battery life of your PSP while you're on the go. Lik Sang (*http://www.lik-sang.com/*) offers both the third-party External 3800mAh Battery Pack for PSP for $24.95 USD (*http://www.lik-sang.com/info.php?category=307&products_id=7027*) and the third-party Clip-on 1800mAh Battery Pack for PSP for $14.95 USD (*http://www.lik-sang.com/info.php?category=307&products_id=7026*). If you speak Japanese, you could probably figure out how to order the My Battery JET for PSP (*http://www.watch.impress.co.jp/game/docs/20050603/jtt.htm*), and if Chinese is your cup of tea, the DragonPlus Rechargeable Handle Pad, which turns your PSP into one big controller (*http://www.chinapsp.net/Default. aspx?tabid=888&DocType=ArticleView&ArticleID=990*).

And, of course, you could always invest in another Sony battery for the PSP and swap them out while you are on the go.

As I write this hack, these are just a few of the commercially available options to extend the battery life of your PSP. There will surely be more and more options in the weeks and months to come.

But, you're reading *PSP Hacks*. You want to do something "hackish." Wouldn't you rather just grab an old AC adapter and some other odds and ends from around the house to hack together your own battery charger for the PSP? Me too.

My sister-in-law, Maggie, just recently received her Biomedical Engineering B.S. with a concentration in electrical work from Columbia University, so I enlisted her help for this hack. Overkill? Of course.

This is the ugliest way possible to hack together an external battery pack for your PSP. Maggie and I decided to make it intentionally basic, using parts we found lying around the house so that I could talk up possible improvements you can make along the way if you want to improve upon this hack. I recommend that you do.

Consider this a basic run-through for the beginners among you. As for you 1337 hackers who scoff at how basic this hack is, consider it a challenge. If you don't want to be bothered with the basics, skip ahead to the "Hacking the Hack" section of the hack.

Things You'll Need

- Some AA batteries (three or more)
- A battery holder (we used the AA Battery Holder part #270-407A from RadioShack, but if you have another lying around, it'll probably do)
- An old DC power cord with a connector that fits in your PSP (the one we used was from an old, broken Aiwa CD player and rated for 6V)
- Wire strippers
- Some electrical tape and/or some solder and a soldering iron
- A multimeter (for testing the connections)

The Theory Behind the Hack

The transformer in the PSP's AC/DC converter adjusts your regular household voltage down to a whopping five volts, which trickles slowly into your PSP, charging the internal, Sony-supplied battery. Why don't they beef up this voltage into the machine so that the charging goes faster, you ask? Well, mini power surges aside, any voltage higher than five volts could very quickly, with a sizzle and a burnt smell, fry up your PlayStation Portable into a very handy PlayStation doorstop or paperweight.

Setting Things Up

The battery holder we had on hand was designed to hold eight AA batteries in series, putting out a whopping 12 volts of power, which is much higher than the 5 volts needed by the PSP and would risk frying our little gaming wonder. Each AA battery puts out 1.5 volts, so some quick math told us that three AA batteries would get us up to 4.5 volts, which is the ballpark we need to be playing in.

We looked at the connected flow of the batteries through the battery holder and stacked two on one side, and then one alone on the adjacent side. Three 1.5-volt AA batteries in a line tested at 4.86 volts with the multimeter, which was perfect, falling just shy of the five volts indicated on the PSP.

Next, we found an AC adapter from an old, broken CD player that was lying around the house. The AC adapter was rated at six volts, and the plug fit perfectly into the PSP.

The voltage of the plug doesn't actually matter for the hack. Just find an old AC adapter with a plug that fits easily in your PSP; however, when wiring, make sure to use your multimeter to correctly match the inner and outer part of the plug to the polarity needed by the PSP. The polarity is indicated on your PSP's 5V socket where you plug the adapter in.

We then took our wire strippers and cut the AC cord from the plug, several inches away from the piece that would be plugged into the PSP. Make sure that you give yourself enough length to work with here. Remember, you can always cut more off, but you can't add back on without some ugly line splicing.

The line coming from the plug is actually two different wires stuck together: one to carry the negative current and the other to carry the positive. Pull the two wires apart. After they are separated, strip off about a quarter inch of plastic from the ends. For each of the wires, twist the little copper wires together so they look more like a solid wire without any stray hairs sticking out.

Assembling the Pack

Now, take the battery holder and put three batteries in so that the current will flow from negative to positive. Where the batteries will need to be placed will vary depending upon the battery holder you have, so pay attention to the connection between the different sections. For our battery holder, we had two batteries stacked in a row on one side, while one sat alone on the adjacent corner.

To make a complete circuit that will charge the PSP, the negative line from the adapter plug (the negative wire will usually have a white stripe down the side of it) will need to be attached to the negative end of the line of batteries, and the positive line from the adapter (which will sometimes be red) will need to be attached to the positive end of the line of batteries.

Make sure to conduct a continuity test to make sure you have the correct wire mapped to the correct pin of your plug.

For both of these connections, we used simple electrical tape. For the negative connection, we attached the wire to the negative contact on the outside of the battery holder (see Figure 2-39).

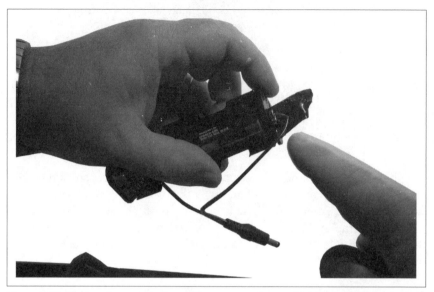

Figure 2-39. Taping the negative line to the negative plug on the battery holder

Then, for the positive connection, we simply taped the wire to the positive top of the AA battery that was sitting solo on the other side and shoved it in with the tape, which helped hold it in place (see Figure 2-40).

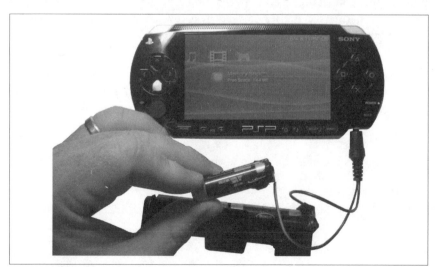

Figure 2-40. Popping the battery into place

When we plugged it in, a nice orange light showed up on the PSP and the battery indicator light began to flash on and off on the PSP's screen, indicating that it was receiving a charge.

Hacking the Hack

Now, our battery pack works, but the current coming from it isn't enough to power the PSP if the internal battery runs out. It is an ugly, horrible shadow hack of what it could be. When the PSP is turned on, it isn't actually managing to charge the PSP; rather, it is working as a battery extender of sorts, extending the length of the internal battery's charge by subsidizing the energy that is powering the PSP. If the PSP is turned off, however, this pack will push energy into the PSP, albeit slowly.

Ideally, if we were building a battery pack out of three AAs, which we were, we'd get a holder made for three AA batteries rather than one built to hold eight. With a fully loaded holder, we could actually solder the positive and negative wires onto the positive and negative outputs from the holder to ensure a tight circuit through which the power can flow.

As is, depending upon how much electrical tape we used on the last battery to thicken it up and how nicely we wedged it into place, from time to time the battery will shift out on the spring that it is resting up against, and the circuit will disconnect until we get it back into place. Also, since we chose to use electrical tape rather than hardwiring everything together nicely, there is the ever-present possibility of the wires ripping free.

 RadioShack also sells battery holders that already have the positive and negative wires attached, making them easier to work with and more aesthetically pleasing.

Now, beyond these physical concerns, the flow of current coming from this battery pack is far below what the PSP ideally needs. If we really wanted to make a professional battery pack, we would grab a battery with larger voltage, such as a 9-volt remote control car battery. In order to prevent the nine volts from frying the 5-volt plug in the PSP, we'd need to attach a 5-volt regulator (like a +5V Fixed-Voltage Regulator 7805 from RadioShack, catalog part # 276-1770, which is capable of a maximum input of 35VDC and puts out +5V at up to 1 amp) between the battery and the wires leading to the plug. The larger battery voltage would in turn provide higher amperage and, therefore, a higher flow of current, and the 5-volt regulator would keep the current capped at five volts, which would protect us from frying our PSP.

If you opt for this setup, you should probably stick a heat sink on the regulator, since regulators tend to fry and the heat sink will keep the regulator from overheating. Be careful to properly connect input, output, and the ground connectors on the regulator, and if you're not too good with soldering, either grab a solderless breadboard from RadioShack or find a guru friend to do it for you, since you could accidentally short the regulator in the process. Soldering will ensure connections, but the breadboard will allow for easy replacement of the regulator should it short out (which, as mentioned previously, they are prone to do). Choose wisely.

HACK #16 Amplify Your PSP

Want to bring the noise with your PSP, but your speakers don't quite manage the bump that you need? Time to learn the basics of audio amplification and apply them.

The speakers on the PSP are okay, as are the headphones, but wouldn't you like a little bit more oomph to your audio? Sure, you could spend some money and buy a nice audio amplifier, but wouldn't it be more fun to build your own?

This hack walks you through putting together a very basic audio amp for your PSP. Since I'm using a solderless breadboard to make all the connections clear, this isn't a permanent solution. However, if you can follow along with these instructions to get the amp up and running, it won't be that difficult to purchase a small circuit board and, with some careful soldering, put together a smaller version of this that could easily be shoved into a rather small container (such as an Altoids tin [Hack #13]). Once you've tested the waters with this hack, a quick Google search will turn up various other audio amp instructions that have materialized online, such as the CMoy Pocket Amplifier HowTo (*http://tangentsoft.net/audio/cmoy-tutorial/*).

Most of these instructions tout themselves as beginner DIY projects, but still have a learning curve that will scare away some beginners. This hack will avoid the shock factor and ease you slowly into the world of audio DIY.

Things You'll Need

Before you get started, make sure you have all these components handy:

- Basic 8 ohm speaker for testing (RadioShack 8-ohm Mini Speaker 273-092, $2.59 USD; small, portable speaker, but not the best sound)
- Audio amp (RadioShack part #LM386, $1.39 USD)
- 4–12V DC source
- Solderless breadboard

- Some wires for connections
- Some electrical tape or some solder and a soldering iron
- An old audio cable to plug into the PSP and wire to the board for testing, or an audio cable with alligator clips

Assemble the Circuit

If you are familiar with circuit diagrams, then you can refer to Figure 2-41 as you work on this basic amplifier.

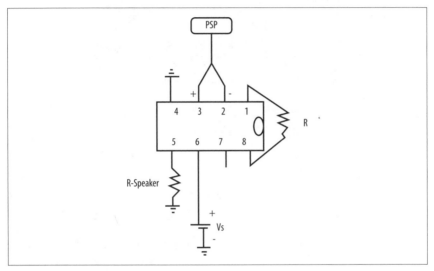

Figure 2-41. Diagram of the circuit

The first step is to place the audio amp chip in the breadboard and designate a line for ground, as shown in Figure 2-42.

Keep in mind that the chip has to be placed on the board so that none of the pins are shorted with one another. This usually means straddling it across the division in the middle of the breadboard.

Locate the notch on one end of the chip and make sure the notch is facing to the right. The pins on the chip number around the chip, starting from the top right near the notch, which is pin 1, and going around the chip in a C-shape to come back to the bottom right near the notch, which is pin 8. If you consult the diagram on the back of the box the chip came in, you will know the purpose for each pin.

On this particular chip (RadioShack part #LM386), pins 1 and 8 are gain pins, pin 2 is negative audio input and pin 3 is positive audio input, pin 4 is ground, pin 5 is audio output, pin 6 is the Vs or voltage source pin, and pin 7 is the bypass pin.

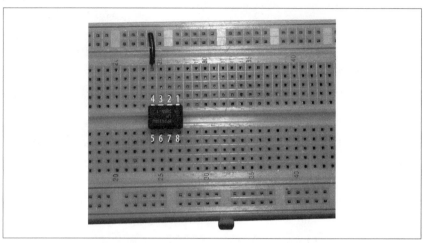

Figure 2-42. Circuit with ground pin wired to ground on the breadboard

Connect the ground pin (pin 4) to the line you previously designated for ground. Put the wire that will serve as the audio input from the PSP into the proper pins of the audio amp chip (pins 2 and 3, negative and positive respectively; these appear as the two wires to the right of the ground wire above the chip in Figure 2-43). Connect the positive wire from the voltage source into the Vs pin (pin 6) of the audio amp chip (the wire on the bottom right in Figure 2-43). Connect the negative speaker terminal to ground (this is the top wire coming from off the board in Figure 2-43). Connect the positive speaker terminal to the output of the audio amp chip (this is the bottom wire attached to pin 5, coming from off the board in Figure 2-43).

Now you have the completed setup for the circuit. If you bought a bare speaker sans wires, make sure that the two wires are soldered correctly onto the speaker. Attach the negative and positive alligator clips from the audio input cable to the two audio input wires you have connected to pins 2 and 3.

Gain is already set to 20, but for a larger gain, you could connect a resistor across the gain pins (pins 1 and 8: the top and bottom pins on the right in Figure 2-43); the larger the resistor, the larger the gain, but the larger the gain, the more audio distortion you will encounter.

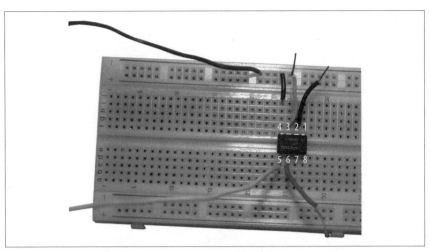

Figure 2-43. Wiring the chip

Once everything is in place, it's time to add the power. For this hack, I used the same battery holder that I used in "Make a Battery Pack for Your PSP" [Hack #15] as the power source for the amp. The chip can handle voltage from roughly 4–15 volts, but it's better to keep the voltage closer to 5 volts, since the chip tends to run hot and can easily burn out. Attach the negative wire from your battery pack to ground, and attach the positive wire to the voltage source wire connected to the Vs pin to turn it on (Figure 2-44).

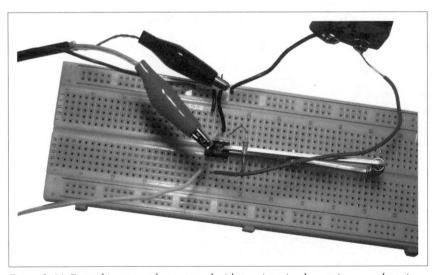

Figure 2-44. Everything properly connected with a resistor in place to increase the gain, and a heat sink clamped onto the chip

Test the Amp

After all your connections are made, plug the audio cable into your PSP and start up something with audio at a moderate volume level (to ensure that you don't blow the speaker). Since you're using a single speaker, the audio will be coming out in mono, but it will be noticeably louder than the PSP alone. As you increase the volume, you will notice that there is an increase in distortion. If you hear nothing, check all your connections again.

Problems and Easy Improvements

The sound quality of this particular amp won't be amazing because I used rather cheap parts. Using better parts, especially a better quality 8-ohm speaker, would improve the sound quality.

This setup is also reliant on the inexpensive audio chip used, which has a tendency to occasionally overheat and can even burn out if left running for too long. Using a more powerful and more expensive amplifier chip in the design would result in a better amp. Simply adding a heat sink will help prevent the current chip from burning out as quickly. Adding a capacitor between the output pin of the chip and the speaker's positive terminal will essentially create a "high pass filter" and cut down on distortion and noise from the power supply by blocking lower frequency signals.

There's also no on and off switch. The design currently works by connecting or disconnecting the power. Adding a switch in between the Vs pin wire and the positive wire from the battery pack would give you the ability to turn this amplifier on or off.

Hacking the Hack

After successfully building this very basic audio amplifier for your PSP, you should be ready to tackle a slightly more complex project. As you can see in Figure 2-45, the size and portability of the completed project isn't very useful. Redesigning this amplifier on a smaller circuit board, you could easily fit the entire circuit inside a very small container for protection and portability. Rather than hardwiring the connections to an audio line to the PSP and the speaker, you could attach a female audio port to both the input and output for the audio, using a male-to-male cord to pull the input from the PSP and running a cord to your headphones or any speaker you have from the other output port. If you really want to hack this hack, build a new and better amplifier to include as part of "Portable PSP Speakers" [Hack #31].

Figure 2-45. The completed project with a capacitor added to help reduce the distortion as the volume is increased

HACK #17 Add an External Wireless Antenna

This modification will not only increase the range and strength of your wireless signal for better online gaming, but it also will earn you major geek points when you pull out a foot-high, omnidirectional antenna at the next PSP-a-thon.

The PSP comes with built-in wireless networking support that allows you to connect to other players for true multiplayer action [Hack #5]. In addition to this, your PSP can also be used to surf the Net, serve up web pages, and more. For all this, you need to be sure your wireless connection is strong and solid.

Unfortunately, the internal wireless antenna is limited by both power and size. As a result, your connection weakens rather quickly the further you get from the access point. To help overcome this weakness, I have worked out the details and steps you need in order to upgrade the PSP wireless abilities by adding in an external antenna that not only gives you extra range and strength, but also turns your PSP into a device that won't be overlooked.

Finding a Replacement

The first step in this process is to find a viable replacement antenna that will make your signal stronger, without tying you to a large and weighty antenna that you need a suitcase to carry. This will require you to deal with various acronyms and cryptic terms, since the FCC has made it annoying to upgrade wireless antennas on any particular device.

First, on the network card, you will find a U.FL connector. Fortunately, these are fairly standard and you can easily find an antenna with a matching U.FL connector that will just plug into the PSP WNIC. However, this is not the best method, even if it is the one I use for this particular hack.

The reason I mention this is that once the hack is in place, you will not be able to easily remove it. That said, if you purchase and install a single component wireless antenna-pigtail-U.FL connector, you will be forced to lug the entire contraption around wherever you take the PSP. Therefore, I recommend you first purchase a U.FL to N Male pigtail, then purchase an omnidirectional antenna with an attached N Female connector. This two-part solution not only allows greater portability, but if you desire a satellite dish antenna upgrade (35+ mile range) at a future date, it is as easy as disconnecting the omni-direction and screwing the N Female pigtail on the dish. In general, a U.FL to N Male pigtail should run about $10 USD and an N Female omni-directional antenna should run $15+ USD, depending on size.

For this replacement, I used a simple pigtail with 5dBi combination. I purchased this antenna for about $20 USD with shipping off of eBay (*http://www.ebay.com*), and it even came with a stand for easy mounting.

Out with the Old

Next, you need to remove the original antenna from the PSP. This presents a bit of a problem, because the antenna connector is buried at the bottom of the device and requires you to completely disassemble the device [Hack #8].

When taking the PSP apart, you will see the antenna and its associated wiring once you remove the LCD tray. As Figure 2-46 illustrates, the antenna is located on the right side of the PSP, under the controller pad. From the antenna, you can see a black wire that trails across the entire width of the PSP and disappears beneath the left controller pad. If you lift the left controller, you can see that the wire actually drops down into the PSP case and connects to the network card buried below the main circuit board. Once you have the PSP completely disassembled, you will need to remove the network card and attached antenna wire from the case. Figure 2-47 illustrates what this component looks like.

Two items are of interest at this point. First, the wire used to connect the WNIC (Wireless Network Interface Card) with the antenna is not of a high quality. As a result, the signal will experience some loss when passing

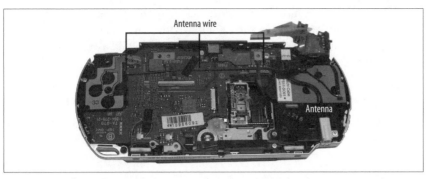

Figure 2-46. The PSP's antenna wire

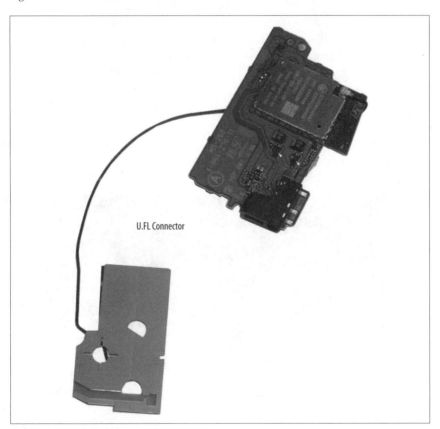

Figure 2-47. NIC with antenna

through the wire and the electronics of the PSP. Second, the actual antenna is no more than a couple of inches long and is located in the brown flat plastic piece found under the right-side controller. These two attributes of the antenna provide a good indicator as to its limits. I am confused as to why the PSP designers would put the antenna in such a location, because the water in the human body causes signal attenuation. Since your hand basically wraps around the antenna when playing the PSP, your signal suffers about a 10db loss.

Once you get the network card out of the PSP, you will need to remove the original antenna from the U.FL socket. This is accomplished by firmly levering the original antenna U.FL connector out of the U.FL socket. Be sure to use perpendicular force, because the connector is quite fragile.

In with the New

At this point, you are ready to start the antenna upgrade. The first thing you will need to do is to create a hole in the PSP case through which you will pass the new pigtail. The location of this hole is important, because the PSP is such a tightly designed device that there is really only one option for this hole. In addition, the PSP case itself will support the new U.FL connector by applying counterpressure against the connector to keep it in place.

Figure 2-48 illustrates where you should cut, melt, or drill the hole. For my trial run of this hack, I chose to melt a hole in the PSP's case using a soldering iron. While this worked, the result was a little messy. I recommend using a drill to make a clean, round, and more professional-looking hole.

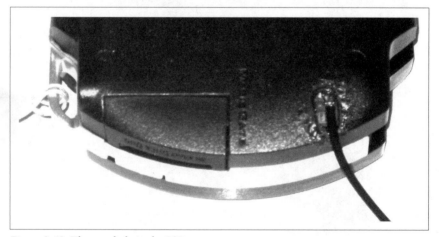

Figure 2-48. The new hole in the PSP

Once the case is updated, take the U.FL pigtail upgrade and slip the U.FL connector through the hole, and seat it firmly into the circuit board's U.FL socket. Then carefully reinsert the network card back into the PSP case and be sure the new pigtail and U.FL connector fits. If it does, you then need to put the entire PSP back together again **[Hack #9]**. Figure 2-49 provides you with a shot of the completed hack.

Figure 2-49. The final product

Testing the Mod

Modifications are great, but they are only of value if they actually enhance a certain feature of a product. In this case, you want to enhance the wireless signal strength, which means you need to compare the original antenna with the upgrade to see if there is really a benefit. For this test, I used a program called AirMagnet (*http://www.airmagnet.com/*) that, among other things, has a nice signal strength graphic output. Figure 2-50 illustrates very clearly the difference between the two signals.

Table 2-1 lists the signal strength versus noise ratio (SNR). What is most interesting about these results is that the new antenna obtained a much greater increase (13db) than I expected from a 5db antenna. From this, I can only assume that moving the antenna outside the PSP body and using a higher-grade wire helped to reduce the signal loss. When combined with the greater gain of the antenna, the increase is much greater than can be credited to the new hardware.

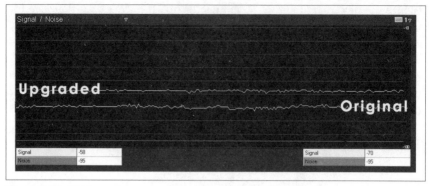

Figure 2-50. AirMagnet

Table 2-1. Comparison of pre-hack and post-hack signal performance

	Signal	Noise	SNR
Original	70	95	25
Upgraded	58	95	37

Hacking the Hack

With this hack, it would be possible in theory to play PSP to PSP with someone miles away with the right antenna. You could also add an amplifier to
your setup and have the FCC come hollering. The sky is really the limit, if
you start with a pigtail attachment. Keeping a common N Male connector
on the end means you will have many options when it comes to selecting the
antenna.

—Seth Fogie

HACK #18   PSP Hands Free

Build a low-cost, hands-free holder for your PSP in a short amount of time.

Movies, movies, movies. You love movies, and so do I. Watching movies on
the PSP is a great feature. The only problem is that you have to hold the PSP
for the length of the movie, due to the size of the screen. Sure, you could buy
a low-cost DVD player for around $150 USD with an LCD, but that's not
the point. You would need to carry around a second device, when you have
a fantastic and very portable screen with the PSP.

One day, while researching how to repair a gas line at the house, I found
myself in the piping area of a large home improvement store. There were
numerous types of pipes: copper, steel, black, white, drain, gas line, and

water pipes—you name it, it was there. I got to thinking: you could create a lot of things from simple PVC pipe. You could buy straight pieces, cut them, and connect them using elbows. One thing led to another, and I had an epiphany at the store. I suddenly grabbed a handful of half-inch PVC pipe off the shelves (both angle pieces and straight pieces) and mixed and matched until I had assembled what I thought would be enough pieces for this project.

Things You'll Need

- PSP Stand (*http://www.joytech.net/*)
- One 4-foot length of white PVC pipe
- Two S-shaped PVC pipes
- Six PVC pipe elbows
- Cleaning compound
- Black enamel spray paint
- PVC pipe cutter or hack saw
- Blowtorch
- Gorilla PVC glue

The Theory Behind the Hack

The PSP is a great entertainment center. For movie viewing, that means having to hold the unit continuously. One option is to use the simple dock solutions that are available, but then you would not be able to watch your movie while you did other things around the house, or while lying in bed. And, of course, there wouldn't be this hack. The dock also requires you to be very close, bent over in an uncomfortable position while trying to watch the movie.

Setting Things Up

PVC pipes are very easy to handle and manipulate to your needs. The first step is to make some simple measurements for the length of pipes you will cut for the down length and the out length. The width of the unit is also critical, as it will need to fit over your head and rest comfortably on your neck. The measurements I used were:

- Two curved pieces of 12 inches in length (accounting for the curve; the piece before the curve was 14.5 inches in length). These will be used to fit over your shoulders.

- Four straight pieces, each 8 inches in length. These form the main part of the frame that connects the curved pieces at an angle, allowing for your PSP to be mounted.

From these pieces I assembled a rectangle, using the elbow joints (you need six) to connect the pieces together. You need to be careful in measuring, since the four straight pieces need to be exactly the same length, as do the pieces you will use to create the curve. If you don't feel comfortable creating a curve, you can also purchase pre-bent PVC in some Lowe's and Home Depot stores, but the curves may be too big and need to be bent slightly more.

Assembling the Holder

After measuring, you now need to make the cuts. I used a $9 USD PVC pipe cutter, but you could use a simple hacksaw. Using a hacksaw will make a mess, so make sure you put paper down beforehand for easy cleanup. I found some PVC that was in a slight "S" form, and then used a blowtorch to bend the PVC slightly to where I wanted it to be. Kids, do not try using a blowtorch without adult supervision. I first tried using a hair dryer, but there was not enough heat generated by it to bend the PVC.

The first time you connect everything together (see Figure 2-51), you may find it is not "true." This will require you to make small cuts with your PVC pipe cutter (see, it's easier than a hacksaw) to shorten as needed.

After you have ensured everything fits together, you can use PVC glue and glue the pieces together.

> Make sure that you are in a properly ventilated area, prefera-bly outside.
>
> If you glue the unit at this stage, you will not be able to sepa-rate the pieces again. If you want to add on to the system later, (e.g., wiring for headphones/speakers or batteries), you will have to cut it open. Skip gluing if you are unsure.

After allowing the proper time for the glue to set (follow instructions on the PVC glue container closely) you can now wipe the PVC down with a cleaning compound. Follow the instructions for your cleaning compound closely. You can now paint the system. Allow drying time for the paint. Do *not* try to mount the dock to the painted surface until the paint is completely dry (see Figure 2-52).

Figure 2-51. Snapped together unit for fitting. Notice the "burned" areas caused by the blowtorch

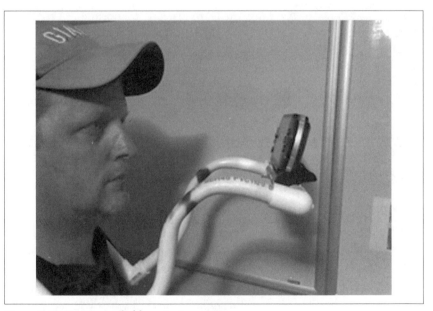

Figure 2-52. Testing out holder prior to painting

There are many ways you can mount the dock to the system. I chose to use a screw. You can also use Velcro from the base of the dock to the PVC, but I could not find a strong-enough Velcro that would hold the dock with the PSP in it properly and securely enough. After mounting the dock to the system, you now need to add a small piece of Velcro to the dock and the PSP. This is so the PSP does not drop out of the dock while you are moving.

Hacking the Hack

This simple, hands-free holder can be greatly expanded upon. You could, for one thing, route the headset wire **[Hack #14]** through the PVC. Or you could add on a battery holder within the PVC and modify the dock slightly. You could also add a beer holder and straw, or maybe even a snack holder.

—James McMurray

Turn Your PSP into a Radio Station
HACK #19   What happens when a PSP and Griffin's iTrip get together?

The iTrip is an FM transmitter designed for the iPod. It allows you to listen to your iPod via an FM radio (87.9 MHz to 107.9 MHz).

There is a good reason for using the iTrip instead of a normal FM transmitter that plugs into the headphone jack. A standard FM transmitter uses switches or a large LCD screen to change frequencies, whereas the iTrip uses digital tones played by the PSP's MP3 player to change the output frequencies. Therefore, with no switches or LCD screens, the circuit board is very small and doesn't get in your way.

To make this work, you're going to need to gut the iTrip (see Figure 2-53) and fuse it into your PSP. Removal of the iTrip's circuitry is simple: take an Xacto blade and separate the two plastic halves that sandwich the circuit board between them, as shown in Figure 2-54.

Making It Work

This hack involves disassembly of your Sony PSP **[Hack #8]**. Use your digital camera to take many photos throughout this process so that you can refer to them later.

After disassembling the PSP, put the iTrip transmitter between the outer case and audio/WiFi card (you'll recognize this card when you see that the headphone jack is fixed to it). This is an ideal place for it, because it is near the audio points that you have to solder wires to.

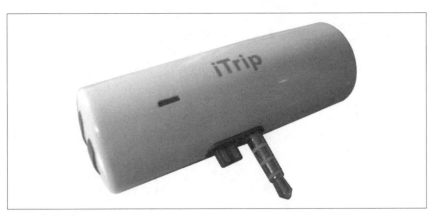

Figure 2-53. iTrip

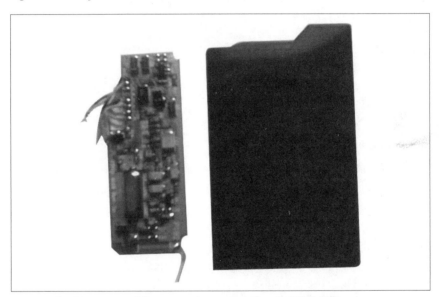

Figure 2-54. iTrip removed from its casing compared to the PSP's battery

The iTrip was never intended to be placed inside of a Japanese handheld gaming console, so you'll need to make some adjustments. With the iTrip in place, you'll see that the crystal oscillator (a subcomponent of the iTrip used to define the frequency range of the transmitter) will not fit. Using a hand-held rotary drill (a Dremel, for example), make an oscillator-shaped hole in the back side of the plastic casing—the oscillator will fit into the hole to allow clearance.

The iTrip has a basic wiring setup. All it needs is +3 volts DC, ground, and an audio signal to turn it on. All of these voltages and audio signals can be found inside the handheld (see Figure 2-55 for the pinout). The audio signal used for playing MP3s, games, and movies is the same one used for playing unique tones to select the iTrip's frequency. Because the iTrip has an audio sensing circuit to turn itself on (a battery-saving feature for the iPod), a dummy headphone plug that connects to nothing will turn on the transmitter when you need it. With no dummy headphone plug inserted, the PSP is in normal operation.

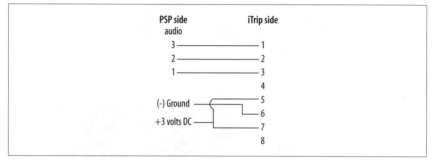

Figure 2-55. Pinout from PSP to iTrip

Finding Power

The PSP runs off of a 3.6-volt DC battery, which is perfect for powering the iTrip.

Figure 2-56 shows the locations of the voltage points on the main board.

Reassembling and Final Steps

Now it's time to put it all back together [Hack #9]. The only deviation from the "Reassemble Hack" is a grounding plate that's discarded to make a better fit. This should not affect the PSP in any way. The last thing to do is to load the audio files that will allow the iTrip to change frequencies. Insert your iTrip CD into your computer. Go to the \Setup\US folder (this will vary based on which country you live in; for example, it will be \Setup\ JP if you live in Japan) and copy these files to a folder in your music directory on the PSP. You could label it "Change Freqs" or whatever is convenient for you.

Using the PSP's Interface to Change Frequencies

This hack would not be interesting if it involved pressing buttons to change frequencies. You can now impress your friends by demonstrating that you can transmit your music on any FM channel you choose. Simply go to the

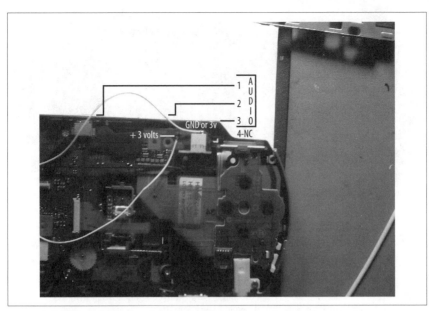

Figure 2-56. The left wire is +3 volts, and the right wire is ground

PSP's own user interface and select the audio player. Then go to the folder you labeled "Change Freqs." Scroll through the 100+ frequencies you have at your disposal, as shown in Figure 2-57, and select one. The unique digital tone will play for five seconds. After it has played that tone, pause the player, because the PSP's player thinks these files are songs and will go on to the next file. If you let it play without stopping, it will change your frequency from 99.5 MHz to 99.7 MHz, and so on. Once the frequency is set, go back to your game, movie, or MP3s, and enjoy listening to your PSP on your home theater or in the car on your way to work.

Hacking the Hack

In order to comply with the FCC's rules on interfering with other consumer electronics, the iTrip is set to transmit at a low level. You can de-solder the equipped antenna and solder in a small RF connector. A pigtail could connect the iTrip to an external antenna or RF amplifier for better range, as long as it stayed within the guidelines set out by the FCC. And, if not, you could always look into a Low Power FM (*http://www.fcc.gov/mb/audio/lpfm/*) license!

—*David Julian*

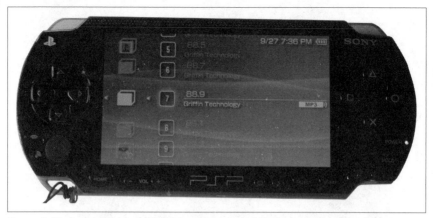

Figure 2-57. Audio files to change frequency accessed through PSP's music player

 ## HACK #20 Make a USB-Powered Charger

The PSP ships with the usual bulky charger, needing to be plugged into the walls to get its juice. With a simple mod, you can make your own USB charger and charge the PSP with your computer.

To build your USB charger, you'll need everything shown in Figure 2-58. In addition to your PSP, you'll need a USB/USB mini cable and a 5V charger (I used one from an old CD player). Wire cutters and electrical tape will also be a big help.

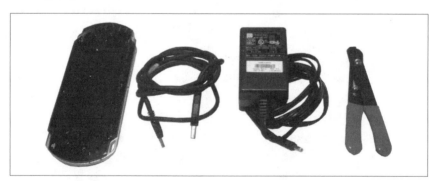

Figure 2-58. The ingredients for this hack

I usually keep a box full of old gear, power chargers, and especially USB cables; they always come in handy for projects like this.

To get started, chop the USB cable in half, spreading and stripping all the wires. You should have four wires: red, black, white, and green.

Some USB cables may have different colored wire, in which case, a little trial and error may be required. I use a voltmeter to determine which wires carry power and to determine their polarity (+ or –). This eliminates the other two wires (data, which we don't care about for this hack). Here's what your wires probably look like:

- USB Ground is the black wire.
- USB +5V power is the red wire.
- USB Data + is the green wire.
- USB Data – is the white wire.

Twist the white, green, and black wires together as shown in Figure 2-59.

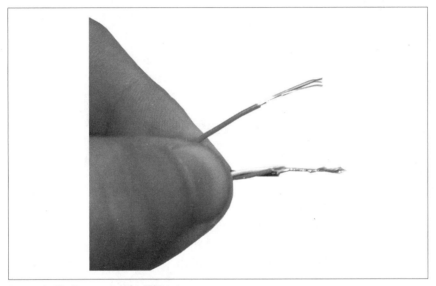

Figure 2-59. Connecting the USB wires

Make sure the power cable is unplugged, and chop the tip off the 5V power cable to expose the wires, as shown in Figure 2-60. The wire with the white writing or lettering usually is positive (+), but examine the power charger you are cannibalizing or use a continuity test to verify that the center of the charger is positive (there's a small diagram on the PSP itself showing the polarity of the power plug; check this to be sure you know where the positive should go).

Twist the red wire on the USB cable to the positive on the power cable, and the remaining bundle of wires to the ground, as shown in Figure 2-61.

Plug the USB cable into your computer, then test the voltage with a voltmeter on the exposed wires, as shown in Figure 2-62.

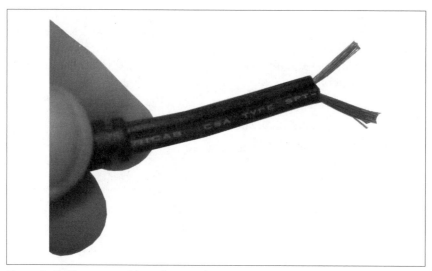

Figure 2-60. The power cable with exposed wires

Figure 2-61. Connecting the USB and power cables

Make sure you're only getting 5V or a little less, but never more. If you're not, double-check the wiring. You can pick up a voltmeter at just about any RadioShack or electronics store, or even on eBay for under $20 USD or so.

Use electrical tape to protect the wiring [Hack #15], wrapping the tape around the positive and negative wires separately or soldering the wires together.

That's it—throw this cable in your bag and you'll never need to look for an outlet again, as long as you have a USB port handy!

Hacking the Hack

Wouldn't you rather have a single cable that functions as both a data cable and a USB power cable?

Get a USB to USB mini cable that you'd normally use for data transfer and chop it in half. One is included with the PSP, or you can usually find one for a couple bucks.

Strip the wires on both sides of the chop, as shown in Figure 2-63.

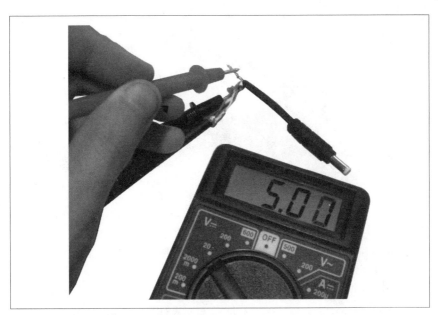

Figure 2-62. Testing the output

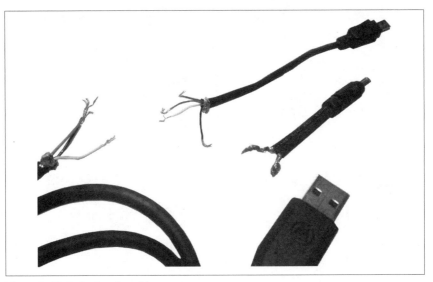

Figure 2-63. Stripping the cables

Wire them together, as shown in Figure 2-64. Use the 5V tip from the USB power cable hack and wire the positive red (+) to the red wires of the USB data cable. Wire the black (–) to the black wires on the USB cable.

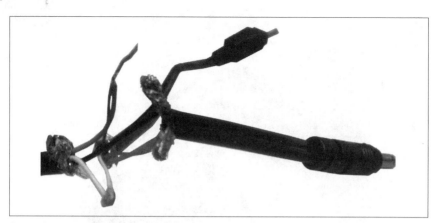

Figure 2-64. Connecting data to data and power to power

Plug the cable into a computer and test the voltage; it's important that the polarity be correct. If in doubt, compare to the diagram on the PSP's power plug to determine where positive and negative should be delivered.

That's it! You now have a dual cable! You can either solder it up or make a small enclosure to house it all.

—Phillip Torrone

## CHAPTER THREE

Multimedia
Hacks 21–35

All the power that goes into making stunning games is there for other purposes, too. Whether you're watching movies, showing off your photos, or listening to music, you'll find that the PSP's graphical and audio capabilities are taken full advantage of by games and multimedia alike. And if you've upgraded to the Version 2.0 firmware, you'll have the pleasure of using a powerful web browser whose graphics are every bit as stunning as the rest of the system's.

HACK #21   Watch UMD Movies

Cut down on the glare without ruining the sharpness of the screen, navigate through your movie with ease, and keep track of where you were in *Spider-Man 2* before you took that break to play *Metal Gear Ac!d*.

Watching UMD movies on your PSP is very similar to watching DVDs on your home system in a lot of ways. However, there are drastic differences that make the experience a little more akin to watching a DVD on your laptop. Even this comparison falls short because you can take the PSP with you anywhere. Portability makes the pauseability of the PSP as a movie-watching medium more important than in other movie-viewing situations. Just as in "Quit a Game Quickly" [Hack #1], Sony did a good job of accounting for the on-the-go nature of PSP movie watching. You can simply put the PSP to sleep at any moment, and continue watching later with a few clicks of the X button.

This hack will cover the basics and some tips and tricks for making the most out of viewing UMD Movies.

Setting up and Starting the Movie

When you first insert a UMD Movie into the PSP, you simply have to navigate to Video → UMD in the PSP's main interface. Keep the UMD icon selected for a moment, and the background of the PSP will change into a graphic for the movie, and a small preview window featuring a repeated video clip from the movie, most likely with some accompanying music, will replace the generic UMD icon. See Figure 3-1.

Figure 3-1. When you select the UMD icon for Hero, the background on the PSP changes and a small video clip begins to loop

Hitting the Start button or the X button on the PSP will take you to the menu screen for the movie, or it will immediately begin playing the movie. If after listening to some MP3s on your PSP or playing a game, you go back to a UMD movie, it will usually return you to the place where you left off.

This isn't always the case. For the most part, the PSP is effective at keeping track of where you were in a UMD movie the next time you go to watch it, but not always.

Because of this, it is a good idea to make a note of where you are in a movie before switching away to another activity on the PSP.

If you've been watching a movie, but you've not really been able to give it the attention it deserves, there's a quick trick here to start over from the beginning. Hitting the Triangle button on the PSP will bring up a small informational menu on the right-hand side of the screen with "Play," "Play from Beginning," and "Information" as options (see Figure 3-2). Choose

"Play" if you want to try to skip past the UMD disks menu and immediately begin playing the movie from the last point you left off (assuming you haven't removed the UMD disk), choose "Play from Beginning" to start over from the beginning of the film, and choose "Information" to see any metadata connected to the movie, including the parental settings.

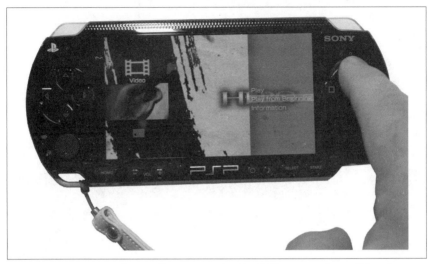

Figure 3-2. Select Triangle to pull up a menu for the UMD movie. Choose "Play from Beginning" to start the movie over

Navigating the Movie

The title screen for the UMD contains many of the usual options that you are most likely familiar with from watching DVDs. Through this interface, you can set up the audio options and subtitles, view any included bonus materials (like trailers, cut scenes, and sometimes even little behind-the-scenes documentaries), make scene or chapter selections to start watching a movie from a specific scene, or simply play the movie.

By default, the title screen is usually where you are taken on a UMD movie the first time it is inserted into your PSP. If, while watching the film, you would like to return to the title screen, hit the Square button on the PSP.

> If you hit the Square button by accident while watching a film, select Play Movie and hit X to return to the same spot you were before mistakenly hitting the Square button.
>
> Sony did a good job of designing a portable interface that lets you quickly get out of a game or movie, but which is also very forgiving should you accidentally hit the wrong button.

One of the cool things about the PSP is that nearly all of these options are available from anywhere within the movie without returning to the title screen. If you hit the Triangle button while a movie is playing, a control panel in the form of an overlay graphic with a variety of options will pop up onscreen (see Figure 3-3). In this figure, I used the keypad to highlight the ? (or Help) option and am about to hit X to bring up the Help menu.

Figure 3-3. Hitting Triangle while a movie is playing brings up an in-movie control panel

The movie will continue playing in the background (unless you paused it before pulling up this menu). Use the keypad to navigate through the different menu options available. I'll go over some of these in a moment, but first I want to take a look at the Help menu. Highlight the ? icon and hit the X button. The movie will pause, and a quick guide to the PSP's basic movie navigation functions will be displayed (see Figure 3-4).

The Video Help screen displays all the basic navigational features for viewing a UMD movie on the PSP. Take some time to familiarize yourself with these basics. To return to the movie, hit O.

The only information about these basic controls that isn't covered by this screen involves the Fastforward and Fast Reverse controls. If you pause the movie by hitting the Start button and then hit the Forward button on the keypad once, the movie will play in slow motion frame by frame. If you hit Forward/Reverse on the keypad during regular play, the movie will begin fastforwarding/rewinding with a 1 next to the arrows. If you tap the button again, the speed will increase and a 2 will be displayed. A third tap will display a 3 and the movie will fastforward/rewind at its quickest viewable speed.

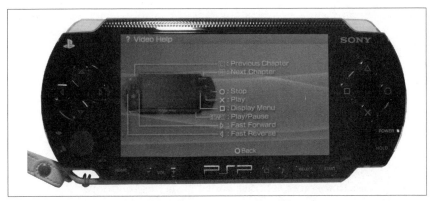

Figure 3-4. The Video Help screen displays all the basic navigational features for watching a UMD movie

To jump forward or back to another section of the movie, simply use the L and R triggers on the PSP.

Let me repeat that: the L and R triggers take you back a chapter and forward a chapter in the movie, respectively.

This is quite possibly the most annoying part of watching a UMD movie on the PSP, because you *will* accidentally hit these buttons and skip ahead or back in the movie from time to time.

Since you know this, consider holding the PSP differently while watching a movie than you normally would hold it while playing games. Also, be hyper-aware of these buttons whenever you are moving around. I've become pretty good at avoiding them, but every once in a while, I'll be shifting in my chair or in bed and *click!* I'm suddenly out of the dramatic love scene and into an intense battle sequence.

Use the Control Panel

While you are watching a movie, hit the Triangle button to display the control panel. This control panel gives you immediate control over the movie you are watching without jumping back to the UMD's Menu. The control panel also allows you to change certain settings, such as UMD Video Volume that normally would only be accessible via the PSP's main control panel under Settings. Perhaps the best thing about the control panel is that it gives you access to extra features of your UMD movie that the movie's main menu doesn't provide.

I'm not going to go into every single feature of this control panel, as that would become tedious and is already covered in the manual to the PSP.

However, I am going to cover a few bits of control panel goodness that I think can help you optimize your UMD movie-watching experience.

Use subtitles. If you are on a PSP running Version 1.0–1.52 of the firmware, the fourth icon in the top row of the control panel controls your subtitles; if you are on a PSP running Version 2.0 of the firmware, the fifth icon in the top row of the control panel controls your subtitles. Highlighting it and hitting X will switch the subtitles. Continuing to hit X will cycle you through all the available subtitles, as well as the Off setting.

What I've discovered in a few of the UMD movie titles that I own is that there are sometimes more subtitles available via this control panel pane than are offered through the main menu to the movie.

For example, the *House of Flying Daggers* UMD disk features two English subtitle tracks, although only one is readily available from the Menu screen (the Menu screen also fails to provide access to the French subtitle track, which is also available via this control panel). The first English subtitle track is a basic track that provides you with a translation of the entire movie. The second English track, however, only provides subtitles for the songs in the movie, which remain untranslated when listening to the English audio track of the movie.

Since your PSP provides portable movie watching, you are often going to find yourself watching a movie in areas with different levels of noise.

I often keep the English subtitle track of any movie I am watching going, just in case the dialogue gets drowned out by the sound of the subway as a new train arrives or for watching in situations where I don't want to wear my headphones but can't hear everything clearly.

Knowing how to quickly access the subtitles is useful if you can't quite make out a bit of whispered dialogue. Simply rewind the movie a little bit by hitting the left arrow on the keypad, pause the movie by hitting the Start button, then pull up the control panel by hitting Triangle, navigate over to subtitles, hit X until you hit the track you need, and hit Start to resume play of the movie. Now you can quickly read the snippet of dialogue you missed, and then switch the subtitles back off and get rid of the control panel to continue viewing.

Frame Advance. In addition to the same controls that are available via the PSP's default controls, the control panel features a few more controls, including Frame Advance. This is the sixth icon in the second row and it simply does what it says, advancing frame by frame through the movie each time you hit X while it is highlighted.

A-B Repeat, Repeat, and Clear. The third row of icons in the control panel features the A-B Repeat (Version 2.0 firmware only), Repeat, and Clear controls. With A-B Repeat, you can mark the movie at point A and then again at point B, and the section between these two points will continually repeat until you either hit A-B Repeat again or hit Clear. With Repeat, you can select to repeat the entire movie or the current chapter. Clear simply clears whatever repeat setting you have selected and sets it back to normal play.

Display. The next to the last icon on the top row, immediately next to the Help panel, is the Display control panel. Highlighting this control panel and hitting X will bring up the name of the movie you are currently watching in the top-left corner of the screen and a thin blue and white strip at the bottom-right corner of the screen that indicates your progression through the movie and the time remaining (see Figure 3-5).

Figure 3-5. The Display control panel places the name of the movie in a bar across the top and a progress bar along the bottom

Most notably, the Display option is useful if you want to keep track of your progress through a movie and how much of a movie remains. Once you activate it, you can leave it running after closing out the control panel. This is very nonintrusive in movies that are letterboxed and leave black bars on the top and bottom of the screen, but if you are watching a movie that takes full advantage of the PSP's screen, you may find the Display distracting or even annoying.

Nevertheless, since the PSP doesn't always remember where you last were in a movie (it usually does, but sometimes it doesn't), I recommend activating this feature whenever you know you are going to stop watching a movie for a while, or if you intend to switch out the UMD disk for a while. If you can remember that the blue progress bar was up to about the middle of the S in the PSP logo, it'll be easier to find where you left off when you come back to it later. Consider jotting this information down on a piece of paper you keep with your PSP.

> This information is even more useful with Version 2.0 of the firmware, which includes chapter and timestamp displays for the UMD that are much easier to mark down.
>
> Firmware 2.0 also adds the Go To command (the second item on the top row of the control panel), whereby you can select the exact chapter or timestamp location where you want to go.

Cutting Down on the Glare

The PlayStation Portable comes with a gorgeous screen, capable of displaying wonderful graphics while playing video games or DVD-quality video while watching a UMD movie. Unfortunately, this beautiful, shiny screen can also be the PSP's Achilles' heel in certain lighting situations, as it is highly reflective.

> One good thing about the highly reflective nature of the PSP's screen is that it can be used as a makeshift mirror whenever the console is switched off.

Here's a short list of things you can do to help keep the reflective glare from being too much of a distraction while watching your UMD movies:

- Hold the PSP at a slight angle, directed at something uniformly colored, such as the ceiling. If you are staring straight into your PSP's screen, you're going to see a reflection of your ugly mug every time a light hits your face or the movie features a particularly dark scene.

- Keep the back of the PSP to the light. The less light hitting the PSP's screen, the less of a reflection that you'll see. However, keep the previous suggestion in mind: if you are facing the blaring sun and looking straight on at the PSP, that light is going to ricochet off of your face and onto its screen.

- Try to watch movies in uniformly lit situations. If everything is lit equally in a room, there will be less distracting reflections on the PSP screen, should they occur. A bright lamp reflecting in a dark room can seriously impede your movie-watching fun.

- Try to watch in the dark. There's a reason that movie theaters turn out all the lights before a movie.

- Use the PSP's brightness control. There's a button with a slightly square icon immediately to the right of the PSP icon sitting under your gorgeous PSP screen. Hitting it a few times cycles through the different brightness settings for the screen. Switch as the occasion warrants.

This short list of five tips will get you started. For more advanced ways of avoiding the glare, you'll want to keep your PSP clean [Hack #7].

Hacking the Hack

This hack discussed the basics of viewing UMD movies on the PSP. If you want to really trick out your movie-watching experience on the PSP, however, you're going to want to check out some of the more advanced hacks in this book, such as "Make an Articulating PSP Stand" [Hack #14] and "PSP Hands Free" [Hack #18].

Get Video on Your PSP

HACK #22

Got video? Here's a variety of different ways you can squeeze that video onto your Memory Stick Duo card.

Besides being able to watch UMD Video disks on your PSP [Hack #21], you can also store MPEG4 video files on your Memory Stick Duo card for watching movies on the go. This feature of the device is one of the things that has had many people online referring to the PSP as "the Video iPod" (before Apple released their video-capable iPod). With a little effort and a big enough memory stick, you can cram all the video you like on your PSP. I'm going to walk you through a variety of different ways you can go about enjoying video on the go on your PSP.

Get a Bigger Memory Stick

Unfortunately, Sony only includes a 32MB Memory Stick Duo card with the PSP. This is fine for saving games, keeping a few pictures, and even storing a few MP3s. If you try to put your own video content on your PSP, however, you'll quickly find that 32MB is simply not enough.

I recommend that you get the largest Memory Stick that you can afford and that you settle for nothing smaller than 256MB. You can get Memory Stick Duo cards in sizes as large as 2GB, but those are still a bit pricey. Fortunately, since the introduction of the 2GB Memory Stick Duo cards, the 1GB cards have fallen drastically in price. You can easily find one available online in the $125–150 USD range, but if you are patient and watch sites like Deal-News (*http://www.dealnews.com*), you can probably snag one for under $100 USD. If you sign up for a free account with DealNews, you can create an alert for Memory Stick Duo cards, and they will email you whenever any new deals are listed. Recently, I've seen a 1GB Memory Stick Duo card for as low as $76 USD.

Once you have a larger Memory Stick with some room to spare, it's time to find out how and where to put your videos on the stick.

The Basics

In order to view video using your PSP's Memory Stick Duo card, you will need to set a few things up first. Either connect your PSP to your computer or mount your Memory Stick Duo card on your computer **[Hack #2]**. Once the Memory Stick shows up on your computer, you will need to create a new folder in the root directory of the Memory Stick, called MP_ROOT. Inside the MP_ROOT folder, you will then need to create another folder and name it either 101MNV01 or 100MNV01. The manual that came with your PSP tells you to name the folder 100MNV01, but if you use iPSP or PSPware to automatically manage your videos, they will create a folder named 101MNV01. Both folders seem to work for watching video. Whichever name you go with, this folder is where all of your MPEG4 videos must go.

The PSP cannot play MPEG4 video encoded at anything higher than 768kbps, so certain high-quality MPEG4 files will need to be converted to a lower bit rate, and the PSP will not recognize the file unless it has a name in the format of *M4V10001.MP4*. The file needs to start with M4V followed by five numbers, and then it must end in *.MP4*.

> For MPEG4 files that have been specially formatted for the PSP, there will usually be another file alongside it. If your movie file's name is *M4V10001.MP4*, this file will be named *M4V10001.THM*. The THM file is a simple 160×120 thumbnail saved in JPEG format at 72dpi that is associated with the video file. As long as the name of the THM file is the same as the MP4 file, this picture will be displayed along-side the video file in the PSP's Video interface.

Once you have the proper directories set up on your PSP's Memory Stick, drop some videos into either */MP_ROOT/100MNV01/* or */MP_ROOT/ 101MNV01/*, disconnect from your computer, and navigate to Video on your PSP, select Memory Stick, hit the X button, select the video you want to watch, and hit the X button again. Sit back and enjoy. If you don't have any video yet, then read on to find some free content online and to learn how to convert your own videos to PSP-friendly MPEG4s.

> Version 2.0 of the firmware added support for another video file format: AVC. These files follow a similar naming convention to the regular *.MP4* files, as they are named *MAQxxxxx. MP4*, where xxxxx is five numbers. AVC edges out MP4 in the image quality department.

Videos Online

Fortunately, a wide variety of videos are already available online, and some of them are even preformatted for the PSP. This is just a short list of places you should consider looking for free content for your PSP. Don't be afraid to jump on your favorite search engine and find some others. Some popular search engines have specialized video searches, such as *http://video.search. yahoo.com/* and *http://video.google.com/*.

> If you are running Version 2.0 of the firmware, then you can use the PSP's browser to navigate to video files, and if they are hosted online without any compression (.ZIP, for example), you can download the video directly to your */MP_ ROOT/100MNV01/* or */MP_ROOT/101MNV01/* folder. To do this, select the link to the file, then hit the Triangle button, navigate to the File menu, hit the X button, select Save Link Target, and hit the X button again. Make sure you save the file in the correct video folder. After it finishes downloading, you can immediately navigate to the video and watch it on your PSP.

PSP Connect. The first place that you'll want to look for free video content is Sony's PSP Connect page (*http://psp.connect.com/*). This site features a video tutorial that autoloads when you visit; this video covers the basics of getting video onto your PSP. Since you already know these basics, just click the Stop Video link underneath the virtual PSP and scroll down to the next section on the web page. If you like the tutorial video and want to share it with friends, there is a PDF version of the tutorial available (*http://psp.connect.com/ tutorial/tutorial.pdf*).

Here you will find an assortment of videos that have been prepared for the PSP by Sony. To the right of each video, there is a small graphic indicating the space that the video will take up on your Memory Stick, as well as what size Memory Stick is needed for each video. If you just opened up your brand new PlayStation Portable or simply haven't yet had the chance to grab a larger Memory Stick, you'll be pleased to find that a few of the provided sample videos are geared to fit on the included measly 32MB card. Download a few, drop them on your Memory Stick, and watch away. Here are some other sources of video for your PSP:

Atom Films

For a little more than a month's time after the North American release of the PSP, Atom Films (*http://www.atomfilms.com*) offered three of their short films preformatted for the PSP. Unfortunately, this trend was short-lived, and neither the films nor new ones like them are available from the site. Nevertheless, they could change their minds, so keep checking back. Even if they don't offer any content specifically geared for the PSP, there are several videos available in downloadable formats on their site, so it is a good place to check for files that you may want to download and convert into PSP-compatible MPEG4 files.

Creative Commons Video

The Creative Commons Video page (*http://creativecommons.org/video/*) is a good place where you can both share your videos freely with the world and find videos online that others have decided to share.

Internet Archive: Moving Image Archive

If you're not familiar with the Internet Archive, you should take a careful look at the entire site, but, for our purposes, make sure that you look at the Moving Image Archive (*http://www.archive.org/details/movies*). Here you will find a wide array of video content that is either in the public domain or released under a Creative Commons, License (*http://creativecommons.org/*) and that you may freely download. There's even a section of freely available feature films (*http://www.archive.org/details/feature_films*). Nearly all of the videos offered through the Internet Archive come encoded in both 64Kb and 256Kb MPEG4 variants. Unfortunately, although these files are MPEG4, they were encoded with 3ivx (*http://www.3ivx.com/*) at a setting that isn't readable by the PSP, so you'll still have to convert the files you find on this site.

PSP Hacking 101

PSP Hacking 101 (*http://www.psphacking101.com/*) is indicative of the kind of cool free content that the PSP is inspiring across the Internet. This site features a downloadable, preformatted-for-the-PSP *videocast* (think podcast [Hack #32] and add video) that covers the basics of what's going on in the PSP homebrew scene [Hack #40]. As of this writing, they've released four videocasts, so make sure you check them out.

Rocketboom

Rocketboom (*http://www.rocketboom.com/vlog/*) with Amanda Congdon is one of the most widely known videoblogs (a weblog that consists of videocasts) on the Internet. There's a short, three-minute show released daily during the week, featuring a mix of parodies, interviews, and oddly mixed video fun, alongside snarky op-ed glances at current events. Even cooler, they now offer PSP-formatted ports of each show (*http://www.rocketboom.com/port/*). You can get the regular video of their shows delivered automatically via your RSS feed reader or via iTunes as a video podcast **[Hack #32]**, but unfortunately, the ease of automatic download is only available for the QuickTime Movie file version of their show; if you choose to download the show this way, you're still going to need to convert it to MPEG4.

BitTorrent

BitTorrent (*http://www.bittorrent.com/*) has clients for Windows, Mac OS X, and Linux. If you're not familiar with BitTorrent, it's a peer-to-peer file-sharing technology that distributes the load of downloading large files between all the people currently downloading the file. You can find a plethora of video content online via BitTorrent through various tracker sites. Few of these files will be preformatted for the PSP, but conversion, as you will see in the next section, is easy enough.

iPSP Movie Loader

iPSP Movie Loader (*http://ipsp.kaisakura.com/ipspmovie.php*) is a cool little free program that promises to allow you to download PSP compatible movie files directly to your PSP. Unfortunately, not many content providers have jumped onboard with this program. As of the writing of this hack, the only content provider linked to on the iPSP Movie Loader site is 29HD Networks (*http://www.29hdnetwork.com/psp_guide.html*).

Convert Video to PSP-Compatible MPEG4

Fortunately, there is a variety of tools available for converting your video files to PSP-compatible MPEG4. This section will cover the main players.

Keep in mind that depending upon the encoding options used on the original file, some files will not want to convert nicely into MPEG4 or AVC. If you run into any files like this, try first converting the files into some other format, like AVI or MOV, and then reconverting into MPEG4.

iPSP and PSPWare. Both PSPWare (*http://www.nullriver.com/index/products/pspware*; $15 USD) and iPSP (*http://ipsp.kaisakura.com/*; $19.99 USD) are available for both Mac OS X and Windows, and both programs do a very good job of automating the process of converting your movie files into a properly formatted MPEG4 format for your PSP and automatically transferring these files to your PSP. Both of these products offer a variety of options for encoding your video, so you can choose to either have a higher-quality video taking up a large footprint on your Memory Stick or to squeeze numerous lower-quality videos onto your Memory Stick. Figure 3-6 shows iPSP converting a video downloaded from the Creative Commons web site.

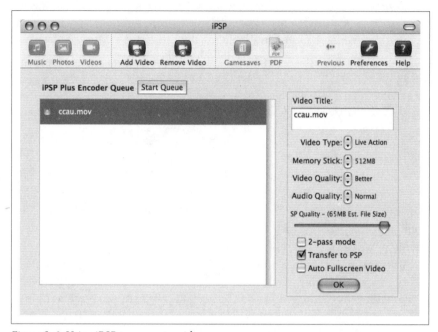

Figure 3-6. Using iPSP to convert a video

PSP Video 9. PSP Video 9 (*http://www.pspvideo9.com/*) is a free, Windows-only program for converting videos into MPEG4 files properly formatted for the PSP. PSP Video 9 can also be used to automatically transfer converted videos from your PC to your PSP, and can be used in conjunction with Videora (*http://www.videora.com/*) to automatically download, convert, and transfer videoblogs (such as Rocketboom) to your PSP.

ffmpeg. The magic key to all the video compression at work in iPSP, PSP-Ware, and PSP Video 9 is actually a little bit of open source goodness that is developed under Linux, but which can be downloaded and compiled for either Windows or Macintosh: *ffmpeg* (*http://ffmpeg.sourceforge.net/index. php*). There are a variety of options you can set for encoding files with ffmpeg, but the basic procedure for converting your videos to PSP-compatible MPEG4 files via ffmpeg is:

```
ffmpeg -i example.mov -b 300 -s 320x240 -vcodec xvid \
  -ab 32 -ar 24000 -acodec aac example.MP4
```

The file following -i is the source file, so replace *example.mov* with the location and name of the file you are converting. -b 300 sets the bit rate to 300kbps. You can make this number higher if you want higher-quality video, but keep in mind that the higher quality the encoding, the larger the file size, and if you go over 768kbps, the file won't play on your PSP. -s 320x240 sets the pixel size for the video, and -vcodec xvid forces the codec to be used to xvid.

The next set of instructions contains the audio settings for the encoded file. -ab 32 sets the audio bit rate to 32kbps, and -ar 24000 sets the frequency to 24000 Hz, while -acodec aac sets the codec to be used to aac. Finally, you need to specify the path to the new file (*example.MP4*).

If you're on Mac OS X and you don't like the idea of compiling ffmpeg, you can always use ffmpegX (*http://homepage.mac.com/major4/*; Shareware $15 USD), which provides a GUI front end for ffmpeg and automates all these settings for you. Its most recent version, shown in Figure 3-7, even includes a PSP MPEG4 preset to make things easier.

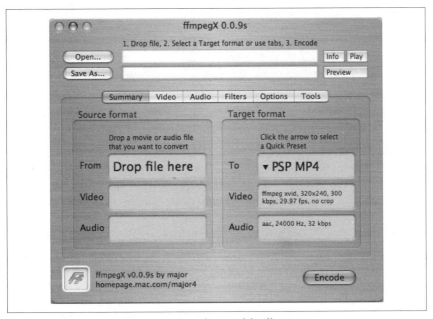

Figure 3-7. ffmpegX, the Mac OS X GUI front end for ffmpeg

Kinoma Producer. If you're looking to batch convert a large number of video files from a variety of formats, then Kinoma Producer (*http://www.kinoma.com/products.html?producer*; $29.99 USD) might be the PSP video-encoding solution for you. Kinoma Producer can convert dozens of files simultaneously and is available in both Windows and Mac OS X flavors. Figure 3-8 shows Kinoma Producer converting a Creative Commons video into MPEG4.

Figure 3-8. Kinoma Producer

Hacking the Hack

You can encode any video you've filmed yourself or downloaded off the Internet, but one of the things that really adds value to your portable PSP viewing is the ability to time-shift your favorite TV shows onto it for portable viewing.

If you have a newer model TiVo with TiVo-to-go or any ReplayTV with an Ethernet port, you can easily transfer video from your digital video recorder to your computer over a local network connection.

With a lot of time and a modicum of effort, you can copy the contents of your DVDs to your computer and recompress your favorite videos into MPEG4 for watching on your PSP.

Of course, for each DVD you want to convert to MPEG4, you can expect to spend a good 5–12 hours of intensive processing time on your computer (depending upon your processor's speed). If you have the patience and the time to spare, then go for it. If not, consider going out to your local media outlet and buying the movie on UMD **[Hack #21]** to help support the growth of the PSP platform.

> Most DVDs use DeCSS encryption as a form of Digital Rights Management (DRM) to prevent widespread piracy. The problem with this solution is that besides not really being an effective means of preventing piracy, the DRM also gets in the way of law-abiding consumers like you and me, who only wish to exercise our fair use rights with a product we've purchased and own. This is a particularly nasty catch-22, and I recommend that you get involved with trying to undo this bad law. See the web site for the Electronic Frontier Foundation (*http://www.eff.org/*) for more information about DRM, and current and proposed laws that essentially (or potentially) infringe on your rights. Examples of potential threats include the "broadcast flag," which involves use of encoded signals in the content that trigger anti-copying features inside your very own home devices. Although an FCC rule requiring manufacturers to implement broadcast flag technology was overturned in court, its supporters are committed to resurrecting it. See Wikipedia for more information: *http://en.wikipedia.org/wiki/Broadcast_flag*.

H A C K #23 Get Music on Your PSP

Don't have an iPod? Get yourself a decent-sized Memory Stick, and you're set to listen to your favorite music on your PSP.

Did you spend all the money that you would have used on a new iPod or MP3 player on your PSP and various games for it? No reason to fret. Your PSP can double as a music player. This hack will show you how to streamline the process of getting tunes on and off of your PSP.

The Basics

While you can cram a few MP3s on the 32MB Memory Stick Duo card that came with the PSP, you are going to need to invest in a larger Memory Stick to really get the most out of the PSP as an MP3 player. I recommend keeping an eye on Memory Stick pricing at DealNews (*http://www.dealnews.com*) or their sister site DealRam (*http://www.dealram.com*), since they regularly have links to 1GB sticks for less than $100 USD.

Once you have the extra space, you need to know where to put your tunes. If you mount your PSP on your computer (attach the PSP via a USB cable, navigate to Settings → USB Mode, then hit the X button) you can simply copy the songs from wherever they reside on your computer to the *MUSIC* folder inside the *PSP* folder at the root level of the Memory Stick.

If you have a PSP with Version 1.0–1.52 of the firmware, then your PSP will recognize any MP3s placed within this folder. If you have a PSP with Version 2.0 of the firmware, your PSP will recognize any MP3s, songs in Sony's ATRAC3plus file format (although these files need to be in */OMGAUDIO/*), and even files you have encoded with Apple's AAC format (although DRM-protected tracks purchased from the iTunes Music Store will not play on your PSP, and you will need to change the file extension of the AAC files you have encoded to *.MP4* for the PSP to recognize these files).

> Are you looking for a quick way to convert your iTMS-purchased songs to DRM-free AAC tracks? Simply burn the tracks to audio CD and then rip them back to your computer, making sure that you have AAC selected under the encoding section of the Advanced menu in iTunes.

If you want, you can use this method to manually manage the songs on your PSP: mount your PSP, copy the songs over to the MUSIC folder inside the PSP folder, dismount your PSP and navigate to Music → Memory Stick, hit the X button, then select the song you want to hear and again hit the X button. There are, fortunately, easier ways to do this, described next.

Automate the Process

Both PSPWare (*http://www.nullriver.com/index/products/pspware*; $15 USD) and iPSP (*http://ipsp.kaisakura.com/*; $19.99 USD)—two of the more popular media managers for the PSP—offer automatic syncing of music to the PSP, using a playlist of your choosing from your iTunes Music Library. This is great if you use iTunes, but if you prefer to use different music managing software on your computer, these two solutions may not be ideal.

> Again, keep in mind: these tools will only be able to manage iTunes playlists containing MP3s or AAC files that are DRM-free and have had their file extensions changed to *.MP4*.

Firmware Version 2.0

If you are running a PSP with Version 2.0 of the firmware, then you can download music from the Internet directly to your PSP's Memory Stick. This is particularly useful for grabbing new music and podcasts **[Hack #32]** from various web sites while you're on the go and connected to a wireless network.

To do this, simply launch the web browser by navigating to Network →
Browser on your PSP, and hit the X button. After your browser launches,
navigate to a page that contains links to audio files in a PSP-compatible format. Unfortunately, the PSP cannot handle compressed files, BitTorrent, or
WMA (Microsoft with DRM format)—unless you are running Version 2.6
firmware or later—so the files will need to be in uncompressed and unprotected MP3 or AAC format. When you click on the link to the corresponding audio file, an overlay screen will pop up asking whether you want to
download the linked file. Hit the X button, as shown in Figure 3-9.

*Figure 3-9. After selecting a link to a song file and hitting the X button, a confirmation
screen will appear*

If, for some reason, the PSP doesn't recognize the file type
and tries to open the file as a web site, cancel the loading of
the page (hit the Triangle button and then select Cancel) and
then go back to the original page (by hitting the L trigger).
This time, place your cursor over the linked file, but instead
of hitting the X button, hit the Triangle button and navigate
to File, then hit the X button. A menu will pop up, as in
Figure 3-10. Select Save Link Target from this menu and hit
the X button.

Another overlay will appear asking for confirmation of the location where
you'd like to save the file and the name you would like to give the file (see
Figure 3-11). If the location did not default to */PSP/MUSIC/*, select that field,
and hit the X button to select this folder (or a subfolder inside the MUSIC

Figure 3-10. Select Save Link Target to download the file

folder). Feel free to change the name of the file to something you will recognize. Just remember to keep the proper extension at the end of the file. If the file you are downloading is an AAC file, go ahead and change the extension on the file to *.MP4* so that your PSP will recognize it.

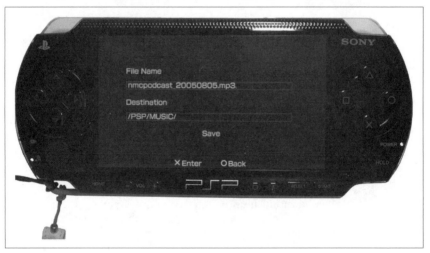

Figure 3-11. After confirming the download, the PSP prompts you for the file name and destination for the file

After downloading the files, hit the Home button on your PSP to exit out of the browser. If you hit the button by mistake, you can either hit it again or hit the X button to return to the browser. Navigate to Music, select Memory

Stick, and hit the X button. You should see your freshly downloaded audio files in the list of available tracks.

This method of grabbing songs can be particularly useful for serving up songs from your networked music collection on your home network. All you need to do is set up a networked folder containing any music files you would like to have ready for your PSP, then direct your PSP's web browser to this folder. For example, if your computer has an IP address of 192.168.1.4 on your local network, and you have a folder called PSPMUSIC that you have set up to be available to other computers on your network, you can launch the PSP's web browser and navigate to *http://192.168.1.4/PSPMUSIC/ nameofthesongyouwant.mp3* to download that song file. Consider building a music index page that links to all these files.

If you've installed Version 2.6 of the firmware, you now have an option called RSS Channel under Network. Now any RSS 2.0 feed containing embedded MP3s can be subscribed to through the PSP's browser, and all the songs on that feed can be streamed to your PSP over a live Internet connection through the RSS browser interface.

PSP as MP3 Player

Once you have your music on your PSP, it's time to listen. Here's a quick overview of the PSP's controls and functionality as an MP3 player.

To keep your music organized into albums, all you need to do is keep a group of audio files in a single folder by the name of the album placed within */PSP/MUSIC/* on your Memory Stick. The preview image associated with the Album folder will be taken from the image associated with the first file in the list of tracks contained within the folder (see Figure 3-12).

Unfortunately, the PSP can only see folders one level deep here, so you cannot do things like create a folder called *The Beatles*, which you then fill with separate folders for each of The Beatles' albums. So, if you want to categorize by artist, make sure you keep all the song files within that main artist folder, rather than embedding folders within folders.

Navigate to Music → Memory Stick and hit the X button to see a list of all the songs and albums located inside your */PSP/MUSIC/* folder. The folders will be listed alphabetically, followed by an alphabetical listing of any lone files in this root Music folder. Select the album you want to listen to and hit the X button.

Figure 3-12. Selecting an album

A list of songs will appear, as shown in Figure 3-13. As you scroll through the different songs, you will notice that certain bits of metadata associated with the song files will be displayed, including the name of the song, the artist, and any album artwork associated with the song file. As with all the other files on your PSP, if you select one of the tracks and hit the Triangle button, a menu will appear on the right side of the screen with options for Play, Delete, or Information. If you select Information and hit the X button, the full list of all metadata associated with the track will be displayed, including the title, artist, album, genre, size, date and time it was updated, Length, Sampling Frequency, and Codec at which the track was compressed.

Otherwise, simply hit the X button to play the song.

Once the song is playing, you have a variety of options. If you hit the Triangle button while the song is playing, the control panel will open, displaying all the available controls (see Figure 3-14).

> The control panel in Figure 3-14 is from Version 2.0 of the firmware. If you are running a previous version of the firmware, some of the controls discussed in this section will not be available to you, although many of them will be identical.

The controls available in the control panel of Version 2.0 of the firmware are Previous Group, Next Group, Previous Track, Next Track, Fast Reverse, Fast Forward, Play, Pause, Stop, Group Mode, A-B Repeat, Play Mode, Clear, Display, and Help. Selecting the Display option adds an overlay along

Figure 3-13. Selecting a song

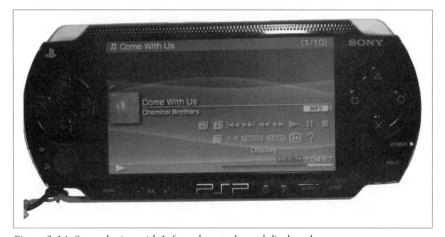

Figure 3-14. Song playing with Info and control panel displayed

the top of the screen with the name of the track in the upper-left corner and the number of the track next to how many tracks are in this group in the upper-right corner of the screen. Selecting the Help option (the question mark) will display the basic Music Help screen in Figure 3-15. This screen shows you all the basic controls on the PSP for navigating through your songs. The L trigger goes to the previous track or the beginning of the current track, the R trigger goes to the next track, the O button stops play, the X button plays, the Start button either plays or pauses the track, and the left and right buttons on the directional keypad rewind or fast forward the track.

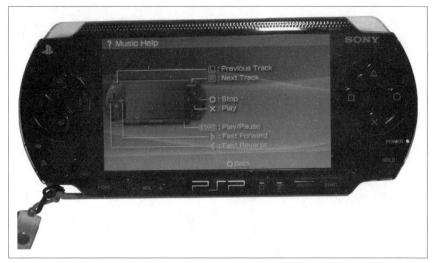

Figure 3-15. Music Help screen

The Group controls all have to do with different albums or folders you have placed inside /PSP/MUSIC/. A-B Mode lets you select first an A point in a track and then a B point in the track, which will continue looping until you choose Clear. The Play Mode control lets you choose either Repeat One, Repeat All, Shuffle, or Repeat Shuffle, and if you toggle the Group mode selection, all of these settings (with the exception of Repeat One) will use all the files in your MUSIC folder rather than just the songs in the current album folder. The other options available in the control panel are mostly self-explanatory.

Hacking the Hack

If you are on a Mac running OS X 10.4, make sure you check out "Automate Mac OS X File Transfers" [Hack #25] for instructions on writing an Apple-Script to automate moving your tunes to your PSP. If you're savvy in other scripting languages, you may want to look over that hack, as well, for some ideas for your own automated script.

If you're running Version 2.0 of the firmware and you want to take full advantage of your networked music collection, you'll want to create a Music page that contains an index and links to all the files within your PSPMUSIC folder. This will allow for easy picking and choosing of songs you want to grab off of your network for on-the-go listening on your PSP. Why not build the same support system for a few videos, too?

Also, if you are homebrew savvy [Hack #40], make sure you check out some of the homebrew MP3 players available for the PSP.

HACK
#24

Convert Text to Audio for Your PSP

Why buy audiobooks for your PSP when you can make your own?

You like books, but you don't particularly like the idea of reading your books on your PSP's screen. (If you do want to read books on your PSP, make sure you check out "Use Your PSP as an E-Book Reader" [Hack #27] and "Create Your Own PSP E-Books" [Hack #29].) You've been considering buying some audiobooks and listening to them on your PSP, but you'd rather spend those hard-earned dollars on games for your PSP. Why not simply make your own audiobooks for the PSP?

Don't worry. I'm not suggesting you sit down and read James Joyce's *Ulysses* out loud while recording it to MP3. Instead, just grab the text of *Ulysses* from Project Gutenberg (*http://www.gutenberg.org/*) for free and have your computer read the text to audio files.

Get the Text

You can do this with any plain text file you have lying around, so don't be afraid to take that business report your boss wants you to review, convert it into plain text, and change it over to audio. Since the PSP is a recreational device, however, I am going to assume that you are looking for some actual reading entertainment.

If that's the case, a wide variety of options are readily available to you via the Internet. Both Project Gutenberg (*http://www.gutenberg.org*) and the Electronic Text Center at the University of Virginia Library (*http://etext.lib. virginia.edu/*) freely offer a variety of literary titles that have fallen out of copyright and entered into the public domain. The text section of the Internet Archive (*http://www.archive.org/details/texts*) contains texts that have entered into the public domain and others that have been released under Creative Commons licenses or are free from any sort of copyright. The Creative Commons web site itself features a text section (*http:// creativecommons.org/text/*) that regularly highlights texts that have been released under Creative Commons licenses.

In addition to these resources, you can easily copy and paste the text of any web document into a *.txt* file, or even use an online RSS feed reading tool like Bloglines (*http://www.bloglines.com*) to display your daily dose of news items on one web page where you can select all, copy, and paste into a *.txt* file.

Text to Speech

After you've picked out a text that you'd like to listen to, it's time to convert that document to MP3.

Now, if you've picked out a particularly long document, such as the afore-mentioned *Ulysses* by James Joyce, you will most likely need to break the text up into separate documents to be made into separate audio files for manageable listening. You could either follow the natural structure of the book, separating the document into individual chapter text files, or do something more arbitrary, like breaking the document into separate files every 30–50 pages.

Once you have your documents ready to go, you need a tool to convert them to MP3 format. A quick search of VersionTracker (*http://www.versiontracker.com*) will turn up a variety of shareware and commercial titles for Windows that will convert text files to audio files. If you conduct the same search on the Mac OS X end of things, you'll find several freeware titles in the mix. This is because Mac OS X has integrated text-to-speech support built into the OS. Here's how you can convert text to speech under Windows, Linux, and Mac OS X. Your end result will be an audio file that you can convert as described in the next section.

Windows. If you are on Windows, use a third-party text-to-audio program such as VoiceMX Studio (*http://www.tanseon.com/products/voicemx.htm*), load the text, and generate your output file (in the case of VoiceMX Studio, you'll get a *.wav* file). Next, convert the file to MP3 as described later in this hack, then take the resulting file and drop it in */PSP/MUSIC/* on your Memory Stick to listen.

Linux. The open source *Festival* (*http://www.festvox.org*) includes an application called *text2wave*, which reads in a text file and outputs a *.wav* file. You may be able to find Festival in your Linux distribution's package repository, so check there before installing from the source.

Once you've got the *.wav* file out of text2wav, you can convert it and drop it into */PSP/MUSIC/* on your Memory Stick. By default, text2wave will read from standard input and dump its *.wav* to standard output. You can create a file with a command such as text2wave input.txt -o output.wav.

You can change text2wave's settings by evaling a valid festival command. For example, to change the voice to *voice_kal_diphone*, you'd do this:

```
text2wave input.txt -o output.wav -eval "(voice_kal_diphone)"
```

Mac OS X. Launch your Terminal (located in */Applications/Utilities/*). Now, assuming the text file that you want to convert is called *text.txt* and is located on your Desktop, at the command line, type the following:

```
say -f ~/Desktop/text.txt -o ~/Desktop/text.aiff
```

This string will read the *text.txt* file on your Desktop to a new AIFF file on your Desktop called *text.aiff,* using the default System voice settings you have defined in the "Text to Speech" section of your Speech control panel (System Preferences → Speech → Text to Speech).

Unfortunately, when I say that the *say* command will read your text file to an AIFF file, I'm being literal. You won't hear it, but the process will happen in real time. If you are converting a long piece of text to audio, be ready to leave your computer running and do something else for a good half hour or more.

Converting Your Speech File

Now all you have to do is take the resulting AIFF or WAV file and drop it into iTunes, then select the file and choose Advanced → Convert Selection to MP3 to let iTunes convert the file to an MP3.

Make sure that under Importing in iTunes' Preferences, you have the encoder set to MP3 Encoder. Since this is a very basic audio track, you may want to play around with the settings of the encoder to create a smaller file, making more space for other files on your Memory Stick.

If you don't have iTunes, then you can use a free program such as LAME (*http://lame.sourceforge.net/*) or Audacity (*http://audacity.sourceforge.net*, which uses LAME under the hood to perform the conversions) to convert the file to MP3.

After converting the file, select the freshly converted version of the file and select File → Show Song File to display the MP3 in the Finder. Simply drag the file over to your PSP's mounted Memory Stick and drop it into */PSP/ MUSIC/*, so that you can listen to it on the PSP.

Hacking the Hack

Automation is the way to hack this hack. Mac users can create an Apple-Script droplet that takes any *.txt* file that you drop onto it, and uses do shell script to run the appropriate *say* command, then grab the resulting file, import it into iTunes, convert it to MP3, and move the resulting file to the Music folder on your PSP. Such a script is beyond my novice AppleScripting skills. If you're interested in this, but not sure how to pull it off, may I suggest O'Reilly's *AppleScript: The Definitive Guide*?

Of course, if you have Mac OS X 10.4 Tiger, you could easily do this with an Automator action [Hack #25].

Since LAME and text2wave are both command-line tools, it's easy to automate this process on Linux. For example, you can make your MP3 with one command line:

```
text2wave input.txt | lame - output.mp3
```

HACK #25 Automate Mac OS X File Transfers

If you're running Mac OS X Tiger, then you can set up Automator to move all your media files onto your PSP.

I spent a little time in Automator (located in the Applications folder) and put together some basic applications to move my files from my Mac to my PSP. I'll walk you through each of them. Each of these can be saved as either an Automator action or a standalone application. Please excuse the cheesy names I've given to these little apps.

PSP Playlist2PSP

The first and easiest of these little apps is built with just a few actions, but you have to set it up first. Open iTunes and create a Playlist called "Transfer to PSP." On your PSP, create a folder inside the Music folder (located inside the PSP folder), and name this folder "from iTunes."

Open up Automator. Choose iTunes from the Application pane and drag the Find iTunes Items action over to the workflow. Under Find, choose Songs and under Whose, choose "Playlist," then "Is" and "Transfer to PSP." Now, choose Finder in the Application pane and drag the Move Finder Items over to the workflow. Under To: set the location to the "from iTunes" folder you created on your PSP and check the Replacing Existing Files box. Figure 3-16 shows the completed workflow.

That's it. Save as either a workflow or application. Make sure that your PSP is connected and mounted and that the songs in the "Transfer to PSP" playlist are in PSP-compatible formats before you run it.

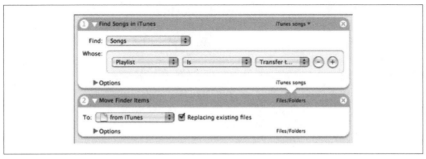

Figure 3-16. PSP Playlist2PSP workflow

Movies2PSP

Now, the previous Automator workflow was dead-on simple. This one is about the same. This time, open up Automator and choose Spotlight from the Application pane. Drag the Find Finder Items action over to the workflow. Under Where, choose your Movies folder and under Whose, choose "Name" and "Ends With," and enter **.MP4** in the field.

Choose Finder in the Application pane and drag the Move Finder Items action to the workflow. Set To: to the 101MNV01 folder inside the MP_ ROOT folder on your Memory Stick and check the Replacing Existing Files box. See Figure 3-17.

That's it. Save as either a workflow or application and make sure you have your PSP connected and mounted before you run it.

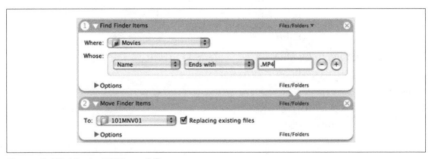

Figure 3-17. Movies2PSP workflow

Audiobook2PSP

Here's something slightly more complex to automate the processes discussed in "Convert Text to Audio for Your PSP" [Hack #24]. This will be a three-part workflow: it will first prompt the user to select a text file; it will then read the text file to AIFF and convert it to MP3; and it will finish by moving the created audiobook to the proper place on your PSP.

Choose a text file. Open Automator and select the Finder from the Applications pane. Drag the "Ask for Finder Items" action and the "Open Finder Items" action into your workflow. In the first action, set "Type:" to Files and "Start at:" to Desktop, then type **Choose a text file to convert to MP3:** in the "Prompt:" field. Leave the Allow Multiple Selection box unchecked. This part of the workflow will open up a dialog prompting the user to select a text file for conversion to MP3 and then pass that text file along to the next action.

In the second action, set "Open with:" to TextEdit. The text file selected in the first part of the action will open in TextEdit. That's it for the first section of this workflow (see Figure 3-18).

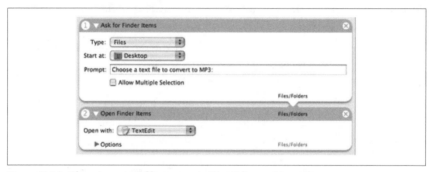

Figure 3-18. Choosing a text file to open in TextEdit

Convert the text file to an MP3. Next, select TextEdit in the Automator Application pane. Drag the "Get Contents of TextEdit…" action into the workflow. This action simply scrapes the text from the front-most page (the page that the first part of this workflow just opened) in TextEdit and passes this text along to the next action.

Next, drag the "Text to Audio File" action over to the workflow. Here you can choose whichever System Voice you prefer; it will default to whatever voice you have set in System Preferences → Speech → Text to Speech. Whatever name you give the audio file under the Save As: field will be the same name (minus the *.aiff*) as the final track as it appears on your PSP. I went for the generic *audiobook.aiff*, but feel free to name your track whatever you like. Set Where: to the Desktop.

Select iTunes in the Application pane of Automator and drag the Import Audio File, Start iTunes Playing, and Pause iTunes actions into the workflow. Make sure you set the Import Audio File action to use MP3 Encoder and check the "Delete source files after encoding" box to neatly remove the *audiobook.aiff* file that was created on the desktop in the previous step. The next two actions simply ensure that the recently encoded *audiobook.mp3* file is the file currently selected in iTunes before going on to the next section of the workflow. Figure 3-19 shows the completed workflow.

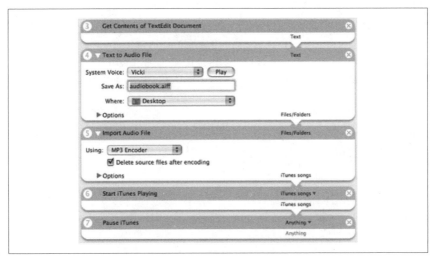

Figure 3-19. Converting text to MP3

Move the MP3 to your PSP. Drag the "Get the Current Song" action from iTunes over to the workflow. This simple action grabs the track currently set to play in iTunes and passes it along to the next action.

Choose Finder in the Application pane of Automator and drag Move Finder Items over to the workflow. Set the To: option to the *MUSIC* folder located inside the *PSP* folder on your Memory Stick and leave the Replacing existing files box unchecked (Figure 3-20).

When you run this complete action, it will prompt you for a text file, which it will then launch in TextEdit and write to an AIFF file on your desktop. Once this file is fully created, iTunes will launch and import the file, converting it to MP3, and then it will pass the track along to the Finder, which will place the file on your Memory Stick. Enjoy.

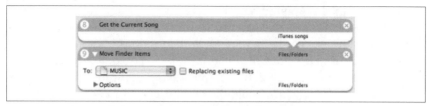

Figure 3-20. Moving the current song to the /PSP/MUSIC/ folder

Hacking the Hack

Now, what's good about these workflows is that they play nicely together. You could easily slap all three of them together into one PSP media management application, either by performing all the same commands in a row with one longer workflow, or by saving them as three separate actions that you call on at different points in a more program-like interface with a dialog prompt asking you what you want to do: move Movies or Audio, or make an Audiobook? If you just want to improve on the Movies2PSP action, you could first convert your movies into the proper format for PSP playback [Hack #22] and then move the converted files to your PSP.

HACK #26 Store Digital Photos on Your PSP

Using your PSP as a portable photo album is easy if you know how to fill the Memory Stick Duo card with images. If you know the different viewing options and controls on your PSP, you'll be showing off your photos in no time.

One of the PSP's most useful functions is also one of its most simple: the ability to display digital images. The majority of the hacks covered in this chapter, and a few from other chapters, hinge on this simple ability. This hack walks you through the basics of managing digital images on your Sony PSP, different ways of getting the images onto the PSP, and navigating the images once they are on your PSP, and points you to some of the more useful ways digital images can be used to add functionality to your PSP.

Put Images in Your PSP

To place images in your PSP, you need to either mount your Memory Stick on your computer using a card reader, or connect your PSP to your computer using a USB mini to USB cable, select Settings → USB Connection from the PSP's Home menu, and hit the X button.

Once the Memory Stick shows up on your computer, you will find a folder called PSP in the card's root directory. Within the PSP folder are four other folders: GAMES, MUSIC, SAVEDATA, and PHOTO. You can simply copy any images that you want to carry around with you on your PSP into the PHOTO directory on the card.

Which Image Format?

If you are running any version of the firmware other than Version 2.0, keep in mind that all images must be in JPEG format and that the PSP is not capable of displaying particularly large JPEG files. Use an image program like Photoshop to save your images into compressed JPEG format. Most likely, your digital camera came with software capable of handling this basic compression of images.

If you are running Version 2.0 of the firmware, then your PSP can handle JPEG, GIF, PNG, TIFF, and BMP images, and you can also download images directly from the Internet using the PSP's Browser. To do this, select the image, then hit the Triangle button, navigate to the File menu, hit the X button, select Save Image, and hit the X button again. After it finishes downloading, you can immediately navigate to the image and view it on your PSP.

Regardless of which image format you use, you can conserve disk space by scaling your image down so that it's close to the PSP's 480×272 pixel screen resolution.

You can also organize the photos on your PSP by grouping them in folders within the PHOTO folder.

Currently, none of the images on my PSP are larger than 250 KB in size, with the majority of the images falling in the 32–64 KB range. You can view larger images on the PSP, but the larger the file size, the longer it will take the files to load, and you won't really see much improvement in image quality after a certain point because of the PSP's screen resolution.

In Figure 3-21, you can see that I have a series of different folders on my PSP. However, the PSP is only capable of reading one level deep into the PHOTO folder, so if you have another folder nested inside a folder inside your PHOTO folder, the PSP will either not see it, or it will show it as being corrupt data.

There are also a variety of programs available that automate organizing your pictures and moving them to your PSP. Two of them are iPSP (*http://www.kaisakura.com/ipsp.php*; $19.99 USD for both OS X and Windows) and

Figure 3-21. Viewing the folders I've placed inside the PHOTO folder

PSPWare (*http://www.nullriver.com/index/products/pspware*; $15 USD for OS X and Windows). Both of these feature abilities beyond simply managing your pictures, and both programs have demo versions, so try before you buy. For example, after clicking on the Photos section of iPSP and choosing a photo album from iPhoto in OS X, iPSP begins automatically converting the images within the album into properly sized JPEGs and importing the images into their own directory within the PHOTO folder on the Memory Stick, as shown in Figure 3-22.

Figure 3-22. iPSP converting the images into properly sized JPEGs

If you own a digital camera that works with a Memory Stick Duo card, then you can simply remove the card from your camera and put it in the PSP to view photos. When you choose Photo → Memory Stick and hit the X button on your PSP, these images will appear in a directory called Digital Camera Images.

Navigate the Photos on Your PSP

On your PSP, navigate to the Photo menu, highlight your Memory Stick, and hit the X button. The folders that you placed inside the PHOTO folder of your Memory Stick will show up in a list, sort of like separate photo albums. Each folder will feature a preview image of the first image in the folder and the name of the folder, and will display the number of images contained in that folder.

Once you have the folder you want to view selected, you can either hit the X button again to bring up another list of all the images contained or hit the Triangle button to bring up the menu featuring Slideshow, Delete, and Information, shown in Figure 3-23.

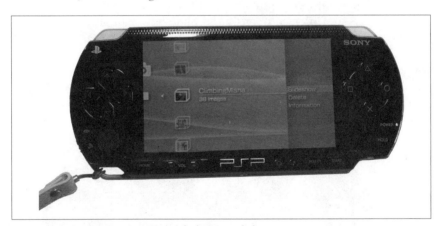

Figure 3-23. Bringing up a menu with the Triangle button

This menu allows you to view a slideshow, delete the entire folder, or display information about the folder. If you choose Information, the only additional information you will discover is the size—displayed in kilobytes—of the folder and its contents.

If you have Version 2.0 of the firmware, you will have the additional option to Receive, which lets you receive a transmitted image from a friend's PSP into the currently selected folder.

Slideshow. If you choose Slideshow and hit the X button, each of the pictures in the folder will be displayed in order, for about four seconds each at Normal speed.

 If this is too fast or too slow for your tastes, you can change the slideshow speed to Fast or Slow. The slideshow speed is set in the PSP's main settings. Navigate to Settings → Photo Settings and hit the X button to bring up Slideshow Speed. Hitting either the X button or the right arrow button on the directional keypad will bring up a menu offering the choices of Fast, Normal, or Slow. Make your selection and hit the X button.

Hitting the Triangle button while the slideshow is running will open up a special slideshow-only control panel as an overlay over the current picture (see Figure 3-24). This menu consists of Slideshow Options, View Mode, Display, and Help on the top row, Previous, Next, Play, Pause, and Stop on the middle row, and Repeat on the bottom row. The middle row, as you can see, consists of basic and rather self-explanatory navigational controls for the slideshow. The Repeat control simply keeps the slideshow going in a continual loop (at least until your battery runs out). The top row of controls needs a bit more explanation.

Figure 3-24. The slideshow control panel

Selecting Slideshow Options and hitting the X button brings a small informational overlay in the bottom-right corner of the screen. This overlay contains an image of a clock indicating the time the picture file was created, the name of the file, the date it was created, and the time it was created.

> Keep in mind that the time and date displayed by the PSP in these informational menus are determined by the time and date that the file was created, rather than the time and date your picture was taken. If you had to convert your pictures into JPEG to be displayed on the PSP, the time and date displayed will correspond with when you made this conversion.

If you select Slideshow Options again, and then again hit the X button, a small preview list of other images in the current slideshow will be displayed at the bottom of the screen, with the one you are currently viewing displayed in the middle. Hitting the X button again while the Slideshow Options control is highlighted will return you back to a regular slideshow, sans all the meta-information. If you don't want to use this control panel, simply hitting the Square button while you are viewing the slideshow will cycle you through these different Slideshow Options.

The View Mode option toggles the slideshow view between Normal (in which the picture is fitted to the screen) and Zoom (in which the picture is made to fill the screen, albeit with some cropping of the image to maintain proportions).

The Display option places an overlay across the top of the screen with the name of the image, the image's number within the slideshow (3/5 would mean that you are viewing the third picture of five), the date the file was created, and the time the file was created.

The Help option displays the Photo Help screen (Figure 3-25) that displays all of the basic controls for navigating photos on the PSP.

Photo view. If, instead of launching a slideshow, you hit X after selecting one of your folders of images (or if you didn't bother with the whole folder aspect in the first place), you will see a list of all the images within that folder. Simply selecting an image and hitting the X button will display it on the PSP. If you hit Triangle instead, an informational menu will pop up with Slideshow, Display, Delete, and Information options (see Figure 3-26), which behave pretty much the same as the similar menu for the image folder.

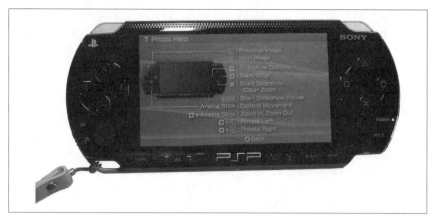

Figure 3-25. Photo Help screen

If you have Version 2.0 of the firmware, you will have additional options, such as Send, which would allow you to transmit the image via infrared to a friend's PSP; and Receive, which lets you receive a transmitted image from a friend's PSP.

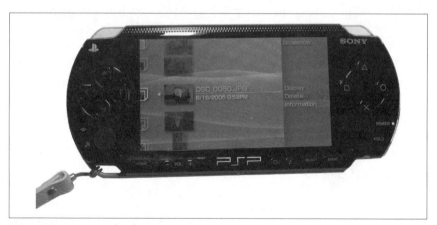

Figure 3-26. Viewing the photo menu

When viewing an image, you can hit the Triangle button to bring forth an overlay control panel. This one is slightly different from the Slideshow control panel. The options include View Mode, Display, and Help on the top row, Clear Zoom, Zoom Out, Zoom In, Rotate Left, Rotate Right, Up, Down, Left, and Right on the middle row, and Previous, Next, and Slideshow on the bottom row.

If you have Version 2.0 of the firmware, you will have two additional controls on the top row of the control panel: Send, which allows you to send the image via IR to a friend, and "Set as Wallpaper," which lets you set the current image as the background image (wallpaper) for your PSP.

Most of these controls function the same as their counterparts in the Slide-show control panel, although there are some slight differences. View Mode toggles between Zoom and Normal view. Display shows the information for the file in an overlay across the top of the screen and a small window indicating the level of zoom (Figure 3-27). The controls on the second row all do what their names imply. The Up, Down, Left, and Right functions won't work if the full image is within view. If you are zoomed in, however, you can use these controls to scan around the image.

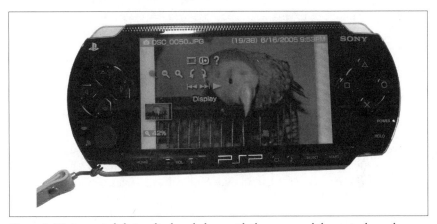

Figure 3-27. Image info being displayed along with the zoom and the control panel

On the other hand, the majority of these functions can be accessed more easily by the PSP's controls themselves. It is much more convenient to simply use the Analog Stick to move around the image when you are zoomed in. The L and R triggers move you back and forward through the images, the square button plus the L and R triggers rotates the image left and right, respectively, the X button clears Zoom, and the Square button used in tandem with the analog stick zooms in and out. Refer to the Photo Help screen for a full list of all of these controls.

If you put your PSP to sleep while viewing pictures, you will be returned to the main menu the next time you wake up your PSP.

Hacking the Hack

This hack consists of very basic instructions for using the image-viewing capabilities of your PSP. These capabilities, however, open up the PSP to a whole slew of neat hacks and tricks that you will find covered in this chapter. Make sure you check out "Use Your PSP as an E-Book Reader" [Hack #27], "Read Web Comics on Your PSP" [Hack #28], and "View Maps" [Hack #34].

H A C K **Use Your PSP as an E-Book Reader**

#27 Use the PSP's picture-viewing capabilities to read e-books.

When you browse the web on your PSP [Hack #41], you'll discover that the PSP's crisp, clear screen presents text clearly and legibly. Why not use the PSP to read e-books?

Several sites online have converted texts and comics into JPEG images specifically designed for viewing in the PSP's photo browser [Hack #26].

Manga

The first PSP "e-books" to emerge online came in the form of Japanese manga comics or graphic novels.

Seven Seas Entertainment's GoManga.com (*http://gomanga.com/pspmanga/ index.php*) has made an entire selection of black and white Manga titles customized for display on the PSP. They are releasing these titles in serialized form, episode by episode. Their current titles include *Amazing Agent Luna*, *Blade for Barter*, *Last Hope*, and *No Man's Land*. Each episode is freely downloadable from their site in a zipped folder. All you have to do is download the files, unzip them, take the folder containing all of the individual page images, and drop it onto your PSP's Memory Stick in */PSP/PHOTO/*. Each picture is 480×297 at a resolution of 72dpi (as you can see in Figure 3-28, the image has been turned on its side so that it will nicely fill the PSP's screen). This is larger than the 480×272 size of your PSP's screen, so you will have to use the analog stick to move around each page of the comic slightly. Holding the PSP on its end with the directional pad and analog stick beneath the screen will let you view the comic properly, and clicking on the R trigger of the PSP moves you ahead to the next page.

A PSP PAK of full-color Manga comics is also freely available from eigo-Manga English Comics (*http://s95330819.onlinehome.us/manga/psppak.htm*). So far, there is only one PSP PAK available, and it contains samples from five different manga comics. These images are set to 480×311 and turned on their side, so again you will need to hold the PSP on end and use the analog stick to move around on the page.

Figure 3-28. Part of the first episode of No Man's Land from Seven Seas Entertainment

PSP Magazines

PSP Magazines (*http://www.pspmagazines.com/*) is a site created and maintained by Jason Schuller, who notes on the site's About page: "I was doing this for myself anyway and figured why not share my work." This site consists of various short articles and selections from various magazines. These selections would all appear to be scraped from the online versions of the magazines and then reformatted for viewing on the PSP by Schuller, who then serves them up for download. There is a rather large selection of magazine snippets available, and the list is updated regularly. There is even a section of independent PSP Magazines listed. All images are set to the default 480×272 size of your PSP's screen and are, for the most part, designed for normal viewing without having to hold your PSP on one end.

Free PSP E-Books

In your search for free e-books for your PSP, you will undoubtedly come across sites offering copies of books without permission from their copyright holders. I suggest that you instead take the time to learn how to make your own PSP e-books **[Hack #29]** from texts freely and legally available to you.

Hacking the Hack

The list of freely available e-books designed for viewing on the PSP is growing daily. Use Google (*http://www.google.com*) to search for PSP e-books and see if any new titles that haven't been mentioned in this brief sampling appear.

Of course, the best way to find content for your PSP that you will be interested in reading is to make your own. Head on over to The Online Books Page (*http://onlineBooks.library.upenn.edu/*) or Project Gutenberg (*http://www.gutenberg.org/*) to grab some books that are freely and legally available in the public domain. Then turn to "Create Your Own PSP E-Books" [Hack #29] for a discussion of the different ways you can go about converting these texts into JPEGs for viewing on your PSP.

HACK #28 Read Web Comics on Your PSP

Grab and convert comics off the Web for portable viewing.

When Jacob first got his USB link cable, he tried a little experiment to see whether he could use his PlayStation Portable to read web comics (*http://en.wikipedia.org/wiki/Webcomic*), and it worked out quite well. This hack will help you to do the same.

Downloading the Comics

The first step will be to download a web comic site of your choosing to your local computer.

Use a web site copier such as HTTrack (*http://www.httrack.com/*) on Windows and Linux or SiteSucker (*http://www.sitesucker.us/index.html*) on Mac OS X.

Download, install, and launch your web site copier. Supply the URL of the web comic that you want to view on your PSP and start the download. Figure 3-29 shows how this is done with SiteSucker. Once you type in the URL, press the download button (the one that looks like a downward-pointed arrow) to begin the download.

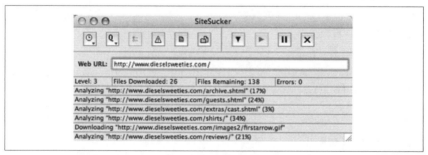

Figure 3-29. Using SiteSucker in OS X to download Diesel Sweeties

Make sure you spend some time adjusting the settings of these web site copiers to exclude downloading any forums associated with your target site, since there are no comics there and forums can add up to quite a lot of HTML pages.

We used Diesel Sweeties (*http://www.dieselsweeties.com/*) and Cat and Girl (*http://www.catandgirl.com/*). Download the web comic site of your choice, starting with the archive where all the comics are located.

Downloading all the images and HTML pages on the web site will take a couple of minutes over broadband. While you are doing this, you should seriously consider buying a T-shirt or other fine products from the web comic authors to thank them for providing their comic goodness for your pleasure. We have both Cat and Girl T-shirts and Diesel Sweeties T-shirts, and they rock ever so hard.

Finding the Images

Once the download has completed, you need to find the directory where all the comic strip images are stored. This may be a simple matter of opening the Images folder inside the site's root folder on your hard drive. However, one of the problems you'll find is that some web comic authors have broken down their comic archives by month and year, so there can be a plethora of folders containing those precious images.

Do a local search for the image file format using your operating system's file search tools (see Figures 3-30 and 3-31). This will generate a list of all the comic strip files in that directory. Now copy the results into a single folder for image processing.

Convert the Images to JPEG

If you're running anything other than Version 2.0 of the firmware, the PSP's Photo capabilities only extend to JPEG files; there are plenty of web comics in GIF and PNG, so you will need to do a batch conversion into JPEG. If you have a PSP with Version 2.0 of the firmware, then you can skip this step. First, make an empty directory called *Cleaned Comics,* where your batch image program can deposit the converted images before loading them onto the PSP.

You don't want to resize the web comics, since most of the fonts are designed to be read at a 1-to-1 onscreen aspect ratio. If you are using Mac

Figure 3-30. Using OS X Tiger's Spotlight to search for images

Figure 3-31. Searching for PNG files within the Comics folder in Windows XP

OS X, we recommend *Easy Batch Photo* (*http://www.yellowmug.com/ easybatchphoto/*) as an inexpensive solution to convert all the comics to JPEG. If you already have a copy on hand, or have been looking to invest some real money in the image-editing arena, Photoshop, Photoshop Elements, or any other major image editor should be able to do a batch conversion on a folder of images with very little difficulty. Another, less expensive solution would be to use the free and open source GIMP (*http:// www.gimp.org*) that is available for Windows, Linux, and many other operating systems, along with the GIMP plug-in, David's Batch Processor (*http://members.ozemail.com.au/~hodsond/dbp.html*).

> Make sure to use an image quality compression ratio better than 50%, so that the comics don't become distorted. Also, don't save a thumbnail in your JPEG file, because the PSP doesn't need the thumbnail and may choke on it, and that thumbnail will just take up more space on your precious Memory Stick.

Put the Comics onto Your PSP

Now that everything is converted, you can copy the images using a PSP file manager such as iPSP (*http://ipsp.kaisakura.com/*) or PSPWare (*http://www. nullriver.com/index/products/pspware*). On Mac OS X, PSPware offers tight Apple iLife integration, so using iPhoto 5, you can simply create a PSP keyword and assign that keyword to all the images that you want to transfer to the PSP.

> The 32MB Memory Stick Duo card that Sony includes with the PSP is just fine for saved games. But if you want to get into transferring JPEGs, MP3s, and movie clips to your PSP, the small 32MB card is just not going to cut it. If you think you'll be carrying lots of web comics around, a bigger Memory Stick Duo card is well worth the investment.

Connect your PSP via a USB to USB mini cable, and use your PSP file manager software to sync the images over to the PSP.

You could also manually drop the pictures off in the directory */PSP/ PHOTOS/WEBCOMICS/* on the Memory Stick if you don't want to use software to manage your PSP.

Viewing the Comics on Your PSP

Once everything has been copied over, disconnect your PSP from your computer, navigate to Photo → Memory Stick, and hit the X button. Select the WEBCOMICS folder that you created and hit the X button to view a list of the comics available. Select one and hit the X button again to open it up (see Figure 3-32).

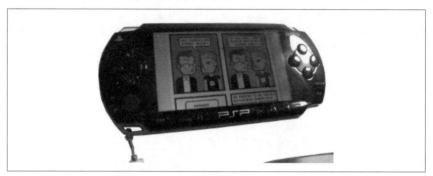

Figure 3-32. A Diesel Sweeties comic loaded on the PSP

When you are in the PSP image viewer, make sure that you are set at 100% (hold down the Square button and move the analog stick up and down to zoom in and out), use the analog stick to pan around the image, and use the R trigger to navigate to the next comic or the L trigger to skip back to a previous comic.

Hacking the Hack

Once you do this, it is pretty simple to do again in the future. If you are a coder, consider writing a script of some sort to automate the entire process.

This isn't something that needs to be done on a daily basis, but it is a great way to read the back issues of your favorite web comic when you are away from your PC and nowhere near a wireless access point. It can be a nice relaxing break from an intense *Wipeout Pure* session.

Also, make sure you check out several of the manga and other comics preformatted for the PSP that are available online [Hack #27].

—*Jacob Metcalf and C.K. Sample III*

Create Your Own PSP E-Books

#29 Prepare your documents for easy viewing as JPEGs on the PSP.

Since you know that it is possible to view JPEG images on the PSP [Hack #26], and that there are already a spattering of e-books in JPEG format available for the PSP [Hack #27], why not make your own e-books out of documents you have on your computer or can download from the Web?

Print Documents to PDF

The easiest way to create e-books is to generate a PDF. Windows, Linux, and Mac OS X have different ways of printing your text files directly to PDF, and as PDF is essentially an image format, it is relatively easy to export the different pages of the PDF files into separate JPEG images for viewing on the PSP.

> If you're on Windows or Linux, rather than spending all your money on Adobe Acrobat, you can grab a free copy of Open Office (*http://www.openoffice.org*), which, besides being a fully functional and free alternative to Microsoft Office, has the ability to convert files to PDF. But if the document you want to convert isn't an office or text document, you may still be in luck: if you can print it to a PostScript file, you can use the ps2pdf utility from GhostScript (*http://www.cs.wisc.edu/~ghost/*) to create your PDF. To print to a PostScript file, configure a generic PostScript printer that outputs to a file rather than a USB or parallel port.

In order to make the pages of your documents easily readable on your PSP with plenty of zoom, I recommend setting the page settings for your PDF printout to 8 inches by 9 inches with 0.3-inch margins and a nice 12 or 14 point font. In Figure 3-33, I have created a special page setting for my printer in Mac OS X that measures 8 inches by 9 inches with 0.1-inch margins around. In the actual document settings, I choose to give the document 0.3-inch margins. Using Mac OS X's built-in PDF support, I print the document directly to PDF.

Converting PDF to JPEGs

After I have my 8 inch by 9 inch PDF file, I need to convert it into a series of JPEGs numbered in sequence and all contained within a folder that I can place inside */PSP/PHOTO/* on my PSP's Memory Stick. For the most part,

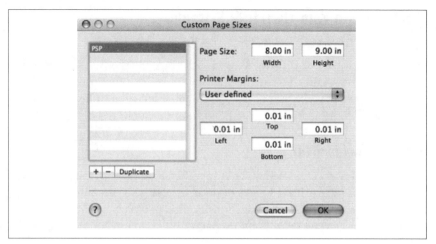

Figure 3-33. Custom paper size for the PSP in Mac OS X

any imaging program capable of working with PDFs can be used to convert PDFs to JPEG, so make sure you look at the following programs before you go searching around the web for a PC version of programs like PDF 2 PSP.

Adobe Acrobat. Most likely, you already have a copy of Adobe Reader or Adobe Acrobat Reader on your computer. They are actually both the same program, only Adobe has recently renamed Acrobat Reader as Adobe Reader. If you don't have either on your computer, you can grab a copy for free directly from Adobe (*http://www.adobe.com*). This program will allow you to view the PDF you have created, but unfortunately it does not support exporting the page images into different formats.

If you own the full version of Adobe Acrobat, you can export the PDF file as a series of JPEGs, and Acrobat will even do the work of naming each separate page as another image in sequence (*Image001.jpg*, *Image002.jpg*, etc.).

Preview.app. If you are on Mac OS X, you can use Preview (included with the operating system and located in the Applications folder). If you open the PDF for your e-book in Preview, you can use File → Save As to manually save each page as a separate JPEG file, as shown in Figure 3-34. For a large document, this can be laborious to say the least, so it is not the ideal solution.

Image-editing programs. Using an image-editing program such as Adobe Photoshop or Photoshop Elements, you can open a selected page of the PDF and resave it as a JPEG with high quality compression. On Mac OS X, Graphic Converter (available from *http://www.lemkesoft.com/en/graphcon.htm*

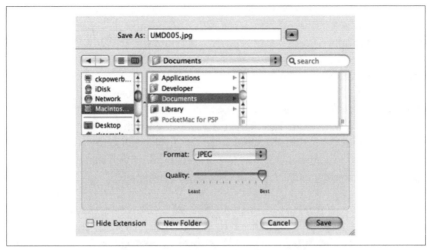

Figure 3-34. Saving the fifth page of a PDF as a JPEG file in Mac OS X's preview

for $30 USD) can do the same. You might already have some sort of image-editing program that came with a digital camera or scanner and is capable of opening PDFs and converting them to JPEGs. The GNU Image Manipulation Program, GIMP (*http://www.gimp.org/*), is available for Windows, Linux, Unix, and Mac OS X, and can handle a wide variety of formats, including PDF and JPEG.

PDF 2 PSP. If you are using a Mac, then you can grab a helpful, free little program called PDF 2 PSP (*http://pdf2psp.sourceforge.net/*), which is shown in Figure 3-35.

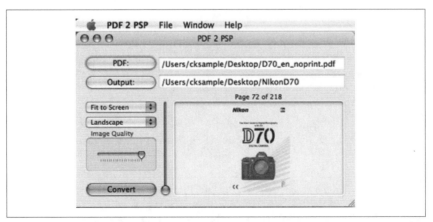

Figure 3-35. PDF 2 PSP set to convert the PDF manual to my Nikon D70 camera into JPEGs

In PDF 2 PSP, you choose the location of the PDF and then a folder where you want the collection of sequenced JPEGs to be stored. If your PSP is connected and mounted on your computer, you can even have the program output directly to */PSP/PHOTO/* on your Memory Stick. You have the option to either adjust the picture to be displayed in portrait or landscape view on the PSP, you can set the quality of the image, and you can set the size of the pages to a variety of options: Original Size, Fit to Screen, Fit to Width, 2x Screen Width, and High Resolution. I recommend choosing Original Size, 2x Screen Width, or High Resolution to ensure legibility of your document on the PSP, and setting the layout to portrait to allow you the ability to both zoom in on the image and pan and scan around the page.

iPSP. iPSP (*http://ipsp.kaisakura.com/*; $19.99 USD) features the ability to convert PDFs to JPEGs formatted to fit on your PSP, but there aren't as many configuration options available as there are with PDF 2 PSP. This isn't necessarily a bad thing, however, as iPSP does a good job of converting PDFs to JPEGs. There are both Mac and PC versions of the program, but at this time, it looks like only the Mac version supports PDF to JPEG conversion. As an example for this hack, I took a PDF copy of the PSP's manual from the PlayStation site (*http://www.playstation.com/manual/pdf/PSP-1001K_1.pdf*) and converted it into a folder of sequenced JPEGs for reading on the PSP (see Figure 3-36). Figure 3-37 shows how the manual appears on my PSP.

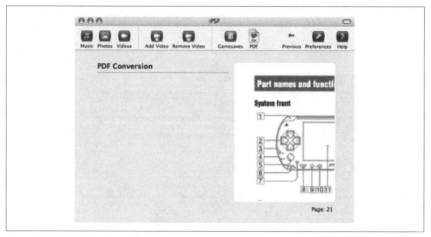

Figure 3-36. iPSP in the process of converting the PDF manual to the PSP to JPEGs

With iPSP, there is no need to locate the folder of converted images and then move them to */PSP/PHOTO/* on your Memory Stick, since the program automatically places the files in the proper location as it converts.

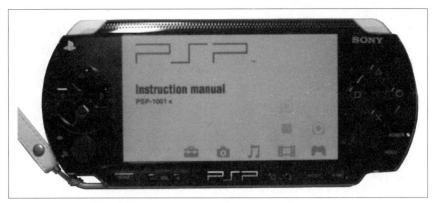

Figure 3-37. The PSP instruction manual on the PSP

The Results

Once you're done converting the PDF to JPEGs, you should have a folder containing images named *Page0001.jpg*, *Page0002.jpg*, etc. Name this folder whatever you want the title of your e-book to be and place the folder inside the PHOTO folder inside the PSP folder on your Memory Stick. After you unmount your PSP from your computer, simply navigate to Photo, make sure the Memory Stick is selected, and hit the X button. Scroll through the images and list of folders until you locate your e-book.

Highlight your e-book and press the X button to load the first page. If you hit the Triangle button to bring up the control panel, you can select the first option on the top row, View Mode, to set the page to be zoomed in, so that you can easily go through all the pages of your book by clicking the R trigger without having to continually rezoom. To scan up and down the page, use the analog stick as shown in Figure 3-38. Most pages will load centered, so you will need to scan up to the top of the page and then scan down as you read. If you need to zoom in on a section of the text, hold down on the square button and move the analog stick up and down to zoom in and out. For more instructions on viewing images on the PSP, make sure you read over "Store Digital Photos on Your PSP" [Hack #26].

Hacking the Hack

The great thing about this hack is that every document that is printable from your computer can be converted into JPEGs for viewing on your PSP on the go. In Figure 3-38, I'm reading through one of the other hacks for this book that I printed to PDF from within Microsoft Word. This opens up a whole new world of possibilities, some of which are covered in other hacks in this book (see "Turn Your PSP into a PDA" [Hack #35], "Read RSS Feeds on Your PSP" [Hack #33], and "View Maps" [Hack #34]).

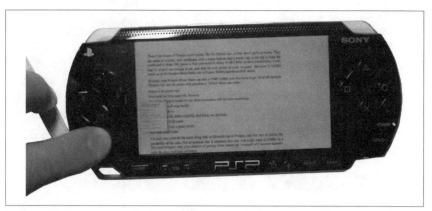

Figure 3-38. Scanning up and down on the page with the analog stick

HACK #30 Create a Portal for Your Memory Stick Files

Why not keep a directory of all the local images and text files on your Version 2.0 PSP in HTML format, for easy access via the browser? Better yet: why not automate the process with Perl and automatically grab all of your psp-tagged del.icio.us bookmarks in there to boot?

Well, you have a PSP with Version 2.0 or later of the firmware, so you don't have all the great homebrew emulators available for the earlier versions. However, unless you downgrade from Version 2.0 [Hack #11], you are making do by loading every JavaScript-capable game or program you can find onto your Memory Stick and converting all your documents to text files for viewing via the nifty little browser that Sony included with Version 2.0 of the firmware.

Let's really trick out your PSP by putting together a Perl script that will run on Windows, Mac OS X, or Linux, with only a few dependencies. This script will automatically scrape the photos contained in your Memory Stick's */PSP/PHOTO/* folder, scrape any text files contained in */PSP/NOTES/*, optionally grab any links on your del.icio.us (*http://del.icio.us*) account that are tagged with "psp," and build an *index.html* file linking to all these files and located at the root directory of your Memory Stick.

Install the Dependencies

This script uses PerlMagick and cURL to work its magic. Since Perl is included in most modern systems, there are only a few bits that you need to make sure are in place before beginning.

Windows. If you are on Windows, first make sure you have Perl installed (we suggest ActivePerl, which you can get from *http://www.activestate.com*). Next, grab PerlMagick, which is part of the ImageMagick package available under the Windows Binary Release section of the ImageMagick site (*http://www.imagemagick.org/script/binary-releases.php*). Next, install cURL from *http://curl.haxx.se/download.html* and put the executable in your PATH. C:\ *Windows* will work, but we suggest you add an entry to your PATH and put it there. If you choose the version of cURL with SSL support, you may need to install additional libraries. This script does not require SSL support.

Mac OS X. If you are on Mac OS X, you need to install ImageMagick. Download the source of ImageMagick (*http://www.imagemagick.org/script/install-source.php*). Extract the source, and then from the Terminal (which is located in */Applications/Utilities/*), type the following commands:

```
cd ImageMagick-<version>
./configure && make
sudo make install
```

Each line is a separate command. Enter the first command, then hit return and wait while a bunch of text flies by in the Terminal window. This will build ImageMagick from the source. If the string of text comes up with any errors at the end after the second command, then try running the command again with sudo at the beginning. After the third command, when sudo is invoked you will be asked for a password (and possibly a warning, if this is the first time you invoke sudo). Enter the Administrator password for your computer.

After ImageMagick successfully compiles, you may need to compile Perl-Magick, if it was not compiled automatically. Enter the following commands to build PerlMagick (the PerlMagick directory is a subdirectory of the *ImageMagick-<version>* directory):

```
cd PerlMagick
perl Makefile.PL
sudo make install
```

Again, if there are any errors in step two, try invoking sudo at the beginning of the command.

Make sure you check the installation documentation that accompanies ImageMagick (in particular, the README and INSTALL files), since you may need some other programs that ImageMagick depends on. For example, on Mac OS X, we needed to install libjpeg (see *http://www.ijg.org/*) from the source tarball (*jpegsrc.v6b.tar.gz*), using the following commands:

```
tar xvfz jpegsrc.v6b.tar.gz
cd jpeg-6b/
```

```
./configure && make
sudo make install
sudo make install-lib
sudo ranlib /usr/local/lib/libjpeg.a
```

UNIX/Linux. Make sure that you have PerlMagick installed. This should be available in your Linux distributions package repository. If not, you can follow the Mac OS X instructions to compile it from source. You will also need cURL.

The Code

```perl
#!/usr/bin/perl -w

use strict;
use Image::Magick;

my $MAXDEPTH = 1; # Maximum depth of photo albums

opendir PSP, "PSP" || die "Could not open PSP: $!\n";
open HTML, (">index.html") || die "Could not open index.html: $!\n";

# Display the top of the HTML file.
#
print HTML <<EOF;
<html>
<head><title>My PSP</title></head>
<body style="width: 480px; height: 272px;">
EOF

# Check the photos and notes subdirectories
#
while (my $dir = readdir(PSP)) {
  if ($dir eq "PHOTO") {
    list_photos("PSP/PHOTO", 0, "<hr><h2>My Pictures</h2>");
  }
  if ($dir eq "NOTES") { list_items("PSP/NOTES", "My Files") };
}
closedir(PSP);

# Import PSP bookmarks from del.icio.us
#
its_delicious();

# Display the end of the HTML file.
#
print HTML "</body>";
close (HTML);

# Enumerate anything found in the notes subdirectory
# and add a link to it.
```

```perl
#
sub list_items {

  my $dirname = shift;
  my $what = shift;

  print HTML qq[<hr><h2>$what</h2>\n<ul>\n];
  opendir DIR, "$dirname" || die "Could not open $dirname: $!\n";
  while (my $item = readdir(DIR)) {

    # Skip things that aren't files.
    #
    next unless -f "$dirname/$item";

    # Construct a hyperlink to the target filename.
    #
    my $target = "$dirname/$item";
    print HTML qq[<li><a href="$target">$item</a></li>\n];
  }
  print HTML qq[</ul>\n];

  closedir (DIR);
}

# Enumerate anything found in the photos subdirectory
# and add a link to it.
#
sub list_photos {

  my $dir = shift;
  my $depth = shift; $depth++;
  my $separator = shift;

  # Create the thumb directory if it does not exist.
  my $thumbdir = "$dir/PSPTHUMBS";
  if (not -d $thumbdir) {
    mkdir ($thumbdir, 0775) || die "Could not mkdir $thumbdir: $!\n";
  }

  print HTML $separator;

  my $handle;
  opendir $handle, "$dir" || die "Could not open $dir: $!\n";
  while (my $file = readdir($handle)) {

    # Skip things that aren't files.
    #
    next if -d "$dir/$file";

    # Scale the photo
    #
    my $thumb = "${file}_sm.jpg";
    my $image = new Image::Magick;
```

```perl
    my $err = $image->Read("$dir/$file");
    if ($err) {
      warn $err;
    } else {
      print STDERR "Processing image $file...\n";
    }
    $image->Scale(height => "32",
                  width =>  "32");
    $image->Write("$thumbdir/$thumb");

    # Construct a hyperlink to the target filename.
    #
    my $img = "$thumbdir/$thumb";
    my $target = "$dir/$file";
    print HTML qq[<img src="$img" />] .
      qq[<a href="$target">$file</a><br/>\n];

  }

  # Collect all the images in subdirectories
  #
  rewinddir($handle);
  while (my $file = readdir($handle)) {
    next if $file eq ".";
    next if $file eq "..";
    next if $file =~ /^pspthumbs$/i;
    if (-d "$dir/$file" && $depth == $MAXDEPTH) {
      list_photos("$dir/$file", $depth, "<p>$file:</p>");
    }
  }

  closedir ($handle);
}

# Import del.icio.us bookmarks tagged PSP
#
sub its_delicious {

  print <<EOF;
http://del.icio.us is a social bookmarking service. If you've
got an account on del.icio.us, I can import your PSP tagged
bookmarks.
EOF

  print "Tell me your del.icio.us username or leave blank to skip: [] ";
  my $username = <STDIN>;
  chomp($username); chomp($username); print "[$username]\n";

  if ($username) {
```

```
my $url = "http://del.icio.us/html/$username/psp" .
          "?count=9999&tags=no&rssbutton=no";
open (CURL, "curl \"$url\" |") || die "Could not launch cURL: $!\n";
print HTML qq[<hr><h2>PSP Bookmarks</h2>\n];
while (<CURL>) {
  print HTML $_;
}
close(CURL);
  }
}
```

Type this code into your text editor of choice and save it as *make_index.pl*. Place this file in the root directory of your PSP's Memory Stick, either by dragging it there or executing one of the following commands:

Unix, Mac OS X, Linux
```
cp make_index.pl /Volumes/Untitled
```

Windows
```
xcopy make_index.pl F:\
```

 If your Memory Stick has a name other than Untitled, Mac OS X users should use the appropriate directory name. If you are on Windows, choose the drive letter (F:, in these examples) that your PSP was assigned. If you are on Linux, be sure to replace */Volumes/Untitled* with the mount point [Hack #3] of your PSP.

To run the script, you must run the following command from the command line.

In Mac OS X, use the Terminal (located in */Applications/Utilities/*) and run the following commands:

```
cd /Volumes/Untitled
perl make_index.pl
```

These are the same commands you will use in UNIX/Linux.

In Windows, open a command prompt and run:

```
F:
cd \
perl make_index.pl
```

Once the script begins running, you will be prompted for your del.icio.us username. If you enter nothing, this step will be skipped. After the command has completed running, you can navigate to the root level of your Memory Stick and you will see a newly created *index.html* file. Double-click on this file to launch it in your computer's web browser and inspect the results of the code.

On Your PSP

Once you have this script created, you can run it every time your PSP is connected to your computer to update the *index.html* file.

On your PSP, make sure that you bookmark *file:/index.html* in the browser, so that you can easily navigate to this index of all of your photos, text files stored in the Notes folder, and your del.icio.us bookmarks tagged with PSP. Consider making it your home page.

Hacking the Hack

In its current form, this script is both rather basic and easily hacked to add more features.

More tags. To grab more tags, you can modify this snippet of code:

```
if ($username) {
    my $url = "http://del.icio.us/html/$username/psp" .
              "?count=9999&tags=no&rssbutton=no";
```

To have the script grab all of your del.icio.us bookmarks regardless of tags, or to add other tags in the form of +games+playstation+whatever to further refine the bookmarks you retrieve, simply remove the /psp.

Automate it even more. On OS X, you could easily create a simple Apple-Script to run each time your PSP is mounted so that you don't have to remember to enter the commands to run the Perl script:

```
Tell Finder
    do shell script "cd /Volumes/Untitled"
    do shell script "perl make_index.pl"
end tell
```

Save this code as an AppleScript app called PSP on your desktop and simply double-click it whenever the PSP is mounted.

Add some more links. Also, if there are a few favorite sites that you always want linked on this page, just add that information in the script. For example, this snippet of code writes the beginning part of the *index.html* file:

```
# Display the top of the HTML file.
#
print HTML <<EOF;
<html>
<head><title>My PSP</title></head>
<body style="width: 480px; height: 272px;">
EOF
```

After the <body> declaration and before the EOF, you can add a whole other section of HTML if you like. For example, something like the following would add links for Google and Yahoo!:

```
# Display the top of the HTML file.
#
print HTML <<EOF;
<html>
<head><title>My PSP</title></head>
<body style="width: 480px; height: 272px;">
<h1>Search Engines</h1>
<a href="http://www.google.com">Google</a><br />
<a href="http://www.yahoo.com">Yahoo!</a><br />
EOF
```

Take the Web with you. To keep it quick and dirty, we used cURL instead of LWP (*http://lwp.linpro.no/lwp/*), a collection of Perl modules for hacking the Web. You could easily change this script to use LWP, although you'd need to make sure you install LWP on each machine you want to run this script. But while you're adding LWP support, you could take advantage of some of LWP's advanced features. For example, in addition to pulling down your del.icio.us bookmarks, you could mirror a few pages from each linked site for offline reading. For more information on hacking with LWP, see *Spidering Hacks* (O'Reilly).

Have fun hacking away at the script.

—Brian Jepson and C.K. Sample III

HACK #31 Portable PSP Speakers

Build a cloth strap or pouch to hold two portable speakers attached to your bag. Plug these speakers into your PSP, then share your tunes with the world.

There has been a substantial increase in specialty speakers for MP3 players, but I still haven't seen anything that is really portable. At least nothing that is strap-on-your-backpack portable. All the ones I see are somewhat bulky and heavy. Headphones are great, but the noise-canceling ones can get you killed if you're riding your bicycle around a busy intersection. Also, with some portable speakers, you can really spread your tunes à la a boom box on the shoulder.

This is probably best done combined with the amp hack [Hack #16]. A little amplification would ensure being able to hear your music when there's a ton of noise from heavy traffic.

Things I Used

- Two old computer speakers
- Velcro
- A needle and thread
- Regular black cotton fabric

Putting It Together

The speakers I used were some old computer speakers that didn't require an AC adapter or any battery power. If you don't have any speakers around, you can go buy some really cheap ones at pretty much any store that sells computer equipment. However, the nicer the speakers you use, the nicer this will be when you're done. Admittedly, I was trying to keep this pretty cheap.

> Unless you want to wire them yourself, you need to make sure your speakers have the right plug-in (3.5mm) before taking them apart. Otherwise, you're either wasting time or have a good deal of rewiring in your future.

Before starting, I plugged the speakers into my PSP and turned up the volume to see whether they would adequately pump up the jam.

If you're using small, old computer speakers like I did, the next step consists of getting the parts (the actual speakers and wire) out of those plastic shells. I removed all the screws I could find in each speaker. I then used my screwdriver to pry open the case. The plastic just sort of snapped open like the battery cover on a remote. This wasn't too bad. After getting them open, however, I realized that the cable going to the speakers went right through a solid little hole in the plastic. I took some pliers and some heavy-duty clippers to cut and tear away at the plastic until I freed the wires. This took a while and was a bit of a pain, but I just had to hack away at that plastic until I got the wire free. Make sure you don't tear up the wire and that it stays attached to both the speaker and plug. If you have to cut the wire, you should be able to splice it back together; if you're careful, this shouldn't be an issue.

After freeing up the speakers, it was time to make the cloth wraps for the speakers. I bought a foot of the cheapest black cotton fabric that I could find (feel free to use whatever color best matches your backpack or messenger bag). I then cut two pieces of fabric at about 11×5 inches each. There's no perfect way to size this, but this size would fit around my backpack straps fine while allowing some wiggle room in the design. These measurements will vary depending on the size of the speakers and where you'll be attaching them. Just make sure to cut them big enough so you can trim off the excess later. Having to sew additional cloth on would make it look like you don't know how to cut and sew, and that's just lame.

I laid one of the speakers on one of the pieces of fabric about one inch high and five inches over. I then folded the fabric over lengthwise and started sewing. I sewed lengthwise and at the ends to keep the cloth together. Make sure not to sew through the wire. It gets a little hard to do when you're trying to keep that speaker in there. Repeat the sewing procedure with the other piece of cloth and speaker. Make sure that you have the wire coming out the right way to meet up with the other one when the speakers are facing the same direction.

Now the speakers need to be secured in the middle so they don't slip out, and the Velcro needs to be attached. Carefully sew around the perimeter of the speakers, again making sure not to accidentally run your needle and thread through the wire. Cut four 3-inch pieces of the rough Velcro, and four 3-inch pieces of the smooth Velcro. I sewed the rough "catchy" pieces of Velcro (the part with the hooks) on the end where the wires were emerging, and I had the wire running between the two pieces of Velcro. I also had them facing the same direction as the back of the speakers. This way, when you wrap the strap around something, the wire will be on the outside. I then put two pieces of smooth Velcro on the opposite side, facing the same way the speaker was facing. After you are done with all this sewing, each speaker should look similar to Figure 3-39.

Figure 3-39. One speaker sewn in place, with Velcro attached

 Make sure that your Velcro is attached so it will line up correctly when wrapping it around something. I accidentally put the rough and smooth Velcro on one of the speaker pouches facing the same way. This resulted in me having to cut that one up—while not cutting the wire—and sewing it back together. It was really a pain.

After the Velcro is attached in the appropriate spots, so that when you wrap these straps around something, it will stay, you're done. If that was confusing, please refer to the picture of the final product to figure out what I'm talking about (see Figure 3-40).

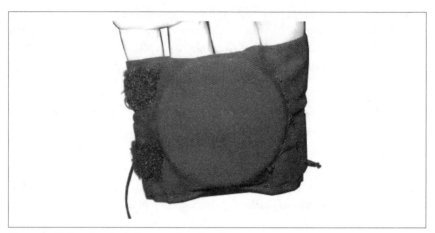

Figure 3-40. Speaker in cloth around my hand

Attaching the Ghetto Blasters

Once the sewing is done, your speakers should be ready to attach to something. I strapped them onto my backpack straps (see Figure 3-41), plugged them into my PSP, and rode around on my bike for a while to test them. They worked pretty well, but they do have a tendency to slip down the straps.

Hacking the Hack

The straps I made are pretty durable, but I do worry about the life of my speakers. They aren't really protected in there, and they definitely have no backing to keep them safe. Depending on the size and quality of your speakers, you might want to put them in some sort of casing before sewing them all up. Just make sure it's nothing that will hamper the sound. You could probably put them in some cardboard [Hack #12]. Just test them out in whatever container you choose before starting all the sewing, and make sure to size the fabric accordingly.

My straps also have a tendency to slide down my backpack straps when biking. The only time they don't is when they are facing straight up. Unfortunately, it is harder to hear them like this since my head is usually bent forward while biking. I still haven't figured out the best way to keep them from sliding down, since I am reluctant to sew more Velcro into the actual

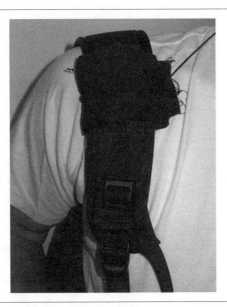

Figure 3-41. Speaker wrapped around backpack strap

straps of my backpack. You could use some sort of unobtrusive clipping mechanism. Mine are light enough that paperclips can keep them in place.

Finally, there are a few things that can be done differently with the fabric and sewing. I just went for some black fabric since my backpack was black. However, you can really personalize your straps with different colors or printed fabric. If you're really trying to keep this cheap, just use an old shirt or something that you never wear anymore. Your straps can also look a lot better if you know how to use and have access to a sewing machine. As you can see from the pictures accompanying this hack, I didn't have this luxury.

—Kevin Sample

HACK #32 Listen to Podcasts on Your PSP

Listen to Podcasts that you've subscribed to using Apple's iTunes.

Podcasting, in its simplest form, is a way of broadcasting online that combines prerecorded audio files with some kind of syndication technology—usually RSS 2.0. What this means for listeners is that they can subscribe to a podcast and automatically be notified when new episodes of the podcast are released. Programs that automate the process (*podcatchers*) have made obtaining and listening to podcasts extremely easy. Because of this, podcasting has taken off as one of the premier forms of online broadcasting.

If you've upgraded to Version 2.6 of the PSP firmware, you'll find that Sony has added a new podcast-savvy (sort of) ability to your PSP: RSS Channel, located alongside your Internet Browser under the Network section of your PSP. Using your browser, you can select RSS 2.0 enclosures for podcasts and subscribe to them on your PSP. The cool or bad part about this, depending on your point of view, is that RSS Channel streams the podcasts to your PSP over a live Internet connection. This is great if you are near an open wireless access point, but it eliminates the portability of podcasts, since there is no way to download the podcasts to your Memory Stick via the RSS Channel. To find out how to do that, keep reading this hack.

There are many programs you can use to obtain podcasts. The most popular podcast-specific program (known as iPodder until Apple persuaded them to change their name) is Juice Receiver (*http://juicereceiver/sourceforge.net/index.php*), a free, multi-platform program that allows you to subscribe to podcasts either through a provided podcast directory or by manually typing in the address of a podcast feed. Once subscribed to a podcast, iPodder can be set to check for and download the latest episodes of a podcast. To listen to downloaded podcasts, you must open the files using a media player such as Windows Media Player or WinAMP.

This hack, however, will use iTunes, because it's slightly more convenient than Juice Receiver. You can both download and listen to podcasts from within iTunes. Furthermore, the Podcasts section of the iTunes Music Store features a large and easy to navigate podcasting directory. However, you can adapt the instructions in this hack to your podcatcher of choice.

Downloading Podcasts

The easiest way to obtain podcasts is via iTunes. Launch iTunes and click on Podcasts in the Source list on the left (see Figure 3-42). Near the bottom of the iTunes window, there will be text reading Podcast Directory with an arrow next to it. Click the arrow and you will be taken to the iTunes Music Store podcast directory.

What you should now see before you are a number of different podcasts that you may download. Pick a podcast you find interesting by clicking on it. You will then be presented with a list of available "episodes" for that particular podcast. In the Price column (most, if not all, of them are free) to the right, you will see a button labeled Get Episode. Click this button and the episode will be downloaded to your music library.

Figure 3-42. A view of the Podcasts section of iTunes

 There are some podcasts that will not play on the PSP. Podcasts that fall into this category are enhanced podcasts and podcasts that are purchased and contain digital rights management. If you find that a podcast you really want to listen to will not play on your PSP, try burning the podcast to an audio CD from iTunes. Then, rip the podcast to your music library as an MP3, using iTunes' CD-ripping features.

Transferring Podcasts to Your PSP

While downloading podcasts using iTunes is pretty straightforward, getting them onto your PSP can be a little tricky. Since iTunes will only sync your music library to an iPod, it is necessary to go outside of iTunes to get the downloaded podcasts onto your PSP.

The first step is to locate where iTunes is keeping your Music Library. If you're using a Mac, launch iTunes and click iTunes → Preferences. Then click the gear icon labeled Advanced. If you're using Windows, launch iTunes and select Edit → Preferences, then click the Advanced tab. The first item on this page of the dialog box labeled "iTunes Music Folder Location" is where you will find your music files. On a Mac, the default location is ~/Music/iTunes Music/ (in your home folder). In Windows, the default is C:\Documents and Settings\username\My Documents\My Music\iTunes\iTunes Music\.

Browse to the folder where your music library is located. You should see a list of folders corresponding with the names of artists in your Music Library, as well as a folder labeled Podcasts. Open this folder and the folder named after the podcast(s) you have just downloaded. In this folder should be the podcast's episode itself, named similarly to what appears in iTunes.

To transfer the podcasts [Hack #23] to your PSP, plug in your PSP to a USB port and from the PSP home screen, select Settings, then USB Connection. On a Mac, a new volume will appear on your desktop. In Windows, a new drive will be mapped under My Computer. Double-click on the volume or drive and then open the PSP folder. Inside, you should see some media folders; open the MUSIC folder.

All you need to do now is to copy the podcasts to your PSP. Simply drag and drop the podcast's episode from the folder in your music library to the MUSIC folder on your PSP. Before unplugging your PSP, make sure to eject it first. On a Mac, drag the volume on your desktop to the trash can in the dock. In Windows, right-click on the drive and select Disconnect.

Exit USB Mode on your PSP and navigate to the Music icon. Then highlight and press X on the Memory Stick icon. You should now see the podcast episode you just transferred to your PSP.

> You may want to create a folder inside the MUSIC folder called "Podcasts" and instead transfer podcasts there. This will not only keep Podcasts separate from the rest of your music, but it will also allow quick access for transferring new podcasts and deleting old ones.

—Jonathan Terleski

Read RSS Feeds on Your PSP

HACK
#33

Either connect wirelessly to Bloglines or save RSS-feed news items as separate JPEGs for offline viewing on the PSP.

Although Sony has hinted at expanding RSS Channel (included with Version 2.6 of the firmware) to be something more than a podcast-streaming feature of the PSP in the future, currently there is no Sony-supported solution for reading your RSS feeds on your PSP. This hack will walk you through several different ways to read your RSS feeds on your PSP. If you're running a PSP with Version 2.0 or newer firmware, then you can use the included browser. If you've managed to get your hands on a PSP running Version 1.0 or 1.5 of the firmware, and you've neglected updating so that you can keep running all the homebrew games and applications out there [Hack #40], then you can either use the *Wipeout Pure* browser hack [Hack #41] to view your RSS feeds or you can convert your feeds to JPEG files for reading on the go.

I've divided this hack into sections that cover each possible firmware configuration, so feel free to jump ahead to the section that corresponds to your PSP's firmware.

If you're not sure which version of the firmware you are running, navigate to Settings → System Settings, hit the X button, select System Information, and hit the X button again. An informational screen will appear on your PSP, listing your PSP's MAC address, the System Software version (this is the firmware), and the nickname of your PSP.

Version 2.0 and Later

If you have Version 2.0 of the firmware, then you have a variety of options for reading your RSS feeds on your PSP.

Online. In order to view your RSS feeds online with your PSP, you will need to set up an account with Bloglines (*http://www.bloglines.com*) or a similar online RSS feed-reading service. Once you have a Bloglines account, turn on your PSP, navigate to Network → Internet Browser, and hit the X button to launch the browser.

Make sure that you have your WLAN switch on, are in range of a WiFi Internet connection, and that you have properly set up such a connection. If you are not sure about these steps, read "Get Your Wireless Network On" [Hack #5] and "Find Yourself a PSP Web Browser" [Hack #41].

Once the browser launches and your PSP connects to the Internet, hit the Triangle button to bring up the Browser's address bar. Navigate to the address bar using the directional keypad and hit the X button. This will bring up the PSP's text entry control panel. Type in the address for Bloglines Mobile (*http://www.bloglines.com/mobile/*) and hit Enter. The Bloglines Mobile page will load, as shown in Figure 3-43.

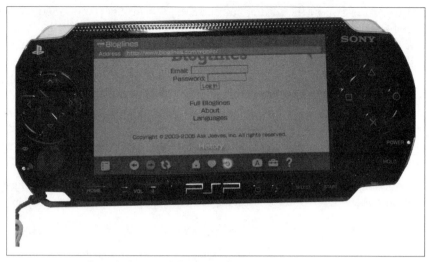

Figure 3-43. Loading Bloglines Mobile via the PSP browser

Hit the Triangle button to leave the browser's control screen and view the web page full-screen. Select the text field next to Email and enter the email address with which you set up your Bloglines account, then enter the appropriate password, select the Enter button, and hit the X button on your PSP. Fortunately, the PSP handles cookies nicely, so the next time you visit Bloglines, your PSP will remember your account information, and you will not have to redo all of this typing. This will take you to a simplified, mobile-ready version of your Bloglines feed page, shown in Figure 3-44, where you can read through all the feeds you have added to your Bloglines account.

> I suggest that you bookmark this page. Hit the Triangle button to bring up the browser's interface, select the heart-shaped icon, which is the Bookmarks control panel, and hit the X button. Choose My Bookmarks, hit the X button again, highlight "Add to Bookmarks," and hit the X button again.

Simply navigate up and down the page, hitting X whenever you want to select a bit you want to read. If you want to visit the page of one of the posts you are reading in Bloglines, but do not want to leave the Bloglines page you are viewing, simply select the link, and press and hold the X button. This will launch the link in one of the browser's three tabs. After you have read the post and want to return to the Bloglines page, simply hold down on the Square button and hit the L trigger to switch back to the first tab.

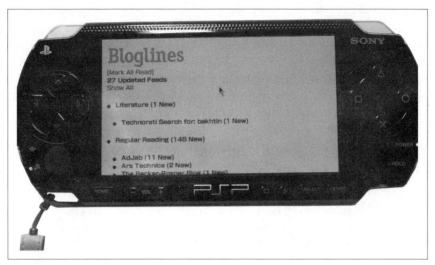

Figure 3-44. Bloglines Mobile's main feed page

If you want, you can always navigate over to the normal Bloglines site by clicking the Full Bloglines link on the Bloglines Mobile page. The PSP is perfectly capable of running the full version of Bloglines, but the right column of the layout tends to get oddly squished in the PSP browser. The mobile version, however, will be quicker and will run a lower risk of returning an out-of-memory error after you've been surfing for a while.

Offline. You have two basic options under the Version 2.0 firmware for viewing your RSS feeds when you are offline. The first option is to follow the methods discussed in "Create Your Own PSP E-Books" [Hack #29] to load your RSS feeds in either Bloglines or some other RSS feed-reading program and then print them out to PDF. You must then convert the PDF you have printed into JPEG files for viewing through the PSP's photo-viewing capabilities. This takes a bit of work and wouldn't be the easiest feat to accomplish before rushing out the door to catch the train.

A much easier option, which will also take up a lot less space on your Memory Stick than all those images would, would be to access your Bloglines account from your computer's web browser. After you have logged into your account, click each group or one overall group of your feeds to display all the posts on one page. Once the page fully loads, right-click in the side panel where all those stories appear. A contextual menu should pop up, giving you an option similar to either Save or Save As.... The wording of this will vary depending upon your system.

I choose Save Frame As… and saved the page as source. You will need to save either as source, HTML, or a *.txt* file, depending upon the options you are offered. If you can save the file directly to text, do so; if not, you will then have to take another step to convert it to text. Take the file and open it up in your computer's web browser; it will appear with all the text intact, although some of the formatting will most likely be off a bit. Choose Edit → Select All, and then select Edit → Copy. Open up your text editor of choice, select Edit → Paste, and save the file as a plain text file. Name it *feeds.txt*.

Take the *feeds.txt* file that you have created and place it in the root directory of your PSP's Memory Stick.

Now, when you are out and about without an open WiFi access point, you can view this feeds file by launching your web browser (if you have a home page configured, you may need to have the WLAN switch turned on for it to launch, and you'll need to cancel out of any attempts to conntect to an access point), hitting the Triangle button, entering **file:/feeds.txt** into the address bar of the PSP's browser, and hitting Enter to launch the file within the browser. It's not a pretty feed-reading solution, but it is very functional, as Figure 3-45 shows.

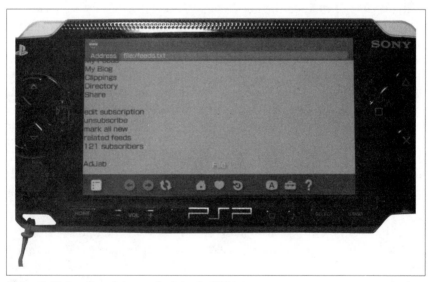

Figure 3-45. Loading plain text feeds in the PSP browser

You could do the same thing with a local HTML file that you saved to the root directory of your PSP, but since Bloglines loads images along with its feeds, if you don't strip the HTML from the page by taking the extra step of resaving it as plain text, the PSP Browser won't properly load the page because it will keep attempting to connect to the access point to grab the images pointed to in the HTML.

However, some browsers give you the option to save the images along with the HTML file. For example, Firefox creates a directory that holds these if you choose the "Web Page, complete" option when you save the page (if your web page is named *myblogs.html*, you'll need to copy the *myblogs_files* subdirectory over to your PSP, along with *myblogs.html*).

Now, just like with the Bloglines Mobile page, make sure you make a bookmark to this *feeds.txt* file. You could even set this page as your home page in the PSP browser, so that every time you launch the PSP Browser, it will go directly to this file. With a little work, it won't be that difficult to set up a regular system through which you can update this file with the latest feeds before heading out the door.

Version 1.0/1.5xx

If you're running an older firmware version, you can read your feeds online or offline.

Online. To read your RSS feeds online with a PSP running Version 1.0 or 1.5xx of the firmware, you will need to set up the same subscription to Bloglines (*http://www.bloglines.com*) or a similar RSS feed-reading service as discussed in the Version 2.0 section. However, since your PSP doesn't come with a browser of its own, you're going to have to find one, either by implementing the *Wipeout Pure* browser hack or by downloading one of the homebrew browsers. Read over "Find Yourself a PSP Web Browser" **[Hack #41]** to find out more about both of these methods.

Once you have everything up and running and you are connected to one of the public portals such as the fujimax PSP Web Portal (*http://67.171.70.72/wipeout/index.html*) or a portal that you have put together yourself **[Hack #42]**, enter the address for Bloglines Mobile (*http://bloglines.com/mobile/*) in the address bar and hit Enter. Select Go and hit the X button. The Bloglines

Mobile site will load, albeit much slower than it does in the Version 2.0 browser. Select the text field next to Email and enter the email address with which you set up your Bloglines account, and then enter the appropriate password, select the Enter button, and hit the X button on your PSP. The page will load and you will be able to read through your different RSS feeds, as shown in Figure 3-46.

> Unfortunately, the *Wipeout Pure* browser doesn't support cookies or bookmarks, so each time you want to check your RSS feeds online, you are going to have to repeat all of these text entry steps. Also, there is no tabbed browsing with this browser, so if you click out of Bloglines, you have to go all the way back through these steps to get back in.

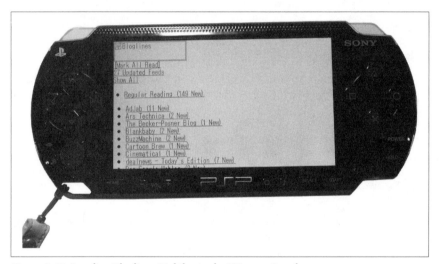

Figure 3-46. Loading Bloglines Mobile via the Wipeout Pure browser

Offline. As mentioned in the Version 2.0 section, you can simply employ the methods discussed in "Create Your Own PSP E-Books" [Hack #29] to load your RSS feeds in either Bloglines or some sort of RSS feed-reading program and then print them out to PDF. You must then convert the PDF you printed into JPEG files for viewing through the PSP's photo-viewing capabilities.

Your other option, assuming you are running Version 1.00 or 1.50 of the firmware, and not 1.51 or 1.52, is to keep an eye on the homebrew scene [Hack #40]. There are several homebrew projects that already allow you to navigate the file structure of your Memory Stick, and I've heard of a few homebrew web browsers and text-viewing projects that are in the works. If you find a good homebrew solution for viewing the files, you can use the methods discussed in the Version 2.0 section to prepare the files for viewing on your PSP.

 ## View Maps

#34 Use your PSP as a makeshift atlas by grabbing images from Google Maps or MapQuest for portable viewing.

As with "Read RSS Feeds on Your PSP" [Hack #33], the details of this hack are going to vary slightly depending upon the firmware in your PSP and whether you're going to be doing this with an active Internet connection or for offline viewing.

I've divided this hack into sections that cover online or offline map viewing, so feel free to jump ahead to the section that you're interested in.

Because neither Google Local (formerly known as Google Maps) nor MapQuest currently work in the *Wipeout Pure* browser [Hack #41], the online section is a Version 2.0–only hack. If you're following the offline section of this hack, there will be virtually no differences between PSPs running different versions of the firmware.

> If you're not sure which version of the firmware you are running, navigate to Settings → System Settings, hit the X button, select System Information, and hit the X button again.

For this section of the hack, I'm going to walk you through connecting to MapQuest (*http://mapquest.com*) using the PSP browser on a PSP running Version 2.0 of the firmware.

> If your PSP is running an earlier version of the firmware, you should skip ahead to the next section, since neither MapQuest nor Google Maps currently loads in the *Wipeout Pure* browser.
>
> As of the writing of this hack, Google Maps is still in beta, and doesn't currently work with either the PSP browser or the *Wipeout Pure* browser. The placeholder page that says that these browsers are not compatible with Google Maps, however, loads nicely and easily in both browsers, so there is a chance this will change soon. If PSP compatibility should happen, the basics that I am covering here with MapQuest can be easily translated over to Google Maps.

Launch your PSP browser and go to MapQuest's main page (*http://mapquest.com*). Once the page loads, scroll down to the address entry fields and enter an address. In Figure 3-47, I entered 1 37th St., New York, NY, because it was an easy address to enter via the PSP's text entry interface.

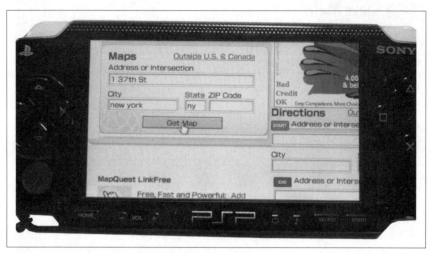

Figure 3-47. Selecting Get Map using the X button

Once the map page loads, you can zoom in or out as you need, using the default MapQuest functions. Once you have the correct map loaded, place the pointer over the image and hit the Triangle button to bring up the PSP browser interface. Use the directional keypad to highlight the File icon (the one in the bottom-left corner of the screen), hit the X button, select Save Image from the menu that appears (see Figure 3-48), and hit the X button again. Figure 3-49 shows the Save dialog that appears.

Make sure that the Destination is set to */PSP/PHOTO/* (you may also want to rename the file's name to something manageable under the File Name field). To change either of these values, use the directional keypad to select the field you need to change and hit the X button. Make your changes, and then hit the X button again. Once you are done, select Save and hit the X button. A progress bar will appear to let you know how much of the file has downloaded. Once the download is complete, the screen will read "Save completed." Hit the O button to return to the PSP browser.

The image you downloaded is now available for viewing on your PSP. Leave the PSP browser and navigate to Photo. Scroll down the list of photos until you find the image you have just downloaded. Select the image and load it on your PSP's screen. Then you can hold down the Square button and use the analog stick to zoom in on the map, and then release the Square button

Figure 3-48. The File menu over a loaded map page in MapQuest

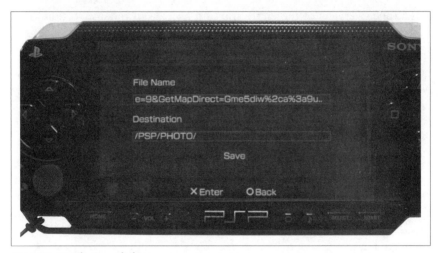

Figure 3-49. The Save dialog

and continue using the analog stick to pan and scan around the map (see Figure 3-50).

If you need directions, use MapQuest's features to get the full directions on the screen, and use the instructions I just covered to grab each of the pictures involved (there is a Map link next to each numbered step) in the directions. Save each file in sequence: *leg01.gif, leg02.gif, leg03.gif*, etc. This way, you can easily track each leg of the trip while you are on the move. Alternately, select Print for what would be the version of the page that you would print out, were you on a computer. There will be two images of your trip

Figure 3-50. Zoomed in on the picture downloaded from MapQuest

listed: one overview of the entire trip and a detail of the last section. Save both of these images.

If you need to grab the text of the directions for viewing while you are on the go and away from a WiFi signal, the best way to do this is to use MapQuest's email feature to email a copy of the directions to a web-accessible email address. Click on the email link and enter TO: and FROM: email addresses (both of which are required). You will be taken to a confirmation page once you are done.

Once your email has been sent, navigate to your web-based email account, log in, and place the cursor over the link that would open the email in a new window. Hit the Triangle button, navigate to the File menu, hit the X button, select Save Link Target (see Figure 3-51), and hit the X button. Rename the file to something such as "directions" and save it to */PSP/COMMON/*, as shown in Figures 3-52 and 3-53.

Now when you are out and about, you can launch the PSP browser and type `file:/psp/common/directions` in the address bar to bring up the text directions you saved. Bookmark this file for easy launch, and you can continually replace it when you need new directions to new places by following these steps.

Offline with MapQuest or Google Maps

If you want to view your directions offline, either from MapQuest or Google Maps, all you have to do is use your computer to navigate to either map provider's version of the directions and print the directions to PDF **[Hack #29]**.

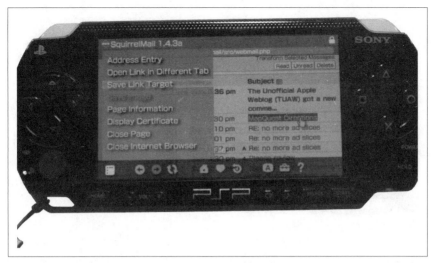

Figure 3-51. Use Save Link Target to save a copy of the email to your Memory Stick

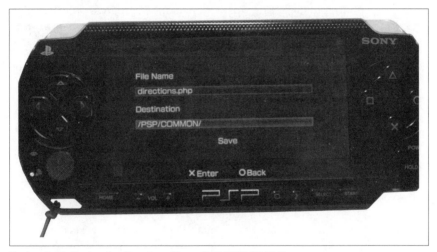

Figure 3-52. Saving the directions file to /PSP/COMMON/

You must then convert the PDF you have printed into JPEG files for viewing through the PSP's photo-viewing capabilities. Alongside this printout, you can save the individual image files from the web site and place all these files in the same folder inside /PSP/PHOTO/ on your Memory Stick.

Hacking the Hack

Now, a really cool hack would be to somehow code a homebrew app that worked together with a hacked GPS receiver to track your whereabouts with

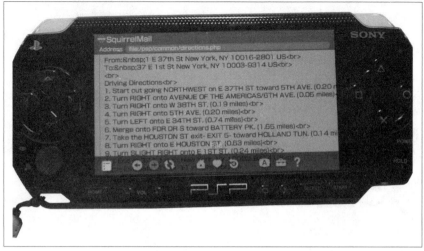

Figure 3-53. The local copy of your directions in file:/psp/common/directions

your PSP. An intrepid hacker has made quite a bit of progress on just such a hack (see *http://pspupdates.qj.net2005/11/gpsp-gps-front-end-program-for-psp. html*).

In the meantime, however, you can email the files you've created to your friends via the webmail discussed earlier in this hack, or even upload the images to Flickr (*http://www.flickr.com*). Have fun!

 HACK
#35

Turn Your PSP into a PDA

With the web capabilities in Version 2.0 of the firmware and all the homebrew options available to people running Version 1.5 of the firmware, you could easily do many of the tasks you would normally do on your PDA on your PSP.

If your boss has agreed to bankroll a new PDA to help you keep track of your busy schedule, you're probably not going to be able to convince him that the PSP is the PDA you need...at least not yet. Many of the rumors and quotes in the media indicate that Sony wants to grow the PlayStation Portable to be the must-have digital device. They have already released Version 2.0 of the firmware that added a browser and opened the platform up to more functionality than it originally had, so there is every chance that future firmware updates will add even more functionality.

Nevertheless, there are several current options, both homebrew and non-homebrew, available for the PSP that can make it a rather attractive make-shift PDA. The text-entry capabilities of the device are currently limited by the lack of a functional keyboard attachment for the PSP, but hopefully either Sony or a third party will fill this need soon. In the meantime, this hack will walk you through the different ways you can trick out your PSP as a PDA.

Address Book

The little black book—an address book, keeping track of the names, phone numbers, and sometimes addresses of important contacts—has been one of the most popular non-digital assistants, surrounded by its own social mythology. And it has become the must-have feature of even the most simplistic PDAs. We have address books on our computers, our cell phones, and our iPods, and ideally we like to keep this information synchronized between these different devices. Why not sync this data to your very sleek PSP?

This section will cover a few options for keeping an address book on your PSP.

Turn addresses into pictures. Before Sony released their browser with Version 2.0 of the firmware, and before people figured out that they could redirect the *Wipeout Pure* browser to view the rest of the Internet [Hack #41], several people realized that you could keep a lot of information on your PSP using the device's built-in picture viewing capabilities. Using the procedure discussed in "Create Your Own PSP E-Books" [Hack #29], you can easily convert your address book to a series of images that you can view on your PSP. Just export your contacts in some sort of textual form, convert to PDF, and then convert the PDF to a series of JPEG images.

This can be time-consuming. Fortunately, if you are using a Macintosh computer running OS X, PocketMac for PSP (*http://www.pocketmac.net/products/pmpsp/index.html*; $9.95 USD), shown in Figure 3-54, synchronizes the contacts in your address book or Entourage address book to an images folder on your PSP, as shown in Figure 3-55. Each contact appears in a separate image, and you can scroll through the names on the PSP (see Figure 3-56) and hit the X button next to any name whose details you need to view. Figure 3-57 shows an address card that's been turned into an image.

PocketMac for PSP can also sync pictures and music from iPhoto and iTunes to your PSP.

Address book through the Web. If you have a web site or server space somewhere, you could serve up your address book as a web page available either via the browser included with Version 2.0 of the firmware or via the *Wipeout Pure* browser. There are also several online services such as Yahoo! (*http://*

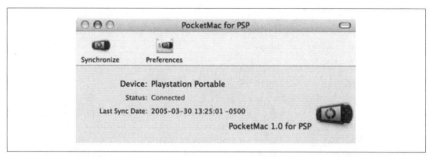

Figure 3-54. PocketMac 1.0 for PSP

Figure 3-55. Contacts folder

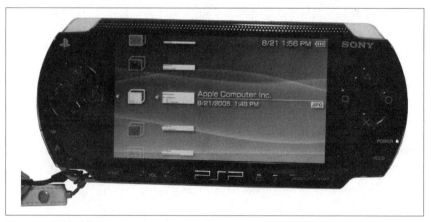

Figure 3-56. Scrolling through the address book

www.yahoo.com) and Apple's .Mac (*http://www.mac.com*) that offer online address book access. PSP Web Browser (*http://www.pspwebbrowser.com/*) is a PSP-specific community portal that offers contacts, along with a whole slew of other services.

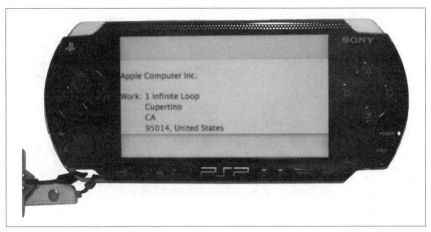

Figure 3-57. Individual address "card"

The browser included with the Version 2.0 firmware is capable of opening plain text and HTML files saved locally on your Memory Stick. You could easily export your address book as HTML, name it something handy like *addressbook.html*, place it in the root directory of your PSP, and navigate to it in the browser by entering *file:/addressbook.html* in the address bar. This would make a nice enhancement to the Memory Stick portal hack **[Hack #30]**. While you're generating a portal for your PSP's Memory Stick, why not convert your address book to HTML?

Address book via homebrew. If you are running Version 1.0 or 1.5 firmware, your PSP can run homebrew applications that the vibrant online community has developed for the PSP **[Hack #40]**. Likewise, if you're running Version 2.0 of the firmware, there are several homebrew options made to run inside the PSP's JavaScript-savvy browser.

One option that has garnered quite a bit of attention is the WinPSPortal (*http://www.winpsportal.com/*), which unfortunately lacks an address book. However, the JavaScript PSP Homebrew Portal (*http://pspupdates.qj.net/2005/ 07/firmware-20-javascript-homebrew-portal.html*) shown in Figure 3-58 has an address book (see Figure 3-59).

Calendar

The PSP displays both date and time in the upper-right corner of its screen, so you can use it to keep track of the time. However, to qualify as an actual PDA, the PSP needs to support a full calendar. As with the address book functionality, you are facing the same choices when setting up a calendar on the PSP: you can either reproduce your own calendar in JPEG form available

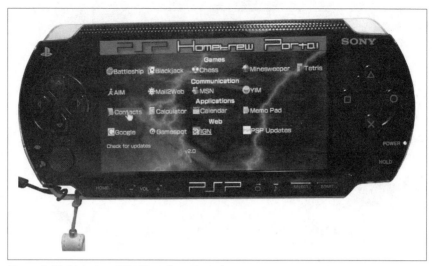

Figure 3-58. Javascript PSP Homebrew Portal

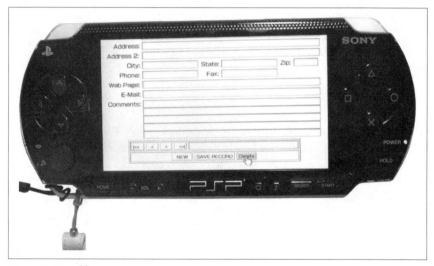

Figure 3-59. Address entry

via the Photo menu, use an online calendar service via a web browser or access a local text or HTML calendar on your PSP, or use one of the homebrew calendar options. WinPSPortal has a very basic calendar (see Figure 3-60), and while the JavaScript PSP Homebrew Portal also has a calendar, it didn't work for me during testing.

Figure 3-60. The WinPSPortal loaded in the browser of a PSP

To-Do List

A to-do list isn't very useful unless you can cross off items as you accomplish them, so while you could set up a to-do list as a single JPEG image, this wouldn't prove very useful. The only way it might work would be to create a separate image file for each item on your to-do list, and save these all in a single To Do folder in the PHOTO folder of your Memory Stick. Then, as you complete each item on the list, you simply have to select that image from the list and hit the Triangle button to pull up the control panel on the right side of the screen. Select Delete and erase the image.

In addition to this makeshift to-do list, you can always use the browser method to access a to-do list over the Internet or locally on your Memory Stick, although a generic *todo.txt* file wouldn't be editable.

For a full-featured to-do list (and more), check out Backpack (*http://www.backpackit.com*). Backpack lets you set up a workspace that you can fill with to-dos, notes, and reminders for free.

Notepad/Portable Office Documents

The lack of notepad and office capability of the PSP is admittedly the weak point of its PDA possibilities. However, this is mostly due to the lack of any sort of quick text-entry device. Mac users can easily export PowerPoint presentations, Excel spreadsheets, and Word documents to PDF and then convert to JPEG for viewing through the photo capabilities of the PSP (if you're on Windows or Linux, you can do the same with Adobe Acrobat or GhostScript, or use the free OpenOffice to open the documents and then generate your PDF). Word documents can be converted to plain text files that are readable by the browser.

Unfortunately, none of these solutions allows you to edit your documents while you are on the go. If you have Internet access and a PSP with Version 2.0 firmware, however, you will find that you can use your PSP to edit most of the popular types of online blogs, wikis, and other editable sites, so if you need to jot down some notes, why not log in to your blogging platform of choice (I use WordPress) via the PSP and save your notes as drafts on the site? You can access these later and flesh out your hastily scrawled notes that you banged out on the PSP's primitive text-entry system. If you want, you can easily configure such software to allow you to view and edit things, but keep the rest of the world from seeing anything.

If you are running Version 1.5 of the firmware, there is a homebrew solution called "Notepad for the PSP" (see "Run Homebrewed Software" [Hack #40]).

Email and Beyond

If you're not sure about basic Internet access on your PSP, make sure you check out "Get Your Wireless Network On" [Hack #5] and "Find Yourself a PSP Web Browser" [Hack #41]. Fortunately, once you have an Internet connection via one of the available PSP browsers, the entire world of webmail and other web-based services is open to you.

Hacking the Hack

As you can see, the PSP is still lacking in some of the key PDA areas. I wouldn't be surprised if future firmware upgrades add some of this functionality, and I hope that a workable keyboard attachment of some sort is also in the works. In the meantime, stay tuned to the homebrew scene [Hack #40] and consider developing a solution of your own [Hack #47].

## CHAPTER FOUR

Games

Hacks 36–40

The PSP is a gaming machine, first and foremost. The hacks collected in this chapter show you how to do a few things that Sony never intended you to do when they first released the PSP.

Play Multiplayer on the PSP with Only One UMD Disk

Share one UMD disk between multiple PSPs in an ad hoc multiplayer WiFi game.

You've just bought a brand new PSP and so has your best friend. You are both eager to play head-to-head, using the PSP's wireless gaming capabilities. Unfortunately, you and your friend have differing tastes in games and, as a result, you don't have two copies of any one game between the both of you. Before you run out to rent or buy a duplicate game from your combined lists, try this little method to trick your PlayStation Portables into thinking that you have two copies of your game.

How It Works

Shortly after the North American release of the PSP, several different sites and online forums began simultaneously reporting that people could play multiplayer ad hoc games among multiple Playstation Portables using only one UMD disk. Here's the basic procedure:

1. Load up an ad hoc multiplayer game on your PSP.
2. Eject the UMD disk.
3. The PSP will ask "Are you sure you want to quit this game?" Quickly select No and hit the X button.
4. Hand the disk to your friend.

5. Your friend puts the UMD disk in her PSP, loads up the game, and connects to the ad hoc multiplayer game you started.

6. Now, either both PSPs will freeze (if this happens, proceed to the next set of steps) or you both will start playing.

 Alternately, you can at this point start again from step 2 to invite yet another friend to play.

If both PSPs froze at step 6, then it's time to troubleshoot the swap by doing some more swapping:

1. Your friend ejects the UMD disk and selects not to quit the game.

2. You put the UMD disk back in your PSP.

3. You both start playing. If, yet again, both PSPs freeze at this point, return to step 1 but reverse who gets the disk. Rinse, repeat.

Unfortunately, this trick only works in certain games, and can be slightly different depending on the game you are using. It's mostly a matter of timing, trial, and error.

To give you an idea of how it works, I'm going to walk you through sharing one *Tony Hawk's Underground 2 Remix* UMD between two PSPs.

Sharing Tony Hawk's Underground 2 Remix

First things first: make sure that you and your friend(s) have the WLAN switch on the bottom-left corner of your PSPs switched on. Assuming that you are playing host to the game, start up *Tony Hawk's Underground 2 Remix*. Once you click through all the beginning bits and load any saved profiles you may want to use, select WiFi Play from the game menu wheel.

Next, select Host Game as you would for any normal WiFi game, and set your server settings per your liking. Then, hit the X key to begin hosting. You will have to wait while the board you selected loads in server mode.

Once it has finished loading, your character will enter Free Skate Mode. Eject your disk, choose No, and hit the X button when the PSP asks whether you want to quit the game. You will return to Free Skate Mode (see Figure 4-1). Make sure you leave the drive door open for now.

Continue free skating as your friend puts the UMD in her PSP and clicks through all the beginning bits. Your friend will select WiFi Play from the game menu wheel, choose Join Game, and select your game from the menu. Once your friend's PSP screen reads "Status: Joining game...," your PSP's

Figure 4-1. Game play resumes without the UMD disk

screen will have an overlay reading that your friend is joining the game (see Figure 4-2) and, in all likelihood, your free skate will freeze. When this happens, have your friend eject the UMD disk and pass it back to you.

Figure 4-2. The second PSP is on top; the host PSP is on bottom

Put the UMD back in your PSP and wait until the screen begins moving again, still with the notification of your friend joining. Now, eject the UMD again and pass it quickly back to your friend. After she reinserts the UMD disk into her machine, the loading screen should appear on the second PSP, while you continue to free skate (see Figure 4-3).

Figure 4-3. The board should begin loading in your friend's PSP while you continue to free skate

If you didn't do all of these steps quickly enough, the connection will time out and you will receive a notification that your friend failed to connect. Your friend's board will still load, however, and inform her that the connection was lost. You can both continue to free skate, or your friend can return to the game's WiFi screen and try the joining process again.

If you do everything quickly enough, you will both be free skating together and can begin playing. Notice in Figure 4-4, I have both PSPs running the game, connected in a WiFi game, and the tray is still open on the host machine.

Depending upon whether you simply free skate, change games, or change boards, you may have to switch several more times after this initial connection is established. You may also try to connect a third PSP by repeating the steps between the PSP hosting the game and this third PSP.

This entire process can take five minutes each time you try, so this little trick, while cool, isn't really a long-term solution for multiplayer WiFi

Figure 4-4. The host machine has no UMD inserted, and the disk tray is open

gaming. If you like the game that you are joining in on, you may want to invest in your own copy to prevent this delayed setup process from becoming aggravating over time.

Hacking the Hack

This hack should work with various games, but there are many games that don't work this way. Although I have tried again and again, I haven't been able to get a group game of *Lumines* going successfully. The connection starts, but then one or the other machine times out. Maybe it needs very precise timing, or maybe it isn't possible. However, I've given up on it, because I figured out another trick: just because you cannot join a WiFi game using only one UMD disk doesn't mean that you cannot all share one UMD disk.

The majority of the games available for the PSP don't actively access the disk during game play (this is how this multiplayer hack works in the first place). Rather, the individual boards are loaded into the PSP's memory and then the disk goes unused until you progress to the next level, need to save, or unlock some new cut scene. So, why not share the game among multiple PSPs?

This trick will work with most board/level-based games. Just before writing this hack, I successfully tried it with both *Lumines* and *DarkStalkers*.

Here's how it works:

1. Load up the game in your PSP and start a single-player game.
2. As soon as it starts, hit the Start button and pause the game.

3. Eject your UMD disk, select No, and hit the X button when the PSP asks whether you want to quit the game. The game will return to the pause screen.

4. Hand your UMD disk to your friend, so that she can load up a single-player game.

5. Once it loads for your friend, have her hit Start, pause the game, and eject the UMD disk, passing it on to another friend.

6. Once everybody is ready to go, unpause and begin playing.

With *Lumines*, you can have a contest between all the players to see who lasts the longest. After a while, the music in the background will stop playing, but the game will continue. In *Wipeout Pure*, you can see who finishes the agreed-upon race first. In *DarkStalkers*, you can see who beats his opponent first. Think about all the different group games and tournaments you could have without the WiFi connectivity, but by sharing a single UMD disk.

The best part about this trick is that once you reach time to switch boards, usually the game just hangs, waiting for the UMD. Retrieve the disk from your friend, load up the next board, hit Pause, and then start passing the disk around. You have hours of shared gaming ahead of you. Have fun!

H A C K   #37   Play Games over the Internet

Connect your computer to the Internet, share the connection with a computer-to-computer network over wireless, and all you need is XLink Kai's free online gaming service to connect to players around the globe with your PSP.

One of the coolest things about playing games on the PlayStation Portable is being able to play wirelessly with your friends. Unfortunately, due to the $250 USD buy-in price of the PSP, finding a friend who has a PSP and is available to play during the same time that you are can be problematic. Since the PSP's networked gaming feature works via 802.11b, why not hook the PSP into your home wireless network and play other eager-to-play gamers online whenever you like? Sony doesn't yet offer a solution to do this, but there is a way.

Things Needed

Here's what you'll need:

- Your PSP.
- High-speed Internet connection (DSL or cable).

- A computer running Linux (x86, MIPS, or PPC), Windows (98/98se/ 2000/ME/XP), or Macintosh OS X (10.3 or newer) hooked into your high-speed Internet connection via Ethernet.

- An 802.11b-compatible WiFi card in your computer that is also compatible with XLink Kai (a list of compatible cards can be found here: *http://www.teamxlink.co.uk/forum/viewtopic.php?t=11469*), or an 802. 11b-compatible router capable of running XLink Kai.

- A free registered account with XLink Kai (*http://www.teamxlink.co.uk*) and a downloaded copy of XLink Kai Evolution for your platform.

- The free Amaryllis (*http://www.nullriver.com/index/products/amaryllis*) from Nullriver Software, the makers of PSPWare (Amaryllis is only required if you are running Mac OS X).

The Way It Works

Your computer connects to your DSL/cable modem via the wired Ethernet connection. Your computer, running XLink Kai, routes the Internet connection coming from its Ethernet port and shares it out via your 802.11b-compatible wireless card. You create a computer-to-computer network between your computer and your PSP, and XLink Kai does all the heavy lifting of convincing your PSP that the games connecting over the Internet and streaming forth from your computer are actually only local PSPs trying to play a friendly game. The procedure described in this hack is the general setup that you will follow, no matter which platform you are using.

The XLink Kai forums have tutorials for using XLink Kai on nearly every platform out there to play PSP games wirelessly over the Internet (*http:// www.teamxlink.co.uk/forum/viewtopic.php?t=5649*). For this hack, I will walk you through the step-by-step process of connecting via Mac OS X, which is one of the more complicated setups. If you are on one of the other platforms, for the most part, the same steps listed here will work for your platform; however, you won't have the added step of installing and running Amaryllis in the mix. I recommend that you read through the entire hack before beginning, since taking the steps in the right order is important.

Set up your PSP

This step universally applies, no matter what type of computer you are running.

Make sure that the wireless switch on your PSP is turned off and that your PSP is also turned off. Turn on your PSP. Go to Settings → Network Settings and click the X button. Select Ad Hoc Mode and hit the X button. You will be prompted to select a channel. Choose Channel 1 and hit the X button, and then hit the X button again to save these settings.

 You could leave the channel set to automatic and everything would still work, and you would most likely find yourself able to play with other people running their PSPs on other channels. However, it's been my own experience, as well as the experience of others online, that playing via Channel 1 works better on the PSP.

Next, load the WiFi-capable game that you would like to play and switch the PSP's wireless switch into the On position. Navigate to a point in the game where you can host a wireless network game. This will differ according to which game you choose to play, so refer to the documentation that came with your game. Once you have started hosting a game, the LED that indicates there is WiFi activity should begin actively flashing. Your PSP is waiting for others to join from the Internet. This is where your computer comes into play.

On Your Computer

Now that your PSP is eagerly awaiting other PSP players, it's time to get your computer to make the Internet connection. Remember, your computer must be getting its Internet connection via Ethernet, since your wireless card will not be able to both receive and send the signal to both your broadband network and your PSP. Make sure that everything is running smoothly as far as the Internet goes on your computer. Assuming that it is, you need to set up a computer-to-computer or ad hoc network over WiFi between your computer and the PSP. If you are on Windows or Linux, make sure that the settings for your wireless connection are set to ad hoc. On Mac OS X, all you need to do is click on the AirPort signal icon in the menu bar, and under Computer-to-Computer Networks, you will see an oddly named computer starting with PSP_, as in Figure 4-5. This is your PSP, which is currently broadcasting, searching to host a multiplayer game. Select the PSP from the list to create a computer-to-computer network between your computer and the PSP.

Connect to XLink Kai

Now that you have established a computer-to-computer network with your PSP, it's time to load XLink Kai.

On a PC, launch Kai, log in to your XLink Kai account, and check Kai's diagnostics to make sure that it is reading your PSP correctly.

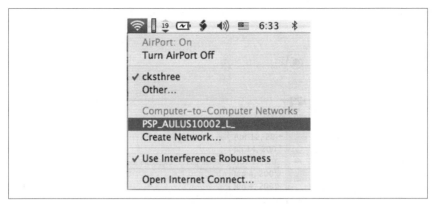

Figure 4-5. The oddly named computer in the Airport's menu bar is your PSP

On a Mac, first launch Kaid, then load Amaryllis and enter the login information to your XLink Kai account. Navigate to the consoles tab in Amaryllis and select the PSP console room (see Figure 4-6).

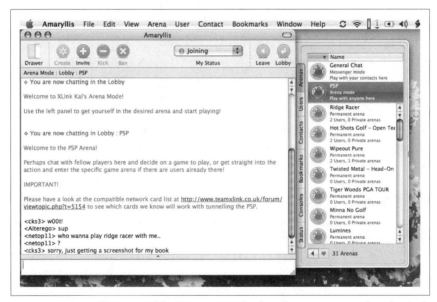

Figure 4-6. Amaryllis's view of the PSP arena with a list of active games in the side panel

Now, back on the PSP, you can at this point stop attempting to host the game that you used to connect the PSP to your computer. You may now begin hosting a new game on your PSP or try to join one of the games being shared out from your computer to your PSP via Kai or Amaryllis.

Enjoy playing online with others!

Wash, Rinse, Repeat

Here's a quick recap of the basic steps:

1. Make sure that your PSP and your PSP's WLAN switch are both turned off.

2. Turn on your PSP and change the network settings to Ad Hoc on Channel 1.

3. Load the game you want to play, switch on the WLAN switch, and begin hosting a wireless game.

4. On your computer, establish a computer-to-computer or ad hoc connection with the PSP.

5. Launch Kai or Kaid. If you are on Mac OS X, launch Amaryllis after launching Kaid.

6. Make sure you are successfully logged in to XLink Kai.

7. Stop hosting the game on your PSP.

8. Start hosting a new game or select a game in Kai/Amaryllis and try to join that game on your PSP.

If you are having trouble connecting, just go through these steps again, and refer to the online tutorials available via the XLink Kai forums (*http://www.teamxlink.co.uk/forum/viewtopic.php?t=5649*). If you switch games, you will have to close everything out and start over from the beginning, as each separate game broadcasts under a different ad hoc or computer-to-computer networked name. The people who are successfully logging in and playing are following the preceding steps to a tee, and starting over from the beginning anytime anything goes wrong.

Game Play

Once you are connected and successfully playing an opponent, one thing you will notice is that there is a noticeable difference between playing with your friend sitting across your living room and playing with your friend in Bangladesh, who you are racing in *Wipeout Pure* over the Internet. Although you can—with only a modicum of work—get the connection between your PSP, your computer, and the XLink Kai network up and running, once you are connected, you will most likely have trouble connecting to games or hosting games from time to time. Keep on trying.

Wipeout Pure connected nicely for me when I was testing this hack, but while *Untold Legends: Brotherhood of the Blade* supports WiFi game play, I could never get it to successfully connect to any other players. I should clarify here: we were able to connect, but we couldn't see each other and, if we weren't headed in the same direction, the game froze, timed out, and we were disconnected.

Also, if you are connected and playing a game successfully, you are still going to encounter all the lag problems that you experience with any other online gaming system. The game will only run as fast as its slowest player. In *Wipeout Pure*, I would sometimes have a good normal race, whereas other times, as soon as the race started, I would find myself racing the ghosts of my opponents and no one would know whether they were winning or not until they finished the race. Several times, my PSP told me I was in first place, but when I jumped through the finish line, thinking I'd won, I suddenly was confronted with the information that I had finished third.

Other Systems

Recently, an alternative to XLink Kai has shown up online; XBConnect, which used to exclusively offer Internet game play to Xbox owners, has opened up a PSP section on their service. XBConnect (*http://www.xbconnect. com/*) is PC-only, so if you are on a Windows machine and frustrated or dissatisfied with XLink Kai, you might want to check out XBConnect.

Whatever you go with, have fun. And if you're online with XLink Kai searching for a quick game, look for cks3. That's me, and I'm always looking for some friendly competition.

Throw a PSP WiFi LAN Party

HACK #38

Use the PSP's built-in ad hoc wireless capabilities to have an on-the-fly LAN party with your PSP-wielding friends.

The PSP is one heck of a little game system that promises sci-fi-like, wireless multiplayer gaming and 3-D graphics that rival top video game consoles. It is now possible to have a networked wireless LAN game with friends without having to carry desktop PCs, string Ethernet all over some dank basement, and worry about some loser cheating by running an aim-bot (a cheat program that automatically aims for you) and ruining the fun. Alas, one of the problems facing many PSP gamers is that not that many of their friends have invested $250 USD (as of December 2005) for a PSP of their very own.

How cool would it be to throw your own public PSP wireless LAN party? With some minor planning and fliers, you could throw the nerd gaming event of the season!

Find the Spot

First, find a good place to have the LAN party. I would suggest a cafe that serves espresso-based drinks, because they have places to sit with power outlets, and they also have drinks and restrooms. Plus, they are all over the place and not as likely to give you the bum's rush as coffee and donut shops that prefer quick turnover to customers who linger. I bet that there is not one place in the Western world without a Starbucks or independent coffee shop less than 10 miles away. Just look for a place with parking that is centrally located around town. If you have a cybercafe or gaming center, then the location is a no-brainer.

> Another idea is to have the LAN party at a local public library. As long as you ask the librarians in advance, bring headphones, and keep it calm, a library would be a great place for a PSP LANfest. They are also smoke-free, open for all ages, and they don't have elevator music pumped over the speakers like some cafes. If you open the gaming to the public, however, you might have trouble keeping things quiet, so talk to the librarian about booking a private room for the event if holding a publicly advertised game is your plan.

First of all, talk to the manager of the place you've picked. Explain that you would like to have a small get-together of gamers who want to play PSP together. Let the manager know that you plan on ordering drinks or food, and she will most likely not have a problem with it. Give yourself about three weeks to plan before the party to get the word out. Give the manager a call a day before the party as a reminder, in case she forgot.

Getting the Word Out

Next, you need to get the word out to potential PSP gamers. Write up a brief flier with the details of what, where, when, and why (see Figure 4-7).

I would put an email address as a point of contact. Make sure to point out that this is not an official function of the cafe. Then you might print out a couple copies and ask whether you can put some up at local game stores that stock PSP games, at the cafe, and other places where you might expect to find fellow gaming candidates. You then might call the local newspaper and ask whether you can get a shout-out in the community calendar or the technology section of the paper. Who knows? They might just run a full article, if it is a slow news day.

Figure 4-7. A possible flier for your LAN party

Set up a dedicated email address, such as *PSPgame_ YourCity@gmail.com,* to coordinate your endeavors and to avoid filling your personal email with LAN party bits and possibly spam.

Then there is this little thing called the Internet. I used to be able to endorse Meetup.com (*http://www.meetup.com/*), but since they are now charging monthly for meetings, it would not be worth it for a PSP party.

If you end up making your own page to promote it, make sure you submit it to the search engines. A Craig's List (*http://www.craigslist.org/*) post for your town could help get the word out. PSP Meets (*http://www.pspmeets.com/*) is a web site that was inspired by the first version of this article that I posted on 8bit Joystick (*http://8bitjoystick.com/*). All you really need is just one other person to play with, but the more, the merrier.

You might plan on about three hours or so for a party, so people could play off one PSP battery charge. I would plan it on a weeknight from 6:00 p.m. to

9:00 p.m., so it would not conflict with work, school, or social life. Make a list of suggested games, and you might want to bring an extra battery pack or AC adapter, in case someone forgets to charge her PSP. This would be a great chance to see and try out new games. You might bring a whiteboard so that if you set up a tournament, you will have something to write the brackets on. You might spare some old PSOne games as a tournament prize. If you have a laptop with a USB Memory Stick Duo reader, bring it so that you can trade and transfer PSP save files **[Hack #2]**. A CD full of MP4 videos and MP3s for the PSP would make a pretty cool party favor. If you make a sign-up sheet, you could collect email addresses for future PSP LAN party announcements.

A Brief Tutorial in Wireless PSP Gaming

Putting together a tutorial on how to set up the wireless game modes of the games you'll be playing might help if some of your players have not gotten down with PSP WiFi networking. But, then again, it is not rocket science.

You should prepare a short handout that applies to all games or write this info on the whiteboard:

- Make sure that you have the WLAN switch on the On position.
- Make sure that you have the PSP set to Ad Hoc Mode rather than Infrastructure Mode. To set up Ad Hoc Mode, navigate to Settings → Network Settings, click the X button, choose Ad Hoc Mode, click the X button, and set to Automatic (or Ch 1, Ch 6, or Ch 11, depending upon what you all agree on). Hit the X button to save the settings.

> If the venue for your WiFi LAN party has its own wireless connection, you may want to check with the owner to find out which channel they are broadcasting on, so that you can set your party to another channel. This should help cut down on interference for all parties involved.

Hacking the Hack

Since the decline of the arcade in the U.S., there has been a void of public community gaming in the same room. It could be pretty cool to get together once a month with total strangers in your community to throw the smack down on the PSP. You could meet new people, play new games, and really get the most of your PSP networking features. Some critics say that video games are a solitary pastime, but they can be a great way to meet new people and zap them over WiFi.

—Jacob Metcalf

Create an Infrared Peripheral Interface

HACK #39

In this article, you will learn how to get a microcontroller to communicate with the PSP and how to use it to make an interface for gamepads and more. Although it won't work with existing games out of the box, you can write your own homebrew games that use these controllers.

If you're lucky enough to own a Sony PSP capable of running homebrew software [Hack #40], you may have tried out some of the countless emulators and ports of older games out there already. The bad thing is that you can't play all the old games in two-player mode. Finding a solution for this was actually my motivation to start with this hack. First, it had to avoid any hardware modifications on the PSP itself, because I don't like to open such an expensive device. Since the PSP already provides infrared and USB ports, this wasn't much of a problem. Secondly, it had to be cheap. Being a student, I was looking for a cheap solution, and so I chose infrared. Aside from IR being cheaper, USB-capable controllers are hard to get.

As the interface consists of parts you can get at most electronic part distributors and doesn't require any special equipment, this project can be handled even by people with little programming and/or soldering experience.

Things You'll Need

- An ATMega8 microcontroller
- A programmer for the AVR (for loading your program onto the microcontroller)
- Two male SUB-D connectors (9-pin)
- 13 resistors, 1 k Ω
- One resistor, 470 Ω
- One infrared diode

If you build your own power supply:

- One LM7805 Voltage Regulator
- One electrolytic capacitor, 10 µF
- Two ceramic capacitors, 100 nFm
- One diode 1N4001

I also recommend downloading the ATMega8 Data Sheet (*http://www.atmel. com/dyn/products/product_card.asp?part_id=2004*) because it provides useful information about the microcontroller.

To create the software for the AVR, I have used AVR-GCC, which is included in the WinAVR Package (*http://winavr.sourceforge.net*). A programmer like the AVR-PG2 from Olimex (*http://www.olimex.com*) will fit your needs. You can either buy them there or build your own one easily with the schematics available for download.

You will also need the newest version of the PSPSDK (*http://www.pspdev. org*). If you haven't already, you have to install Cygwin (*http://www.cygwin. com/*) in order to run PSPSDK on Windows [Hack #47].

Types of Gamepads

With every generation of game console, the gamepads have changed. Until the early 1990s, most gamepads consisted only of some buttons directly connected to the console. Since gamepads were designed with more and more buttons, new ways for reading out the data had to be found. Original PlayStation gamepads, for example, have a small microcontroller inside that handles all the button input, converts the analog stick data to binary values, and communicates with the console over a serial protocol.

For this project, I will use a Sega Master System gamepad, which consists of only six buttons and uses a 9-pin SUB-D connector. Figure 4-8 shows the schematic.

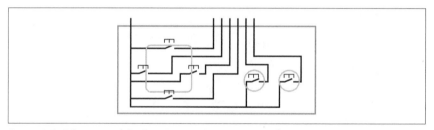

Figure 4-8. Schematic of the Sega Master System gamepad

If your eyes are starting to glaze over right now, don't fret. You just need a crash course. Dan O'Sullivan and Tom Igoe's *Physical Computing* (Course Technology PTR) explains everything involved with projects such as this, from the individual components up to the power supply, to all the skills you need to breadboard up your circuits.

Setting up the AVR

Before you can start with the fun, you have to get the AVR up and running. This isn't really difficult, since you only have to connect the supply voltage and ground, and then upload your program. Being a microcontroller, the AVR doesn't need any periphery.

Power supply. If you take a look at the data sheet, you will see that the ATMega8 accepts any value between 4.5 V and 5.5 V as supply voltage. This means you could either use a battery pack as power supply or build one using an LM7805 Voltage Regulator, which will provide a more stable 5 V supply voltage. Figure 4-9 shows a basic power supply design.

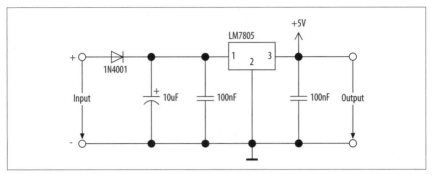

Figure 4-9. A power supply using the 7805 Voltage Regulator

If you decide to build a power supply using the 7805, the only thing you have to do is connect the input voltage, which can be any value between 8V and 35V, between the input and the ground pin. Even though it will work on its own, I strongly recommend that you connect a diode between input and pin 1, a 1 μF and a 100 nF capacitor between Pin 1 and ground, and a 1 μF capacitor between output and ground.

Having built your power supply, connect the output to the VCC pin of the AVR and tie the GND and AGND pins to ground. Connect a 1 kΩ resistor between VCC and RESET to make sure that the AVR isn't in reset mode, if no programmer is connected.

If you don't feel up to building the power supply, you can always fall back on the battery pack, or purchase a power supply that delivers 5 volts DC and use it in this project.

Now you can connect your programmer to the AVR.

Creating the Circuit

You can connect the buttons directly to the microcontroller using pull-down resistors. Pull-down resistors are necessary because each input pin of the microcontroller needs either a low or high state. If you choose the pins where you connect the buttons, you have to be careful bout which ones you can use and which you cannot. For example, the RESET pin is necessary for programming the microcontroller and should not be disabled.

I connected the gamepads to the microcontroller, as shown in Figure 4-10.

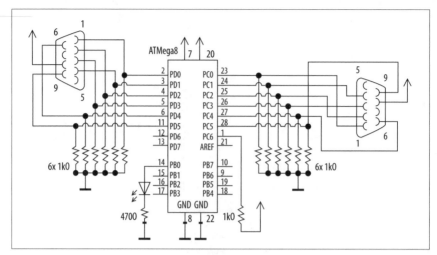

Figure 4-10. A schematic of the interface

The IR diode is directly connected to an I/O pin of the microcontroller with a resistor. The resistance is lower than the one you would use for a standard LED, since the way of using pulses enables the diode to shine brighter (explained previously).

Sending Data to the PSP

Now that the AVR is set up and ready to run your programs, you can start writing the program that sends data to the PSP. To do this, you need to understand how IRDA Data Transfer works.

If you already know a bit about serial data transmission, this should be easy for you to understand, because IRDA is very similar to RS232 transmission. Each frame has a start bit and a stop bit, and the standard baud rate of the PSP is set to 9600 bps. The difference to the standard serial protocol is that bits are determined as short pulses, and the byte to send has to be inverted. Figure 4-11 illustrates this.

Usually the length of the pulses is 3/16 of the bit time. The receiver gets a clearer signal when using pulses because the output power of the diode can be higher over such a short duration. With this information, you can write a function that sends one byte of data to the PSP. First, you have to include the necessary libraries:

```
#include <avr/delay.h>
#include <avr/io.h>

#define F_CPU          1000000UL
```

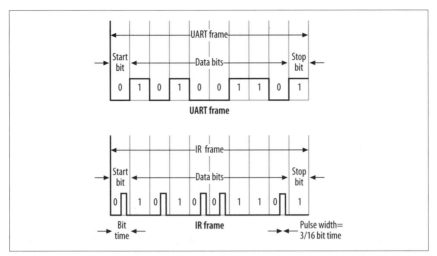

Figure 4-11. An IRDA Data Frame compared to an RS232 Data Frame

The file *delay.h* provides functions for software delays, and *io.h* includes the I/O Port definitions. The delay functions need the clock frequency defined as F_CPU in Hertz in order to work. You must write 1 MHz, since this is the default clock speed of the ATMega8.

Next, you need to define some constants:

```
#define OUT_PORT      PORTB
#define OUT_PIN    PB1
#define OUT_DDR    DDRB

#define DOWN_TIME    78.125
#define PULSE_TIME   18.0288
```

The #defines with the prefix OUT determine which pin of which port is used for the output of the IRDA Signal. This is the pin the IR LED should be connected to.

Next, you need a function to send one bit. To make it more accurate, define it as *inline*. It checks whether the bit to send is 0 and, if so, creates a pulse by setting PB1 high for a short period of time:

```
__inline__ void ir_send_bit(char bit){
    _delay_us(DOWN_TIME);
    if(!bit) {
        PORTB |= 0x01;
    }
    _delay_us(PULSE_TIME);
    PORTB &= !0x01;
}
```

Create an Infrared Peripheral Interface

For sending a byte to the PSP, you need to call the `ir_send_bit` function 10 times. First the start bit, then a loop that sends the byte and, at the end, the stop bit:

```
void ir_send_byte(char byte)
{
    char i = 8;
    ir_send_bit(0); // Start-Bit
    while(i)
    {
        ir_send_bit(byte&0x01);
        byte >>= 1;
        i--;
    }
    ir_send_bit(1); // Stop-Bit
}
```

Now that you're able to send bytes over infrared, the only thing left to do is to detect button changes and send them to the PSP. In each byte you send to the PSP, a byte is used to indicate the state of the gamepad controls (see Figure 4-12).

Figure 4-12. A byte containing button data

The first thing the main function does is to set the Data Direction Registers. All pins, except the first one of PortB, will be defined as input pins. After that, an infinite loop follows, which checks whether any button states have changed:

```
int main(void) {
    DDRB = 0x01;
    DDRD = 0x00;
    DDRC = 0x00;
    unsigned char gp1_old, gp2_old, gp1_new, gp2_new;
    while(1) {
        gp1_new = PINC;
        gp2_new = PIND;
        if(gp1_new != gp1_old){
            ir_send_byte(gp1_new);
        }
        if(gp2_new != gp2_old){
            /* set the GP select bit */
            ir_send_byte(gp2_new | 0b10000000);
        }
```

```
        _delay_us(10);
        gp1_old = gp1_new;
        gp2_old = gp2_new;
    }
}
```

Writing the PSP Application

Now that you are able to send data to the PSP, you just have to write a little library that provides functions for decoding the data and making applications with support for external gamepads.

First, some declarations and imports are necessary:

```
#include <pspkernel.h>
#include <pspdebug.h>
#include <pspctrl.h>
#include <stdlib.h>

/* Define the module info section */
PSP_MODULE_INFO("IRDA Example", 0, 1, 1);

#define printf      pspDebugScreenPrintf

#define     GP_UP           0x0001
#define     GP_RIGHT        0x0002
#define     GP_DOWN         0x0004
#define     GP_LEFT         0x0008
#define     GP_1            0x0010
#define     GP_2            0x0020

SceUID          f;
unsigned char   odata = 0,
                ndata = 0,
                gamepad1,
                gamepad2;
```

Next, initialize the infrared port of the PSP. Write a function that does this work and that has to be called once the application is started. It opens a stream for reading data from the IR port:

```
int GP_Init( )
{
    return (f = sceIoOpen("irda0:", PSP_O_RDWR, 0));
}
```

Now you just need a function that the application can use for checking the button states. As long as there is new data available, the loop assigns it to the variables gamepad1 or gamepad2, depending on the state of the GP select bit:

```
void GP_Update( )
{
```

```
        do
        {
            odata = ndata;
            sceIoRead(f, &ndata, 1);
            if(ndata & 0b10000000)
            {
                gamepad2 = ndata;
            } else {
                gamepad1 = ndata;
            }
        } while( odata != ndata );
    }
```

Having written all the necessary code for receiving data from the interface,
you can test to see whether everything works with this simple test application. It will check for updates every frame and directly print the states on the
screen:

```
    void printStates(unsigned char data)
    {
        printf("UP    : %u\n", (data&GP_UP) != 0);
        printf("DOWN  : %u\n", (data&GP_DOWN) != 0);
        printf("LEFT  : %u\n", (data&GP_LEFT) != 0);
        printf("RIGHT : %u\n", (data&GP_RIGHT) != 0);
        printf("1     : %u\n", (data&GP_1) != 0);
        printf("2     : %u\n", (data&GP_2) != 0);
    }

    int main(void)
    {
        SceCtrlData pad;
        pspDebugScreenInit();
        printf("\nIRDA Test Application\n");
        GP_Init();
        while (1)
        {
            GP_Update();
            pspDebugScreenSetXY(0,3);

            printf("--- Gamepad 1 ---\n");
            printStates(gamepad1);

            printf("\n--- Gamepad 2 ---\n");
            printStates(gamepad2);

            sceCtrlReadBufferPositive(&pad, 1);  // Refresh the PSP
                                                  // Button States
            if(pad.Buttons & PSP_CTRL_CIRCLE)    // If Circle is pressed...
            {
                sceKernelExitGame();             // ...exit the Application
            }
        }
    }
```

This application provides a good base for creating your own gamepad-enabled applications or implementing gamepad support into existing applications, such as emulators.

Hacking the Hack

This is a very simple hack that shows only a small example of what is possible with the PSP, a microcontroller, and infrared. You can connect virtually everything to the microcontroller, send the data to the PSP, and do whatever you want with it inside of your own homebrew applications. Atmel provides useful application notes on their site that show you, for example, how to connect a keyboard to an AVR.

—Thomas Novotny

Run Homebrewed Software

#40   One of the great things about the PSP as a gaming system is the large number of developers and hackers who flocked together to figure out ways to really trick out the system with their own homebrew applications.

If you have a PSP running Version 1.0 or 1.5 of the firmware, don't update to Version 2.0 of the firmware.

If you have a PSP running 1.51 or 1.52 of the firmware, then you might as well go ahead and upgrade to 2.0. Why? Well, all the dutiful hackers have figured out ways of running their own code on PSPs running Versions 1.0 and 1.5 of the firmware. They haven't figured out how to get around the clamps Sony slapped on Versions 1.51, 1.52, or 2.0…at least, not as of this writing.

> If you buy a game that requires you to update to 1.51, 1.52, or 2.0, try grabbing WAB Version Changer (*http://www. psphacks.net/content/view/344*), which will trick the game into thinking you are running a newer version of the firmware and do so without ruining your homebrew. Keep your eyes on the WAB team too, as they are working on a downgrader to help everyone who has already updated their PSPs.

So, if you're running Version 1.0 or 1.5 of the firmware, an entire world of programs and emulators are available to you. If you're running Version 2.0, then you can still run browser-based JavaScript homebrew, but no native code and no emulators. Again, I think this will prove to be a "yet" situation. There are people working right now on breaking the locks Sony has put in the way of all the homebrew. If you're daring, you can try downgrading your firmware [Hack #11].

Feel free to skip ahead to the section that covers your firmware. Not sure what you have? Have you already bought a PSP running Version 2.0, but want to sell it on eBay to buy one running Version 1.5 of the firmware? Read on to find out how to spot a 1.5 PSP among a stack of 2.0s.

Spot Your Firmware

Here's how to make sure you're getting the PSP you really need.

Out of the box. If you have your PSP in your hands, it's pretty easy to find out which firmware you are running. Simply navigate to Settings → System Settings, hit the X button, then scroll down to System Information and hit the X button again. An informational screen will pop up listing your PSP's MAC address, the System Software, and your PSP's nickname. Whatever number follows Version in the System Software row is the version of the firmware you are running.

In the box. If you don't have your PSP yet, or you're in the market for a second one, here's what you need to know to try to avoid grabbing another Version 2.0. The UPC sticker on one end of the box indicates the firmware version. In Figure 4-13, there are two boxes, one without an A under 120V, indicating Version 1.5 boxed with the *Spider-Man 2* UMD, and one with an A, indicating Version 1.5 of the firmware without the free UMD. If the box says something other than *PSP-1001 K* along the top, or it has a B or any other letter than an A underneath the 120V, then you're dealing with 1.51, 1.52, or 2.0 firmware, and you won't be able to run the homebrew.

Figure 4-13. Checking the box for Version 1.5 firmware

Homebrew and Emulators

If you were one of the fortunate few who grabbed a Japanese PSP running Version 1.0 of the firmware, then you have a very nice homebrew machine at your fingertips. There are multiple sites online that serve as repositories for these homebrew applications, where you can download them and then transfer them to the GAMES folder inside the PSP folder on your Memory

Stick. After you copy the homebrew applications and games to this folder, navigate to Games → Memory Stick on your PSP, hit the X button, and then select the homebrew game or application you want to play from the list and hit the X button again to launch it.

> Keep in mind that all these homebrew apps take up space on your Memory Stick. Make sure you watch sites such as deal-news (*http://www.dealnews.com*) to try to get a 1GB or larger Memory Stick Duo card on the cheap.

If you, like most people who purchased their PSP in North America, have Version 1.5 of the firmware on your PSP, then things are only slightly trickier. Originally, the first workaround for running homebrew on Version 1.50 of the firmware involved something called a *swaploit*. For the swaploit, the *EBOOT.PBP* file that contains the main code for each homebrew program had to be split into two parts, placed into two identical folders inside */PSP/ GAMES/* on two different Memory Sticks. You would navigate to the game on the first Memory Stick and hit the X button, then immediately after the PSP flash screen appeared, indicating that the game was launching, you had to quickly eject that first Memory Stick and replace it with the second one. If you timed everything just right, the game or homebrew application would successfully launch.

This swaploit was far from ideal, as the swapping required speed and skill and wasn't very good for the Memory Sticks involved, which—over time— would develop scratches on their contacts (and could also at times be damaged or possibly lost from accidentally shooting them across the room while ejecting them to make way for the second Memory Stick).

Fortunately, another workaround was discovered that eliminated the need to swap the Memory Sticks. Again, the *EBOOT.PBP* file was split in two, but this time, both files were placed on the same Memory Stick inside two different folders. Each folder had the same name, with the first ending with an additional % at the end of the name. When navigating through the Memory Stick via the PSP's Game menu, each homebrew game or application would show up next to another file called Corrupted Data. This file was merely the second folder that didn't appear launchable to the PSP.

Split your EBOOT.PBP files. Most newer homebrew apps come in both Version 1.0 *EBOOT.PBP* format and in split 1.50 format, but in case you run across a homebrew application that is only ready to run on Version 1.0 firmware, there are a few tools available to help you properly prepare the file for running on your PSP.

If you are running Mac OS X, you will want to grab HomebrewPSP Converter (*http://ipsp.kaisakura.com/homebrew.php*), which is available for free from RnSKSoftronics, the makers of iPSP. This easy-to-use application will let you select a recently downloaded *EBOOT.PBP* file, split the file into the necessary two parts, and automatically copy these files to a mounted PSP when you click the Transfer To PSP button (see Figure 4-14).

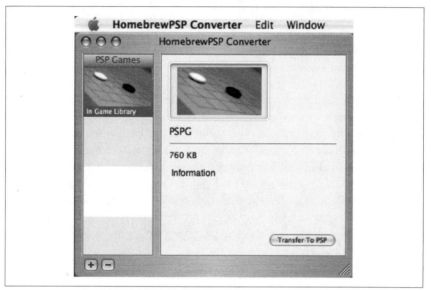

Figure 4-14. HomebrewPSP Converter

If you're running Windows XP, there are several programs that will do the same thing that HomebrewPSP Converter does on OS X. PSP Homebrew 9 (*http://www.pspvideo9.com/homebrew/*), from the makers of PSP Video 9, is a free (although donations are welcomed by the developer, Sajeeth Cherian) Windows solution for converting and moving your homebrew applications to your PSP on a Windows box.

> In most cases, you won't need to worry about this. Most homebrew applications out there come preprepared in both firmware 1.0- and 1.5-savvy versions, so there is really not much need for converting the files anymore. I only supply the information here for the rare file that isn't pre-prepared, and to provide some of the history behind the scene.

Where to find homebrew and emulation applications. So, now that you know how to both prepare the homebrew applications and get them onto your PSP, all you need to do is to find some homebrew to play. A comprehensive list of the ever-changing landscape of homebrew for the PSP is beyond the scope of this hack. Such an endeavor would be an entire book of its own, and a book that probably shouldn't be written for a while longer, as the scene keeps popping up with new apps and sometimes daily improvements of existing applications.

In the meantime, let's spend some time looking at some online sites where you can grab some of the latest homebrew.

At the risk of being self-promotional, I'll first direct you to the PSP category of my blog, Sample the Web (*http://www.sampletheweb.com/categories/ media/psp/*), where I keep track of a lot of the little PSP bits that interest me. You should also check out PSP Fanboy, a PSP blog that I write for, and PSP Hacks: The Book (*http://www.psphacksthebook.com/*), a site that—as I write this—is nothing but a placeholder online, but which I intend to populate with lots of useful links and information to enhance this book. Also, make sure you check O'Reilly's web site page for this book (*http://www.oreilly. com/catalog/psphks*), as we'll be providing corrections to the book from time to time.

None of these sites, however, are hosting the various homebrew applications that you want to get your hands on. There are two places that I've found to be the best repositories for PSP homebrew. One is PSP Updates (*http://www.pspupdates.com/*).

> Unfortunately, for the most part, PSP Updates is hidden behind multiple pop-up- and pop-over-plagued pages that can be more than a bit frustrating at times. The content is both great and free, but if you don't like sites that continually bombard you with advertisements, you may want to consider signing up for a paid account with PSP Updates so that you can browse their files ad-free.
>
> I like free, however, so I'll just continually close the ad windows and click the Skip This Ad links to get to the goods, and diligently empty my browser's cache files after I'm done.

The other, less ad-laden site is PSP-Hacks (*http://www.psp-hacks.com/*), which has an easily accessible Homebrew Download section (*http://www. psp-hacks.com/downloads.php#homebrew*), although not as comprehensive as PSP Updates' selection.

Here's a short list of other useful PSP- and homebrew-related links:

PSPworld (*http://www.pspworld.com/*)
PSP-vault (*http://www.psp-vault.com/*)
PSP Garden (*http://www.pspgarden.com/*)

PSP Spot (*http://www.psp-spot.com/*)
PSP Hacks (*http://www.psphacks.net/*)

If I don't have direct links to any of the homebrew applications I list in this hack, it's because the developer doesn't have a web site of his own, and the file is found regularly updated on one of these sites. Wherever possible, however, I will link directly to the developer's site.

PSP Chess. Christopher Bowron is one of the first and most diligent homebrew developers, releasing PSP Chess (*http://bace.bowron.us/*) and continuing to improve and update the program over time. It's a really nifty and well-designed chess program that I play regularly on my PSP (see Figure 4-15).

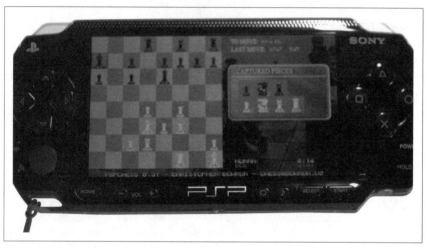

Figure 4-15. PSP Chess

PSP Rhythm Composer and DJSP. The musically inclined amongst you will like PSP Rhythm Composer (*http://www.iturzaeta.com/PSPRhythm/*). This homebrew drum machine for your PSP features a 16-step sequencer, 16 drum instruments with 32 total samples, 16 drum patterns, and a song mode.

If you enjoy listening more than creating, you might prefer DJSP (visit *http://www.handango.com/PlatformProductDetail.jsp?siteId=1&platformId=14&N =4294925759&productId=175143&R=175143*) over the MP3 player that comes preloaded in your PSP (see Figure 4-16).

This Audio Visual MP3 player for the PSP features 10 different visual patterns that play along with your music, a 10-band equalizer that will allow you to increase the volume beyond the loudest volume allowed by the PSP's

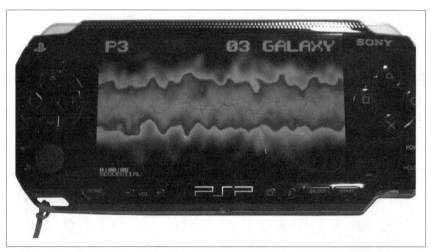

Figure 4-16. DJSP

default MP3 player, and the ability to play tracks of any file length (according to the web site, up to 2 GB, if necessary).

Games and emulators. In addition to the homebrew games such as *PSP Chess* and *PSP Go*, there are various programs copied from other games, in particular a *Bejeweled* clone and games such as *Dr. Mario* (see Figure 4-17). Perhaps one of the most popular forms of homebrew that has the largest following and has persuaded many PSP owners to diligently avoid upgrading their firmware can be found in the form of homebrew emulators that emulate the behavior of other gaming systems.

Figure 4-17. Dr. Mario

Since its initial release, the PSP has become one of the best and most versatile emulation platforms available. There are PSP emulators for the Super Nintendo, Nintendo 64, Sega Genesis, Atari Lynx, and a variety of other platforms. There's even a MAME emulator for the PSP. Many of these are available bundled together in packs, such as the Kxsploit Homebrew Pack (pictured in Figure 4-18).

Figure 4-18. Snes9X as part of the Kxsploit Homebrew Pack

All of these emulators need ROMs to run. You can obtain many excellent homebrew ROMs for a variety of systems at *http://www.pdroms.de/*.

Browser-Based Homebrew

While Version 2.0 of the firmware prevents regular homebrew from running on the PSP, you do at least have an additional web browser (without having to do the *Wipeout Pure* trick) that is capable of running various JavaScript apps and web-based games, such as *PSP Tetris* (*http://webtopsp.com*) and those found at PSP Web Browser.com (*http://www.pspwebbrowser.com/*). Also, most of these games can be downloaded locally to your Memory Stick, so that you don't need a live Internet connection to play them.

Hacking the Hack

If you really want to hack this hack, you're either going to want to learn to develop your own homebrew for the PSP **[Hack #47]** or spend some time scouring the Net for all your favorite JavaScript games that you can port to the PSP.

Networking and the Web
Hacks 41–47

The PSP's built-in 802.11b opens up all sorts of possibilities, and the web browser included in Version 2.0 makes a lot of those possibilities real. Even if you haven't upgraded to 2.0, you can still surf the Web from your PSP, but you'll need to engage in a little trickery to do that. And although running Version 2.0 locks users out of a lot of cool homebrew apps, read on and you'll learn about one kind of homebrew that will work even on Version 2.0: browser-based JavaScript and CSS applications.

HACK #41 Find Yourself a PSP Web Browser

Your PSP has built-in 802.11b wireless capabilities. High-speed, portable Internet access is literally at your fingertips.

The first section of this hack shows everyone with Version 1.0–1.52 of the firmware how to access the browser in *Wipeout Pure* for its intended use, and points you to the basics of redirecting the browser to one of the several PSP-designed web portals that open up these browsers to the full Internet, as well as many of the other hacks covered in this book.

If you are running Version 2.0 of the firmware, skip ahead to the Version 2.0 section to learn all the ins and outs of your browser.

Version 1.x Firmware

In "Create Your Own PSP Web Portal" [Hack #42], Jonathan Terleski discusses in detail how you can set up your own web portal for the PSP. This introductory hack, on the other hand, is going to point you to a few of the existing PSP web portals you can find online, and show you the basics of tricking your PSP into letting you surf the Internet via an embedded browser in *Wipeout Pure*. Here's what you'll need:

- A PSP
- A copy of *Wipeout Pure* (supposedly, a Japanese game, *Derby Time*, also features a built-in web browser and could be used for this hack; I haven't tested this)
- An accessible wireless (802.11b/g) access point (see "Get Your Wireless Network On" **[Hack #5]** for more information on setting up your own wireless network to work with the PSP)
- An active Internet connection (broadband preferred, if not completely necessary)

The history behind the hack. Shortly after the PSP's North American release, several people noticed that there was a very basic browser built into *Wipeout Pure*, accessible via the main menu of the game. When you click on Downloads in this menu, the game attempts to connect to the Internet and access a page that allows you to download new skins and racetracks for the game.

Several people decided to run a scan while this connection was going on and discovered that *Wipeout Pure*'s browser was attempting to reach out to *http://ingame.scea.com/wipeout/index.html*. Setting up a little simple DNS redirection taking any requests for *http://ingame.scea.com* and redirecting them to another server hosting a */wipeout/index.html* file was the next logical step. Fill that *index.html* file with a few of your favorite links, and suddenly the entire Internet is available to you via your PSP.

 If you try to load *http://ingame.scea.com/wipeout/index.html* in your regular web browser on your computer, you will receive a page warning you that you are forbidden to access that page. You could try hacking the user agent identification in your browser to mimic the PSP's browser, but just load it in the PSP if you really want to see it.

The Wipeout Pure browser. Grab your copy of *Wipeout Pure* and stick it in your PSP. Click through all the beginning bits and load any preexisting game profiles. After you do all this, you should be presented with *Wipeout Pure*'s main menu. Select the Download option and hit X (see Figure 5-1).

When you select Download, an overlay screen will pop up saying "Game Experience May Change During Wireless Play." Select OK and press the X

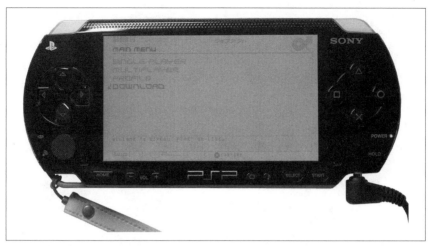

Figure 5-1. The Download option in the game's main menu

button. This will bring up another overlay screen for your Network Connection, prompting you to select from your preconfigured network connections.

Choose your default connection and hit the X button. This will load the *Wipeout Pure* browser, and the default browser page will be displayed with any available downloads. If you get an error message saying, "A connection error has occurred. The WLAN switch is not turned on," go back, switch the WLAN switch (located on the bottom-left side of your PSP) into the on position, and try again. If you get a message that your wireless access point is not available, check to make sure that your wireless network is running and configured properly [Hack #5] and try again.

Once you have the default page loaded, use the directional keypad to select Downloads and hit the X button. A new page will load with a set of PSP download terms and conditions. Use the directional keypad to highlight Accept and hit the X button. A list of available downloads will appear. Highlight the download you want to grab and hit the X button. A more detailed description of the download will appear. Again, use the directional keypad to navigate to the actual download and hit the X button. An overlay progress bar will appear and the download will begin (see Figure 5-2).

Once you are finished using the browser for its default purposes, simply hit the Start button and select Quit to return to *Wipeout Pure*'s main menu.

Now that you've checked out the browser for its intended purposes, you should trick it into doing some real web surfing.

Figure 5-2. The progress bar in the Wipeout Pure browser as Gamma Pack 1 downloads

Redirecting the browser. Repeat all the steps from the last section up until you are ready to select your default connection. Highlight the connection and hit the Triangle button. An overlay menu will appear on the right side of the screen. Use the directional keypad to select Edit from this menu and then hit the X button (see Figure 5-3).

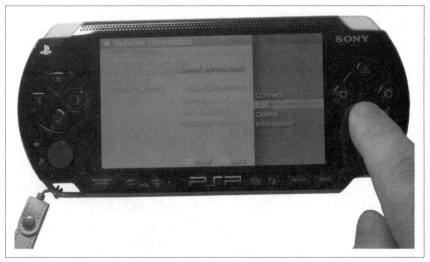

Figure 5-3. Pull up the side menu with which you can edit your default connection

All of these settings can be accessed from the main Settings menu on your PSP (Settings → Network Settings). For the purposes of this hack, I'm showing you how to edit a preexisting connection from within *Wipeout Pure*, but if you think you will be surfing the Web via your PSP on a regular basis, it makes sense to set up a few extra connections.

As you can see in Figure 5-3, I have three connections set up. Connection 1 is just the default connection for game playing over the Internet [Hack #37] and downloading PSP updates and in-game downloads such as the Gamma Pack 1. The other two connections connect to various online portals, which I am about to discuss.

Once you select Edit, you will be presented with a series of screens. The first screen is the connection name. If you want to change it, you can, but I'm leaving it as Connection 1. Simply hit the right directional keypad to move on to the next screen. This is the WLAN Settings screen. Highlight Scan and press X to scan for any networks in range. Pick the one you want and hit X again. You will be returned to the WLAN Settings screen. Hit the right directional key to move on to the next screen. Configure the appropriate WLAN security settings and hit the right directional key again.

Now you will be presented with the Address Settings screen. You have a choice between Easy and Custom. Select Custom and hit the X key. This will immediately bring you to the IP Address Setting screen. You can either leave this set to Automatic and move on to the next screen to make the necessary changes to your DNS Settings to use a public PSP web portal, or you can choose Manual and hit the X button, as I have done in Figure 5-4.

In the Manual Network Connection pane, I gave the PSP an IP address of 192.168.1.18 (so that it would not conflict with the other IP addresses I've assigned on my network), left the subnet to the default 255.255.255.0, and set the Default Router to 192.168.1.1, the address to my wireless access point. To make the changes, you have to hit X on each field you want to change, and then scroll up and down using the directional keypad until you hit the right number, then hit X again to get to the next field. If the network you are connecting to uses automatic (DHCP) assignment for some or all wireless users, you're better off selecting Automatic for the IP address assignment. My manual settings will probably not work for you.

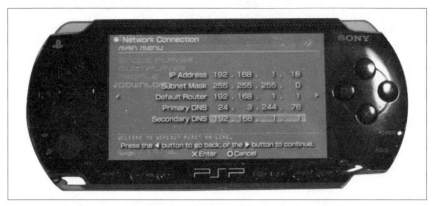

Figure 5-4. In the Manual Settings panel, I have replaced the Primary DNS with 24.3. 244.76, the IP address to the fujimax PSP Web Portal

If you'd rather not spend all this time making sure that the IP and Subnet settings are all perfect, you can skip much of this by selecting Automatic instead of Manual on the Address Settings screen, then when the DNS Settings screen appears, selecting Manual. This will allow you to only change the relevant DNS settings before moving on.

The important change for this hack is the Primary DNS. Even if your network uses DHCP assignment, you must override its default settings. You should make the Primary DNS 24.3.244.76, which is the address of the fujimax PSP Web Portal. If you want to check out the fujimax PSP Web Portal before performing this change on your PSP, visit *http://24.3.244.76/wipeout/ index.html* from your desktop computer. You can, if you'd like, set the Secondary DNS to the DNS server that the wireless access point is configured to hand out. Although this gives you a back up if, for whatever reason, the fujimax PSP Web Portal is down, it won't let you redirect the browser to the PSP Web Portal.

The IP address of the fujimax PSP Web Portal changed once before from 67.171.70.72 to 24.3.244.76. If you try to access it and it doesn't come up, check in the sidebar of the blog associated with the portal (*http://genius.fujumax.com/weblog/ index.html*) to see whether the IP address has changed yet again.

After you have completed all the proper entries, click on the right arrow on the directional keypad to move to the next screen. Make sure that Do Not

Use is highlighted under Proxy Server and then hit the right arrow again to move on to the Setting List screen, which will give you a summary of the settings you have just entered. Hit the right arrow button again and press X to save your settings.

> If you are on Version 2.0 of the firmware, you'll be asked whether you want to launch an Internet browser before you review your settings. You can choose Do Not Start unless you are in a hotspot that requires you to log into a web portal before you can access the Internet. Of course, 2.0 users don't need to use the *Wipeout Pure* hack, but I'm sure some of you want to try it out anyhow!

This will return you to the Select Connection screen. Select the connection that you just edited and hit the X button. When you hit this, the PSP sends out a request for *http://ingame.scea.com/wipeout/index.html*, but since you changed the Domain Name Server to 24.3.244.76, the request for this page is redirected by that DNS server to *http://24.3.244.76/wipeout/index.html*, the address for the fujimax PSP Web Portal. The resulting page should look like Figure 5-5. Click on the X button to enter the portal.

Figure 5-5. The entry page to the PSP Web Portal by fujimax

PSP Web Portal by fujimax. Once you click on X, the main page of the PSP Web Portal will load. Use the directional keypad to jump around between the different hyperlinks on the page.

There is a link to Google (*http://www.google.com*) in the upper-right corner of the screen, and an address bar at the bottom of the screen via which you can pull up any web page you like (see Figure 5-6). Additionally, there is a list of links (tech, news, misc., psp) on the right-hand side of the screen. If you click on one of these links, a series of related links appears below a graphic of the link category. Figure 5-7 shows Google on the PSP.

Figure 5-6. PSP category of PSP Web Portal

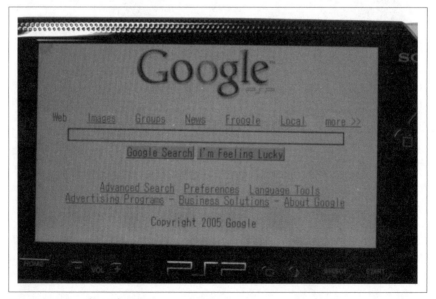

Figure 5-7. Google on the PSP

If you move down to the address bar on the bottom of the page and hit the X button, the PSP's default text-entry screen will appear. In Figure 5-8, you can see where I have entered the address of my blog in this text-entry screen. Highlighting Enter and hitting X brings me back to the PSP Web Portal screen.

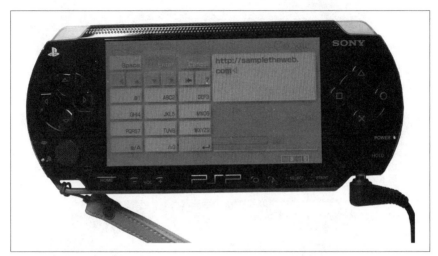

Figure 5-8. Entering the address of my blog in the PSP's text-entry screen

After entering the address on this screen, I highlight the Enter button and hit X. This returns me to the PSP Web Portal with the text I just entered appearing in the address bar at the bottom of the page. Navigating to the Go button next to the address bar and hitting the X button loads the page. If you are used to flawless Web browsing on a broadband connection, prepare for a rude wake-up call. The *Wipeout Pure* browser can move very slowly at times, especially on graphics-rich sites that aren't designed for a small screen. My site loaded, although without the background graphic, and while the text loaded rather quickly, some of the images took some time to load. Figure 5-9 depicts a blog entry featuring a picture of my pet parrot, Misha. As you can see, the site is legible and the picture shows up clearly. However, it took about five minutes to load.

Have some fun exploring all that the PSP Web Portal has to offer. See Figures 5-10 and 5-11 for examples of a few of the links offered under the PSP category and some of the pretty cool things you can actually do with this browser. Whenever you become too lost in the Web, simply hit the Start button and choose "Go to Home Page" to return to the PSP Web Portal or Quit to return to the main menu of *Wipeout Pure*.

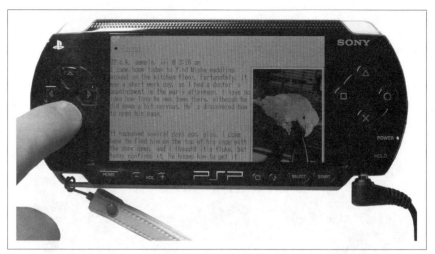

Figure 5-9. An entry from my blog, Sample the Web (http://www.sampletheweb.com)

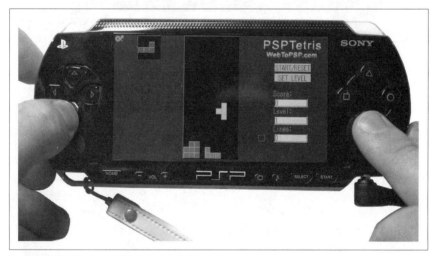

Figure 5-10. Playing PSPTetris via the Internet

PSP browser by Nomad. One of the links that you'll find under the PSP section of the PSP Web Portal's main page is to the PSP browser (*http://www.allxboxskins.com/pspbrowser.php*). This PHP-based page embeds a browser inside the *Wipeout Pure* browser, so that you can surf different sites and keep a handy address bar at the top of the screen with instant access to Google. This solution helps avoid having to return back to the main portal page whenever you want to navigate to a new site that isn't linked on the page you are currently viewing (see Figure 5-12).

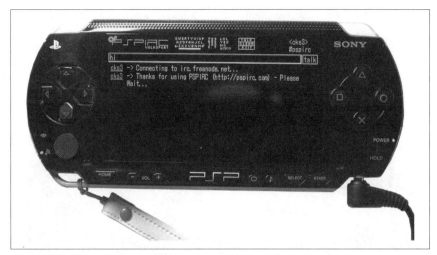

Figure 5-11. Participating in IRC chat via PSP IRC

Figure 5-12. The PSP browser's address bar stays at the top of the page even when you navigate to another page

Firmware Version 2.0

If you have a PSP with Version 2.0 of the firmware, then there are only two steps you need to take to get online and browse the Web with your PSP. First, make sure that you have access to a wireless network [Hack #5], then make sure that your WLAN switch is in the On position, navigate to Network → Browser, and hit the X button. The browser will launch and load the home page. Want to know all the ins and outs of the browser? Read on.

Basic controls. Hitting the Triangle button while the browser is loaded on your PSP displays the browser's full interface, complete with an address bar (see Figure 5-13).

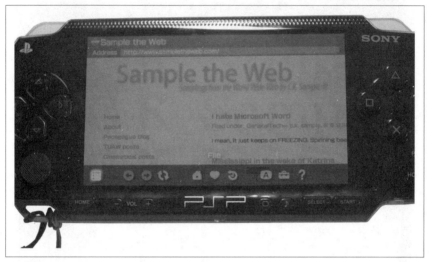

Figure 5-13. Firmware 2.0's browser interface

If you navigate over to the ? (or Help) menu and hit the X button, a screen showing all the basic controls of the browser will be displayed (Figure 5-14).

The L trigger moves back, while the R trigger moves forward. The Triangle displays the menu, the Circle closes the browser, and the X button is enter, and it will also open links you have selected. If you hit the X button and hold on a link, it opens the link in a new tab. Pressing the Square button while moving the analog stick scrolls, using the Square button with the directional keypad scrolls the page, and the Square button plus the triggers moves to the previous or next tab.

Tabbed browsing and JavaScript. One of the really cool things about this browser is that it is a fully functional JavaScript-capable browser with tabbed browsing capabilities. You have three tabs to work with and can switch between them by holding down the Square button and hitting the L or R triggers. You can also run most JavaScript. It can handle complex web sites like Flickr (*http://www.flickr.com*) and Gmail (*http://gmail.google.com*; Figure 5-15). Flash is currently the Achilles' heel of the PSP browser.

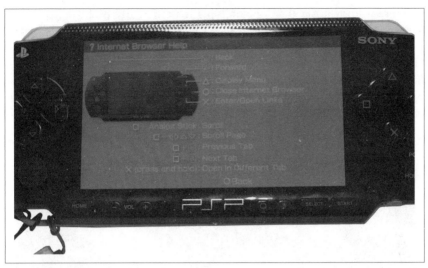

Figure 5-14. Internet Browser Help screen

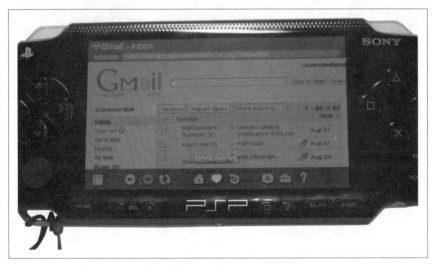

Figure 5-15. Gmail loads easily in the PSP's browser

File menu. The File menu (Figure 5-16) gives you the option to close the browser, close the page, display the page's certificate, display the page information, save an image, save a link target, open a link in different tab, or open an address entry field. The most useful options in this menu are the Close Page option (to close an unwanted tab—close these often to keep from running out of memory), the Save Image option (to save images to your Photo folder for viewing on your PSP), and especially the Save Link Target option. Save Link Target allows you to download files to your PSP, whether they are a known file type or not. This is particularly useful if you come across an important web page that you want to save for later offline viewing. Simply use the L trigger to move back to the linking page, then place the cursor over the page you want to save, hit the Triangle, select the File menu, hit the X button, select Save Link Target, and hit the X button again. Take note of where you save the file, since you can navigate to it again in your web browser by typing *file://filelocation/filename.html*. You can also use this feature to save files that are incorrectly recognized and try to load as text in the browser.

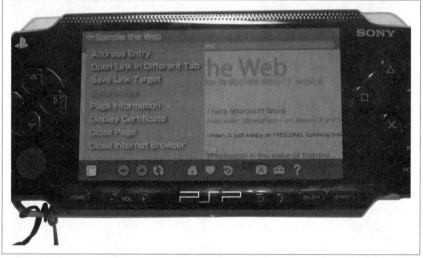

Figure 5-16. File menu

Bookmarks. The heart-shaped icon is the Bookmarks menu, which gives you an option between PSP-branded web sites and your own bookmarks organized under My Bookmarks. The first option in this menu gives you the option to add the current page to your bookmarks (Figure 5-17).

View. The View menu lets you change the different display options for the browser. You can choose text size from small, medium, and large, switch the encoding, and switch between different display modes: Normal, Just-Fit, and Smart-Fit. In Normal display mode, the page width is not adjusted, so you must pan and scan around the web page. This is typically the mode I use, as it tends to best represent the normal experience of web browsing that I am used to from using a computer. Just-Fit adjusts the page width to match the screen width; at least, this is what it is supposed to do. In reality,

Figure 5-17. My Bookmarks

it seems to only manage to shrink the columns of some web pages. Smart-Fit reorganizes web pages so that the different columns are stacked on top of each other and the main content is at the top. This can make for some clunky navigation of some web sites, so I generally avoid this view mode; however, you may prefer scrolling up and down to scrolling side to side and up and down, as in Normal display mode.

Tools. The Tools menu is particularly useful, not only because it is where you need to navigate to set the preferences for the browser, but because it is the first place you want to navigate whenever you are troubleshooting. Selecting Settings from this list opens the Settings screen, where you can set your home page, and under View Settings, you can choose to toggle on and off JavaScript, images, and animations, set proxy settings, and determine your cookie and cache settings. The other options under the Tools menu allow you to delete your cookies, cache, authentication information, and input history, as well as display your current connection status. If you ever get an out-of-memory error while trying to load a page, try navigating to the Tools menu and selecting Delete Cache, then navigating over to Refresh and hitting the X button. I've found that this often corrects the error, and the page loads successfully.

Offline Browsing

One of the best features of the PSP's browser is its ability to view files without a live Internet connection.

If you have a home page set (Tools → Settings → Home Page), your browser will insist on checking for a live Internet connection when you first launch it, and if you have your WLAN switch turned off, it will not launch properly. So make sure that your WLAN switch is in the On position, navigate to Network → Internet Browser, and hit the X button. As the PSP attempts to connect to the Internet, hit the O button to cancel the connection. Now hit the Triangle button to bring up the browser's interface.

You can avoid this problem by setting the home page to be a blank page (or by setting a home page that resides on your memory stick [Hack #30]).

Navigate to the address bar and hit the X button. Here, you can browse the file structure of your PSP's Memory Stick (providing you know where everything is located) and view any files that the browser is capable of displaying (*.html*, *.htm*, *.php*, *.txt*, *.png*, *.gif*, *.jpeg*, *.jpg*, and *.bmp*, to name a few of the most common). For example, if you want to view a picture in your Photo folder, you would simply enter *file:/PSP/PHOTO/nameofpicture.jpg* in the address bar and hit the X button to load the image. For images, this isn't really that useful, but you can save all sorts of documents as text or HTML on your Memory Stick and load these files for reading on the go. This is a very useful little feature that I use for notes and reading on-the-go daily. And after you've finished entering the long text string to get to your important files, don't forget to bookmark the file (Triangle button → Bookmarks → X button → My Bookmarks → X button → Add to Bookmarks → X button) so that you can easily get to the file in the future.

Hacking the Hack

If you haven't upgraded to Version 2.0, and you didn't already know about the *Wipeout Pure* hack, you are probably amazed by being able to surf the Web on your PSP. If you want to take things a step further, however, you're going to want to serve up your own PSP web portal customized with your personal favorite links [Hack #42]. While creating that portal, you might want to embed your own QWERTY keyboard via Javascript that will work in place of the PSP's rather clunky text-entry screen [Hack #46]. There are lots of tricks you can do with this starter hack. Thumb through the table of contents of this book, and you'll spot quite a few.

If you really want to take full advantage of the feature-rich web browser included with Version 2.0 of the firmware, you're going to want to spend some time making an *index.html* file at the root level of your Memory Stick, cataloguing all the files you may want to quickly access while on the go. For help with that, make sure you check out "Create a Portal for Your Memory Stick Files" [Hack #30].

Create Your Own PSP Web Portal

#42 Configure and use your own PSP web portal.

So you've been browsing the Web [Hack #41] with your copy of *Wipeout Pure*, but up until now, you've had to depend on someone else's web portal. You've had to use *his* links, navigate *his* design, and use the functionality *he* provides. All this in addition to worrying about whether or not the portal itself is even currently working.

This hack, however, will free you from the constraints that come with relying on someone else's portal. By setting up a DNS (Domain Name System) and web server on your computer, you will be able to create and use your own customized PSP web portal. The directions given here assume you will be setting up your DNS and web server on the same computer.

The DNS Server

Before you can start serving web pages to your PSP, you need to first trick the PSP into believing that your web server is someone it's not. When you load up the "Downloads" section of *Wipeout Pure*, your PSP attempts to retrieve data from the following domain: *ingame.scea.com*. Normally, the IP address returned by your Internet service provider's DNS server would belong to Sony and would direct you to downloadable *Wipeout Pure* content. However, by setting up your own DNS server, it is possible to "trick" the PSP and return the IP address of a web server of your choice.

The first step in setting up a DNS server is installation. If you are using a Mac or a Unix variant, the most common DNS server used is BIND. If you are using Windows, a good (and free) DNS server is TreeWalk DNS (*http://www.ntcanuck.com*). Installation guides are included with both of these server packages when you download the software, and are pretty straightforward. Further, these are just recommendations; there are dozens of DNS server software packages available for virtually every platform.

Once installed, you now need to configure your DNS server to resolve *ingame.scea.com* to the IP address of your web server. There are two files you will need to create and edit: *scea.zone* and *named.conf*. First, we will create the *scea.zone* file. Using a text editor, create a new file called *scea.zone* (make sure there is no *.txt* appended to the filename) and type in the following:

```
; scea.zone
; scea.com db file
```

```
$TTL 86400

@    IN    SOA    scea.com        dummy.scea.com. (
                        050622          ; Serial
                        10800           ; Refresh
                        3600            ; Retry
                        604800          ; Expire
                        86400           ; Min TTL
                        )

; Addresses for canonical names

              NS    192.168.0.100
              A     192.168.0.100
ingame        A     192.168.0.100
webcluster    A     192.168.0.100


$ORIGIN scea.com.
```

In the preceding example, `192.168.0.100` is used as the IP address of the DNS/web server you are setting up. Replace each occurrence of that IP address with the IP address of the machine you installed the DNS server on.

Where this file must be placed on your computer depends on the DNS server you installed. If you're using BIND, the file should be placed in either */etc/namedb* or */var/named*, depending on how it was installed. If you're using TreeWalk DNS, place the file in *C:\Windows\System32\dns\etc*. If you installed another DNS server, consult the documentation that came with the software to see where DNS Zone files must be stored.

All that's left to do now is to make your DNS server aware of the new DNS Zone you have just created. To do this, locate the *named.conf* file on your computer. If using BIND, this file may be found at */etc/named.conf*. For those using TreeWalk DNS, the file is located at *C:\Windows\System32\dns\ etc\named.conf*. Again, consult the server documentation if you are using another DNS server.

Once you've located the file, simply append this entry to the end and save the file:

```
zone "scea.com" {
    type master;
    file "scea.zone";
};
```

All that is left to do is restart the DNS server so it takes note of the new DNS Zone. If you're using BIND, run the named executable.

This will need to be done via a shell prompt, and most likely will require root privileges. To run the executable with root privileges, type the command **sudo named**. You will then be prompted for the root password to your machine.

If you're using TreeWalk DNS, access the TreeWalk control panel via the Start menu and click "Reload" and then "Start" if the server isn't already running.

That's all for the DNS server; now it's time to set up the web server.

The Web Server

Now that it is possible to have your PSP access the IP address of your choosing, it's time to set up a web server from which you can serve your custom web portal.

Like the DNS server, the first step is to install a web server on your computer. If you're using a Mac, you can turn on the preinstalled Apache web server by going into System Preferences, clicking the Sharing icon, and checking the box next to "Personal Web Sharing." If you're using Windows or Unix, you will need to install a web server such as Apache (Version 2 suggested). Apache is an open source web server that powers many commercial web sites. It can be downloaded at *http://httpd.apache.org/download.cgi*. If you're using Windows, you will want to download the *.msi* install package and follow the instructions that come with it. If installing Apache in a Unix environment, you may be able to find a precompiled install package for your distribution. Otherwise, you'll have to compile the source code yourself and continue installation from there.

Like DNS servers, there are many web servers available. Also, if you have one already installed, there is no reason to install another.

When the PSP makes a request from *Wipeout Pure*, it asks for the */wipeout/ index.html* file. So what we must now do is create a file named *index.html* and place it where the PSP can access it. Open a text editor and type the following:

```
<html>
<head></head>
<body><br><br>
<center>My PSP Web Portal</center>
<br><br>
<a href="http://www.google.com/">Google</a>
</body>
</html>
```

Save this file as *index.html*.

Next, you need to create a directory called "wipeout" in your web server's root directory. On a Mac, the root directory will be */Library/WebServer/Documents*, so you will create the directory */Library/WebServer/Documents/wipeout* (this is not to be confused with the Library folder in your home directory). If you installed Apache in Windows, you will want to create the directory in *C:\Program Files\Apache Group\Apache2\htdocs*. Then, simply place *index.html* in the *wipeout* directory.

If you are using Apache in Unix, or are using another web server, consult the server's documentation to identify the root folder from which web pages are being served.

That's it! Now you can test it using your PSP.

Configuring Your PSP

As detailed in "Find Yourself a PSP Web Browser" **[Hack #41]**, you will now need to configure your PSP to use another DNS server. Follow the instructions discussed in that hack, but instead of entering the IP address of a web portal on the Internet, enter the IP address of your DNS server. Now fire up *Wipeout Pure*, choose the connection you just created/edited, and you should see the web page shown in Figure 5-18. Nothing too fancy, but the more links you add to the HTML, the more impressive and useful your web portal will be.

Figure 5-18. The rendered HTML

Congratulations! You can now create and access custom web pages from your PSP.

Hacking the Hack

If you want your web portal to be accessible to other devices via the Internet, there are a few changes you must make to the method outlined above. First, you will need to change the following entry in *scea.zone*:

```
ingame          A    192.168.0.100
```

to:

```
ingame          A    XX.XXX.X.XXX
```

where XX.XXX.X.XXX is the external IP address given to your computer/router. You can find out what this is by going to *http://www.whatismyip.com*.

The next thing you must do is set up your router to forward incoming traffic on ports 53 and 80 to your DNS/web server. Connecting to a web interface built into your router usually allows you to do this. Consult your router's documentation on how to forward ports to individual machines on your network. You will need to forward ports 53 (UDP) and 80 (TCP) to your web server's internal IP address (i.e., 192.168.0.100, as used earlier).

Finally, change the DNS setting on your PSP [Hack #41] to use your computer/ router's external IP address instead of your web server's internal IP address.

You should now be able to access your web portal from home or anywhere else.

—Jonathan Terleski

Use Your PSP to Control Your Home

Are you one of the lucky few living in the world of tomorrow with an entire home network that actually networks control of your home? If so, wouldn't it be nice to control your home wirelessly with your PSP? Read on to find out how.

When the *Wipeout Pure* browser hack [Hack #41] came out, I saw someone controlling his Xbox Media Center from his PSP browser. It's great that you can control XBMC from your PSP, but what if your Xbox isn't on, and your TV isn't on, and your TV is not on the right input? You still have to get up or find the remote and adjust all of that.

I've come up with my own solution.

> This hack first appeared on LiquidIce's PSP Hacks and quickly spread around to various web sites (go to *http:// psphacks.blogspot.com/2005/04/psp-home-control-10.html*).

Setting up the DNS Hack

The first step was to be able to redirect the *Wipeout Pure* browser to any URL I wanted. To do that, I turned to MooPS (*http://www.layouts.xbox-scene.com/main/filemanager/index.php?action=downloadfile&filename=Setup MooPS_1.0.1.rar&directory=Software&*), which is a DNS/web server that you run on your Windows computer (see Figures 5-19 and 5-20). It automatically forwards requests for *http://ingame.scea.com* to the URL of your choice. For another way to set this up, see "Find Yourself a PSP Web Browser" [Hack #41].

If you have Version 2.0 of the firmware, you can simply navigate to the page you create rather than bothering with this redirect, which is only necessary due to the limitations of the *Wipeout Pure* browser.

Figure 5-19. MooPS

Controlling A/V Equipment

By using a controller device called the WACI NX (*http://www.waciworld. com/*), you could turn on the TV, turn on the Xbox, switch to the correct input on the TV, and send the Play command to XBMC, all in one button press on your PSP (see Figure 5-21).

So far, I have the ability to turn my lights on and off, and I have full control (play, stop, pause, and menu) of my DVD player, TiVo, and high-definition TV, all wirelessly from my PSP. I can also send commands to my pre-2.0 PC running Winamp to tell it to play, stop, and pause my music, or even browse my playlists.

To do most of the controlling, I used this tiny web-server control box called the WACI NX. It's great because it has an HTTP and FTP server and uses regular HTML to issue the commands, making it the perfect match for my pre-2.0 PSP, which does not support any fancy JavaScript or DHTML. The PSP talks to the WACI NX via WiFi through the network. In turn, the

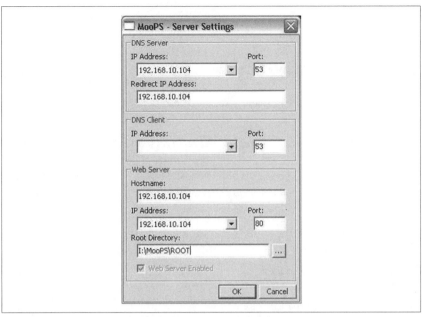

Figure 5-20. MooPS Server Settings

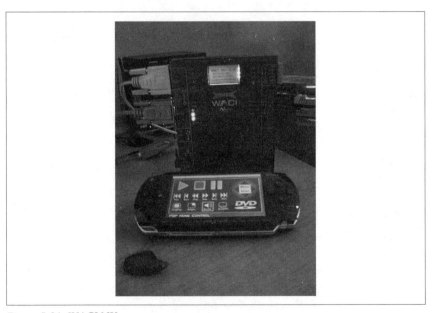

Figure 5-21. WACI NX

WACI emits the IR signal to the TV through one of my IR emitters, just as though I had pressed the button on the remote.

The WACI NX has a built-in IR Learner, so you can grab all of your remotes, learn all the button commands, and save them in the WACI to be played back and emitted later. You could even do macros so it sends out a sequence of button presses with a specified delay between each button press.

The pages it hosts are constructed using layers and <div> tags. I put an image map on the graphics and created some HTML pages with special links, which are crafted so that when the PSP highlights and clicks on a spot on the image map, it instructs the WACI NX server to send an IR signal to my A/V equipment or triggers its relays to cut power on the lights.

The actual links are name value pairs going to a script I made on the WACI NX.

```
http://192.168.1.102/rpcpost.
asp?method=IRSend&Param1=1&Param2=DVD&Param3=Play
```

That script is written to execute the IR Send and then redirect back to the referring page. To change which command I run, I just change the URL string in my link.

I'm sure that if you rigged something up, you could do something similar with special software that runs on your PC. However, by using the WACI, I have a dedicated piece of hardware whose only function is to send commands to my stuff, no matter which interface I create to control it. Unlike Sony, which hides its protocols, the WACI NX has an open protocol that you can access from just about any web programming language. I can program using Flash, ASP, HTML, JavaScript, C#, C++, and Java. It's great for developers, and fairly simple to get started using the provided sample code. For more info on the WACI NX, you could check out WACI World (*http:// www.waciworld.com/*).

Controlling Winamp

Another web server you could set up is a plug-in for Winamp called BrowseAmp (*http://www.browseamp.com/*). This program will set up a mini web server that uses the same kind of special URLs to send commands to the Winamp player running on your computer. I've put together a skin that looks good on the PSP screen. You can find it posted on my site (*http:// psphacks.blogspot.com*).

I have a lot more ideas on how to improve this system. Right now, navigation is clunky because every button press causes the page to refresh. This is the same reason why PSP IRC (*http://pspirc.com/*) keeps refreshing the entire screen. I want to explore sending the commands to the WACI using an *IFrame* or *XMLHTTPRequest* object, but as far as I know, these basic HTML features are not implemented in the *Wipeout Pure* browser.

—*LiquidIce*

  ## Control iTunes from Your PSP

#44 If you are on a Mac, you can use your PSP as a remote control for iTunes.

If you're running Mac OS X, you can easily use your PSP as a remote control for iTunes via a program called PatioTunes (*http://www.mindola.com/patiotunes/*; $15 USD). Unfortunately, no similar package was available for Windows at the time of this writing.

> Originally, I wanted this hack to be a full-fledged remote control, using the PSP's IR port to control my home entertainment system. Unfortunately, so far, this hack has proved to be a bit beyond my abilities. Phillip Torrone has also been working on an IR remote solution for the PSP, and if either of us ever figure it out, we'll post the results on the book's web site.

Download, install, and launch PatioTunes. The program will launch and tell you where you need to point the browser on your PSP (see Figure 5-22). If you're on a PSP running Version 2.0, this will work like a charm. If you're using "Find Yourself a PSP Web Browser" [Hack #41] on another version of the firmware, you'll need to make sure that you've created your own portal [Hack #42] so that you can redirect the browser to a local address on your local area network.

Figure 5-22. PatioTunes

If you launch PatioTunes' Preferences (see Figure 5-23), you can set the refresh rate for the PatioTunes' interface in your PSP's browser. You can also adjust the port over which the connection occurs, in case there are any conflicting ports or special restrictions on your network.

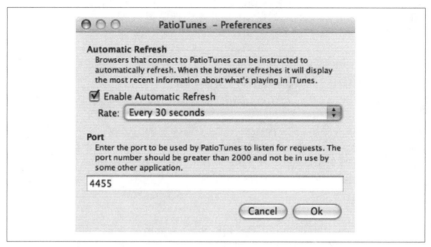

Figure 5-23. PatioTunes' preferences

Launch the browser of your choice on your PSP and navigate to the URL that PatioTunes provided for you. If you are on Version 2.0 firmware, then I recommend that you add a quick bookmark to the PatioTunes main page. There are three tabs in the upper-right corner of the page: Playlists, Artists (Figure 5-24), and Search. Playlists lists all the different playlists in your iTunes Music Library, but no songs will appear until you actually select a playlist and then click the little gray arrow icon to the right of the drop-down menu. The Artist menu displays all the songs by the currently playing artist.

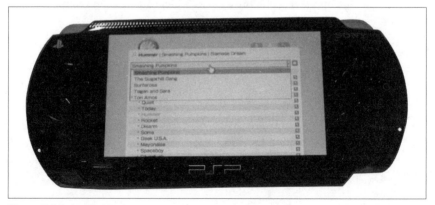

Figure 5-24. Artists view

The Search menu lets you search through your iTunes Music Library, either by song title, artist, album, or a combination of the three. One nice feature is that after you conduct a search, it is added to a temporary playlist called "PatioTunes Search."

There are minimal controls at the bottom of each page, featuring previous track, next track, and play/pause. You can also use PatioTunes to remotely create a playlist or increase the volume in iTunes.

This is a great little application that you can really make shine by either connecting your computer to your entertainment system, or by using AirPort Express and AirTunes to stream music playing from your iTunes Music Library to your stereo. All it's lacking, and a feature that I'd like to see in the next version, is an album artwork feature that would display the album cover associated with the currently playing track.

Now you can stroll around your house, browsing the Web on your PSP, and switch over to PatioTunes whenever you want to change the currently playing track. Have fun!

HACK #45 Generate Dial Tones

Use your PSP to dial telephone numbers.

Since your PSP is a fully capable MP3 player, you can also use it to play back the different tones used by the telephone system to dial numbers. All you need to do is get your hands on some MP3s or WAVs of these audio files and either keep them in a folder inside your */PSP/MUSIC/* folder, or string them together into sequences of numbers to be dialed.

Consider taking the complete numbers of your different friends and recording this sequence of tones as an MP3 file by the name of each friend. This way, whenever you want to dial your friend, just navigate to the MP3 called "Billy 555-555-5555" on your PSP and hit the X button to play the audio either through the PSP's speakers or the headphones that you hold up to a phone receiver.

Charting the Tones

Now that we're in the 21st century, this trick won't always work, since the telephone system has changed somewhat, with more digital bits in the way that prevent dialing by tone. Nevertheless, given the right combination of a public pay phone on an older phone system, you should be able to use your PSP to dial a few numbers over a compatible touch-tone phone via DTMF (Dual Tone Multiple Frequency) tones. Table 5-1 shows the combined tones that make up the touch-tone dialing system. The four alphabet keys are sometimes used internally by the phone system. Table 5-2 shows what you'd use on an international system that supports CCITT.

Table 5-1. DTMF tones

DTMF Chart	1209 Hz	1336 Hz	1477 Hz	1633 Hz
697 Hz	1	2	3	A
770 Hz	4	5	6	B
852 Hz	7	8	9	C
941 Hz	*	0	#	D

Table 5-2. CCITT tones

CCITT	700	900	1100	1300	1500	1700
700	N/A	1	2	4	7	Code 11
900	1	N/A	3	5	8	Code 12
1100	2	3	N/A	6	9	KP
1300	4	5	6	N/A	0	KP2
1500	7	8	9	0	N/A	ST
1700	Code 11	Code 12	KP	KP2	ST	N/A

If you don't want to spend quite a bit of time holding a microphone carefully up to your phone to record the proper dial tones, you can find sample audio files for most of these tones online. Search and you will find. You can easily find all the DTMF tones and CCITT tones. Alternately, you can generate audio files for the numbers you will be dialing, using DialABC.com's Generate DTMF Tones service (*http://www.dialabc.com/sound/generate*).

Once you load all the proper tones needed in your PSP, all you have to do is find a public pay phone that will accept the tones. If you've created a complete string of numbers ready for dialing, using the previously mentioned Generate DTMF Tones service, or if you spent a lot of time (in an audio program like Audacity, Acid, or GarageBand) arranging the different individual tones in the correct order and converting them to MP3, you can simply turn up the PSP's volume to the max, hold your headphones or the PSP's speakers up to the receiver, and click Play to dial the number. This could be an effective way of keeping your address book [Hack #35] on your PSP.

Another option would be to have all the relevant DTMF numbers saved into a particular folder on your PSP with a few extra seconds at the end of each file, or a separate file that is a few seconds of silence. Then, whenever you encounter a particularly dirty-keyed public phone that you don't want to touch, simply "play" the number you want to dial by mixing and matching the corresponding number files in the correct order. Hold the headphones up to the receiver and press the X button to play each tone, pause the tone, and then switch to the next tone you need to play. Theoretically, under the right circumstances, these methods should work; however, the phone system keeps changing and updating, frequencies are slightly different for different areas, and different model pay phones react differently to different tones, so the corresponding tones continue to change as well.

Hacking the Hack

There are certain aspects of this hack that could get you into trouble depending on how you use them, and it's your responsibility to make sure you don't violate any applicable laws. Since this hack is a direct descendant of early hacker activities, I'm going to walk you through a basic history of phreaking. Besides, what can it hurt, considering that this entire hack will be irrelevant once the last analog pay phone dies, everything moves to digital, and we all communicate via VoIP rather than over traditional analog phone systems? Not to mention the implants that will allow us to communicate with others simply by subvocalizing.

An overly concise (and therefore inaccurate) history of phreaking. In the 1970s, there was a blind boy who could whistle a 2600-cycle tone. He discovered that if he whistled this note into a phone, he could make long-distance calls for free. Someone else discovered that a toy whistle included with Cap'n Crunch cereal boxes also produced a 2600-cycle tone. This tone was the same used by the post-live-operator phone company to access the system that controlled the network. This 2600-cycle tone unlocked the ability to make free long-distance calls, and *phreaking* (etymology: a mashed remix of freak + phone + free) was born. It was one of the earliest forms of hacking, and two of the 1337 early hackers and phreakers from the Homebrew Computer Club in California, infamous for building *Blue Boxes*, went by the handles Berkeley Blue and Oak Toebark. You are probably more familiar with them as the two Steves: Jobs and Wozniak, the founders of Apple Computer.

Here are some definitions related to this topic:

Blue Box
   A device used to defeat long distance charges by generating a 2600-cycle tone.

Red Box
   Another device, similar to a Blue Box, which generates tones capable of tricking public phones into thinking that coins have been deposited.

Green Box
> A device that generates tones for Coin Collect, Coin Return, and Ring Back, and must be used by the party receiving the call.

DTMF
> Dual Tone Multiple Frequency, more commonly known as touch-tone, is a dialing system that works by combining two tones simultaneously for each number dialed.

CCITT
> Stands for Comité Consultatif International Télégraphique et Téléphonique. (International Consultative Committee on Telecommunications and Telegraphy). CCITT changed its name to ITU-T in 1993. Similar to DTMF, these tones have to do with international standards of telecommunications.

If you want to find out more information about phreaking, you will need to spend a lot of time online researching which sounds do what and under what systems, and find out as much as you can about the internal workings of the phone system. Start with Wikipedia (*http://en.wikipedia.org/wiki/ Phreaking*).

But, hey, we all know the easiest form of hacking is social hacking. Make friends with someone who works for the phone company, show some interest in his job, ask lots of questions, and buy him a few beers. You never know what useful bits you might discover.

HACK #46 Add a JavaScript Keyboard to Your PSP Web Portal

Make your web surfing activities a whole lot easier by providing an alternate QWERTY keyboard in place of the PSP's internal keypad, making your PSP-based web surfing as simple as Up-X-Down-X-Down-Right-X-Down-Down-Down-X.

"Find Yourself a PSP Web Browser" [Hack #41] provides an extra dimension that allows even the most novice user the ability to surf the Internet from her PSP. However, getting online is the easy part! Once there, you quickly discover that web surfing is not as simple as typing in a URL or clicking on a link. Since the PSP is missing a standard keyboard, you are forced to use its internal keypad that has even less functionality than a cell phone. If you are planning on using the browser hack for more than just goofing around, then this form of data entry quickly gets old.

To help overcome this challenge, I offer you a JavaScript keyboard that not only provides you with an easy-to-use QWERTY keyboard with all your standard alphanumeric characters, but also gives you some extra features, such as one-button http:// entry and a URL checker to make sure that you typed everything correctly before attempting to load the URL.

The Code

You'll have to add some JavaScript to your */wipeout/index.html* page that is loaded when the browser hack is performed using *Wipeout Pure*.

This only works if you are using your own custom *index. html* page for the browser hack. To do this, you will need a personal web server that you control and that is accessible to your PSP when the browser hack is executed **[Hack #42]**.

Open the *index.html* page in your favorite editor and enter the following code. You will need to replace everything between and including the <body> tags, or the script will not work as designed. Feel free to customize the script/html as you see fit. Once the code is pasted in, save the page and upload it to the web server.

```
<body bgcolor="black" onLoad="frmKeypad.http.focus( )">
<script>
var theurl="";
function GO( ){
    window.location=theurl;
}
</script>
<form name="frmKeypad">
    <table><tr><td align="center">
    <input type="button" value="0" onClick="theurl=theurl+'0'">
    <input type="button" value="1" onClick="theurl=theurl+'1'">
    <input type="button" value="2" onClick="theurl=theurl+'2'">
    <input type="button" value="3" onClick="theurl=theurl+'3'">
    <input type="button" value="4" onClick="theurl=theurl+'4'">
    <input type="button" value="5" onClick="theurl=theurl+'5'">
    <input type="button" value="6" onClick="theurl=theurl+'6'">
    <input type="button" value="7" onClick="theurl=theurl+'7'">
    <input type="button" value="8" onClick="theurl=theurl+'8'">
    <input type="button" value="9" onClick="theurl=theurl+'9'"><br>
    <input type="button" value="q" onClick="theurl=theurl+'q'">
    <input type="button" value="w" onClick="theurl=theurl+'w'">
    <input type="button" value="e" onClick="theurl=theurl+'e'">
    <input type="button" value="r" onClick="theurl=theurl+'r'">
    <input type="button" value="t" onClick="theurl=theurl+'t'">
    <input type="button" value="y" onClick="theurl=theurl+'y'">
    <input type="button" value="u" onClick="theurl=theurl+'u'">
    <input type="button" value="i" onClick="theurl=theurl+'i'">
    <input type="button" value="o" onClick="theurl=theurl+'o'">
    <input type="button" value="p" onClick="theurl=theurl+'p'">
    <input type="button" value="q" onClick="theurl=theurl+'q'"><br>
```

```
<input type="button" value="a" onClick="theurl=theurl+'a'">
<input type="button" value="s" onClick="theurl=theurl+'s'">
<input type="button" value="d" onClick="theurl=theurl+'d'">
<input type="button" value="f" onClick="theurl=theurl+'f'">
<input type="button" value="g" onClick="theurl=theurl+'g'">
<input type="button" value="h" onClick="theurl=theurl+'h'">
<input type="button" value="j" onClick="theurl=theurl+'j'">
<input type="button" value="k" onClick="theurl=theurl+'k'">
<input type="button" value="l" onClick="theurl=theurl+'l'"><br>
<input type="button" value="z" onClick="theurl=theurl+'z'">
<input type="button" value="x" onClick="theurl=theurl+'x'">
<input type="button" value="c" onClick="theurl=theurl+'c'">
<input type="button" value="v" onClick="theurl=theurl+'v'">
<input type="button" value="b" onClick="theurl=theurl+'b'">
<input type="button" value="n" onClick="theurl=theurl+'n'">
<input type="button" value="m" onClick="theurl=theurl+'m'">
<input type="button" value="a" onClick="theurl=theurl+'a'"><br>
<input type="button"
  value="http://" name="http" onClick="theurl=theurl+'http://'">
<input type="button" value="." onClick="theurl=theurl+'.'">
<input type="button" value="/" onClick="theurl=theurl+'/'">
<input type="button" value=":" onClick="theurl=theurl+':'"><br>
<input type="button" value="?" onClick="alert('Type the theurls using
your arrows and the X button. Use the URL Check button to be sure you
have the right address. Once complete, hit the GO button.')">
<input type="button" value="Clear" onClick="theurl=''">
<input type="button" value="URL Check" onClick="alert(theurl)">
<input type="button" value="GO!" onClick="window.location=theurl"><br>
<br>
</td></tr></table>
</form>

</body>
```

This script uses the variable theurl to hold the entered characters. Each time
a button is selected, the associated letter is added to theurl via the onClick
JavaScript command (e.g., onClick="theurl=theurl+'a'").

> There are many other JavaScript commands available to you
> when creating your own custom page. However, it is impor-
> tant to note that not every function is supported by the
> *Wipeout Pure* browser. If you intend to hack together some-
> thing more advanced than this script, you will have to work
> out which functions will and will not work.

Once the URL is entered, you can use the URL Check button to view the
entered URL in a pop-up window. Due to the very limited JavaScript support, this is about the only option to view what you have typed. If you
entered the wrong characters, use the Clear button to reset theurl variable,

or the BS button to remove the tail end characters of the URL until you reach the location of the typo. Once everything is typed correctly, the window.location function is called when you hit the GO! button, which sends the browser to the desired location. Figure 5-25 provides you with a screenshot of the keyboard, and Figure 5-26 illustrates the URL checker pop-up window.

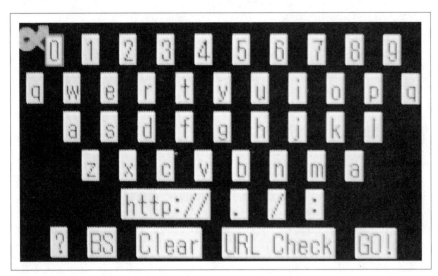

Figure 5-25. PSP JavaScript keyboard

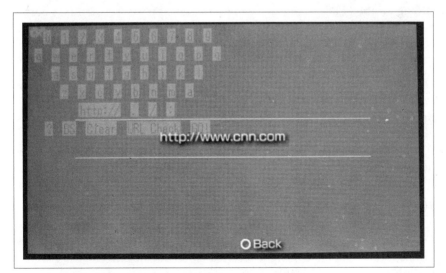

Figure 5-26. The URL checker pop-up window

Hacking the Hack

Once you have the keyboard up and running, it is easy to customize it to your own needs. You can easily add a button-based bookmark menu on the bottom of the screen using the following format. For example, this button would load the Airscanner home page:

```
<input type="button" value="Airscanner!"
onClick="window.location='http://www.airscanner.com'">
```

If you need capital letters, you can easily create an alternate keyboard that includes these ASCII characters. At this point, the options are up to you. Have fun!

—Seth Fogie

HACK #47   Develop for the PSP

If you think you have the chops to code your own app for the PSP, this hack will show you where to get started.

Do you love your PSP, but you're disappointed that it doesn't have a program for easily viewing all of your recipes? A paint-by-numbers program? An advanced statistical analysis tool? A PSP port of *Snood*? Why not code your own application?

Unfortunately, the buy-in price to be a Sony-certified programmer for the PSP is a bit beyond most of us mere mortals, so the only real way to get into coding for the PSP is to dive right in to the homebrew scene **[Hack #40]**. Fortunately, there's lots of very valuable information online for the would-be PSP coder, and there's a very active community of other coders working away in their free time to make the PSP a vibrant homebrew platform.

Homebrew applications can't be loaded on a PSP without some trickery, and it's a given that the most recent (2.0, as of this writing) version of the firmware is immune to such trickery. So, if you want to run true homebrew applications, you're going to need to make sure that you get your hands on a PSP running Version 1.0 or 1.5 of the firmware. If you're a cracking savant, however, please by all means figure out a way to run homebrew on later firmware versions—the Internet will herald your name far and wide.

But, if you're not inclined to invoke the trickery needed to load homebrew, you're running the latest firmware, or you just want to do some elementary programming, you're not out of luck. The PSP web browser is powered by JavaScript, HTML, and CSS, the technologies that come together to give you Dynamic HTML (DHTML). With these, you can write some simple and attractive applications that run right on your PSP's web browser.

PS2Dev.org

The PS2Dev Network (*http://www.ps2dev.org*) has a plethora of information for developing for both the PSP and PS2. When you first start clicking around on the site, you'll probably head straight to the PSP Tutorial section (*http://ps2dev.org/psp/Tutorials*) and find yourself staring at an empty page. Don't panic. Most of the information you would want to find has made its way over to the PS2Dev Network wiki (*http://wiki.ps2dev.org/*). If you navigate to the Programming FAQ section of the wiki (*http://wiki.ps2dev.org/psp:programming_faq*), you'll find a section called "How do I get started in PSP programming?" Here you will be confronted with the cost of entry into the world of PSP programming: familiarity with C or C++.

If you are on Windows, you will need to download Cygwin (*http://www.cygwin.com/*), which will allow you to compile the Unix programs needed to code for the PSP. If you are on Mac OS X or Linux, you should be able to compile the PSPSDK and PSP tool chain, as long as all the necessary dependencies are in place. Both of these tools are available via the PS2Dev Network's PSP Project page (*http://ps2dev.org/psp/Projects*).

ScriptScribbler PSP Programming Tutorials

ScriptScribbler (*http://www.scriptscribbler.com*) currently offers three tutorials by Brad Dwyer on programming for the PSP, and it looks as though there will continue to be more tutorials forthcoming in the future. The first section of the tutorial (*http://www.scriptscribbler.com/psp/tutorials/lesson01.htm*) walks you through setting up a development environment on Windows. The second section walks you through creating your first program (*http://www.scriptscribbler.com/psp/tutorials/lesson02.htm*), a basic "Hello World" program for the PSP. The third section, serving as a programming primer, is currently the most useful (*http://www.scriptscribbler.com/psp/tutorials/lesson03.htm*), as it serves as a "crash course in the basics of C programming for the PSP."

LuaPlayer

If C and C++ aren't your thing, and you're feeling a little rusty in the coding arena, then you'll most likely want to check out the LuaPlayer (*http://www.luaplayer.org/*). To work with LuaPlayer, all you need is a PSP running Version 1.0 or 1.5 of the firmware, and a text editor on your computer. The LuaPlayer site features a rather good step-by-step tutorial (*http://www.luaplayer.org/tutorial/index.html*) to this PSP scripting language that walks you through creating a basic "Hello World" test program, working with images, working with animation, and an introduction to coding for the controls on the PSP. There are several sections not yet complete in the tutorial, but considering the amount of people in the PS2Dev Forums (*http://forums. ps2dev.org/viewforum.php?f=21*) who are using this tool to easily program for the PSP, you can most likely find some guidance with a few carefully placed questions.

One of the advantages of using Lua is that you can test applications on a computer running Windows before you deploy them to your PSP. This eliminates the need to copy your source code over to your PSP every time you make a change. Instead, you can do all your testing and debugging on your PC, and send it to your PSP when you are ready to play it. For more information on the Windows version of Lua Player, see *http://forums.ps2dev.org/ viewtopic.php?p=22332#22332*.

Here's a simple Lua program that runs on the PSP. You should save it as *script.lua*, and follow the instructions included with the Lua Player to run it on your PSP. This is a program that draws an @ character onscreen at the specified x/y coordinates. You can move the directional pad to move the character and leave a trail, as shown in Figure 5-27.

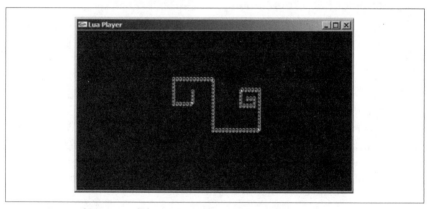

Figure 5-27. Snaking around the screen in the Lua Player for Windows

```
-- starting positions for the character
x = 200
y = 100

-- A nice color
color = Color.new(128, 255, 0)

-- this flag tells whether the program needs to draw
draw_character = true

-- loop forever
```

```
while true do

  if draw_character then
    -- print a rogue at the x/y coordinates
    screen:print(x, y, "@", color)
    screen.flip( )
  end

  -- check whether the user pressed the pad, and move accordingly
  pad = Controls.read( )
  draw_character = true
  if pad:left( ) then
    x = x - 3
  elseif pad:right( ) then
    x = x + 3
  elseif pad:up( ) then
    y = y - 3
  elseif pad:down( ) then
    y = y + 3
  else
    draw_character = false
  end

  -- wait for the next vertical blank
  screen.waitVblankStart( )

end
```

JavaScript

The PSP's web browser is no slouch; although it's not as feature-laden as the latest desktop browsers, it holds its own pretty well. If you know a little HTML, CSS, and JavaScript, you can create DHTML applications that run right in the browser. For example, here's a short program that draws a chunky version of the Mandelbrot Set, one of the most famous *fractals* (objects that exhibit self-similarity at various levels of detail but with an organic irregularity):

```html
<html>
<head><title>Mandelbrot Set</title></head>
<body style="width: 480px; height: 272px;">

<script language="JavaScript">

colors = new Array("black", "aqua", "blue", "fuchsia", "gray",
    "green", "lime", "maroon", "navy", "olive", "purple",
    "red", "silver", "teal", "white", "yellow");

function plot( ) {

  height = 20;
```

```
    width = 150;
    max = 17; // maximum number of iterations.

    document.write('<p style="font-size: 8px">');

    // imaginary axis from -1.25 to 1.25
    for (y = -1.25; y <= 1.25; y += 2.5/height) {

      // real axis from -2.25 to .75
      for (x = -2.25; x <= .75; x += 3/width) {

        a1 = x;
        b1 = y;
        for (cnt = 1; cnt <= max; cnt++) {

          // If the square magnitude of the complex number exceeds
          // the limit, break out of the loop. Otherwise, calculate
          // and loop around again.
          //
          a = a1*a1;
          b = b1*b1;
          if (a + b > 4.0) {
            break;
          } else {
            b1 = 2 * a1 * b1 + y; // imaginary component
            a1 = a - b + x;    // real component
          }

        }
        if (cnt > max) {
          // At this resolution, the point does not appear to be
          // outside the Mandelbrot set, so use color 0 (black).
          cnt = 0;
        }
        style = 'background-color: ' + colors[ cnt % 16 ] + ';';
        document.write('<span style="' + style + '"> </span>');

      }
      document.write('<br/>');
    }
    document.write('</p>');
  }

  plot();

</script>

</body>
</html>
```

You can save this as an HTML file on your PSP's memory stick, navigate to it with the 2.0 firmware's web browser [Hack #41], wait a minute or two, and then see the fractal displayed (albeit rather crudely) on your PSP's screen, as shown in Figure 5-28.

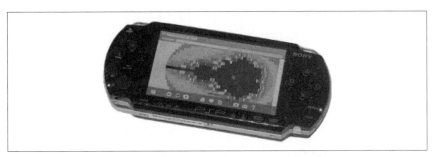

Figure 5-28. Viewing the Mandelbrot Set on the PSP

In fact, you could combine DHTML with Perl [Hack #30] to create a read-only copy of your address book, calendar, or favorite recipes on your PSP. Create some attractive styles to present the data, use JavaScript to create navigation features, and use Perl to extract the data and dump it into an HTML file that acts as the back-end database for your styles and scripts. For more information, see the *JavaScript & DHTML Cookbook* (O'Reilly).

Hacking the Hack

This hack is just an introduction to some of the available information on developing for the PSP. If you really want to delve into PSP programming, you plan to spend many hours talking to other developers on the PS2Dev Forums (*http://forums.ps2dev.org/*). If you really want to make some primo games and programs for the PSP, you're going to need to seriously perfect your C and C++ coding skills. O'Reilly has several books and online articles about these languages, and you can find them all on our C/C++ programming pages (*http://cprog.oreilly.com/*).

—*Brian Jepson and C.K. Sample III*

## CHAPTER SIX

Eye Candy
Hacks 48–50

The PSP is a thing of beauty, from its gorgeous screen to every detail of its buttons, case, and flashing lights. In this chapter, you'll learn how to make that screen a little lovelier, and even do something a little different with those blinking lights.

HACK #48 Hack the PSP's Background Images

You already know how to get your favorite color in the background of your PSP, but wouldn't you rather put your own custom images in there?

Thanks to the great movement of homebrew software for the PSP thriving on the Internet, you can now replace the default color backgrounds [Hack #4] on your Version 1.0–1.5 PSP with pictures of your choosing. Be warned, however, that if you choose to employ this method, there is no turning back. Changing the images is a permanent change. You can replace them later with newer images, if you like, but if you want to return the PSP to its default background set, you're either going to have to do some slightly more advanced hacking to back up the original images before you do this hack, or dig around on the Internet for someone else's copies of the images.

If you have a PSP with Version 2.0 of the firmware, Sony has added a Wallpaper setting to your PSP so that you can do this without any hacking. Simply navigate to Settings → Theme Settings, hit the X button, scroll down to Wallpaper, hit the X button again, and choose Use. Navigate to any picture under Photo on your PSP and hit the X button to view the photo. While viewing, hit the Triangle button to bring up the control panel. Navigate to the second control on the top row, "Set as Wallpaper," and hit the X button. The image you were viewing is now the wallpaper image for your PSP.

Things You'll Need

- A Sony PSP running Version 1.5 of the firmware—until the homebrew community figures a way past the roadblocks Sony put in place in later versions of the firmware, this hack will only work on PSPs running v1.5.

- PSPersonalize—this is the homebrew app that makes the hack work. The file doesn't have a home page on the Web, but you should find it easily enough in the popular PSP homebrew sites; a quick Google search for "PSPersonalize" should turn it up, and you can also look for a link to the files on the site I've set up to go along with this book (*http://www. psphacksthebook.com*).

- A Memory Stick and some way to copy files from your computer to your Memory Stick [Hack #2].

- Some basic image editing software.

- Some images.

Prepare Your Images

For this hack, you're going to need 12 images (one for each month of the year). If you want your background image to stay the same year round, you're still going to need 12 separate, but identical, image files (or you will need to continually keep changing the date on your PSP to the one month containing the background picture you want).

You will need to use whatever image editing software you have on hand to convert your images to 24-bit Windows bitmap files less than or equal to 300×170 resolution. I've seen recommendations online stating that you need to keep the images less than or equal to 150KB in size as well; this is probably the ideal, but I've made this work with a few files weighing in closer to 200KB in size. The main issue here is that larger file sizes will take longer to load on your PSP, and the larger the size, the more you risk the image either not loading or, worse, crashing your PSP.

Once you have converted the images into 300×170 pixel images, you will want to rename them with two digits followed by *.BMP* for each of the 12 months of the year. For example, whatever image you want for January needs to be named *01.BMP*, and whatever file you want for November needs to be *11.BMP*. You should have files named 01–12, all ending in .BMP, when you are finished.

Everything in Its Right Place

Now that you have downloaded and decompressed PSPersonalize, and you have all of your images in the proper format, it's time to get them on the PSP and ready to go for the transfer. Take the two PSPersonalize folders (one should be named "PSPersonalize%" and the other "PSPersonalize)" and place them inside */PSP/GAMES/* on your Memory Stick. Take all of your images and put them in the root directory of your Memory Stick, so that PSPersonalize will be able to find the images.

After you have finished transferring the files to your Memory Stick, either place it back into your PSP or unmount your PSP from your computer and disconnect the USB cable.

PSPersonalize

On the PSP, navigate to Game → Memory Stick and hit the X button. You will see PSPersonalize and a file called Corrupt Data next to it. Ignore the Corrupt Data file, select PSPersonalize, pause for a moment to notice the cool background and audio for PSPersonalize (see Figure 6-1), and then hit the X button.

Figure 6-1. PSPersonalize

The same PSP animated screen that plays whenever you run a game will be displayed. After this graphic is displayed, a black screen with white and yellow text will appear:

    copy
    ms0:/01.bmp

to

flash0:/vsh/resource/01.bmp

are you sure?

O= OK, X = Cancel

The first location, *ms0:/*, is the root directory of your Memory Stick, and the second location, *flash0:/vsh/resource/*, is the folder where the background images are stored on the internal flash memory of your PSP. Hit the O button to replace January's graphic with the picture you have named *01.BMP* and placed in the root directory of your Memory Stick.

After you hit the O button, "please wait..." will appear momentarily in the upper-left corner of the screen while the file is copied over, and then you will be returned to the previous screen, only now it will read *02.bmp* as the file is being copied over. Continue hitting O at each screen until you have replaced all 12 files. Once this is done, a small note will appear in the upper-right corner of the screen, reading "finished...". Hit the Home button on your PSP. A prompt will come up asking "Are you sure you want to quit the game?" Select Yes and hit the X button. You will be returned to the main menu of your PSP.

Now all the new images should be copied over to your PSP's internal flash memory, so the next time you mount your Memory Stick on your computer, you can feel free to delete all the *.BMP* files that you placed there for the transfer.

Remember, if you want the same background year-round, simply make 12 copies of the same file and name them *01. BMP* through *12.BMP*. Likewise, if you want the background graphic to change only in July, make just one file, *07. BMP*, and hit X each time you are prompted by PSPersonalize to copy the file until it asks whether you want to copy *ms0:/07.bmp*. Now that you know how to use PSPersonalize, you can replace the images of individual months whenever you like.

View the New Backgrounds

The background of the current month should already appear changed when you return to the PSP's main menu. If it doesn't, or if you want to test to make sure that all of your images work, navigate over to Settings → Date & Time Settings and hit the X button. Select Date and Time from the list and hit the X button again. Change the month and hit the X button.

If the screen turns bright white, don't panic (see Figure 6-2). The PSP is only allotted so much memory for displaying the background images, so if the image that is currently loaded is a little larger than normal, and the new image that you are trying to load is also a little too large, the PSP won't be able to handle both images simultaneously, and the bright white screen can be the result of its failure to load the image. This shouldn't happen when the date normally changes between months—only when you force a change using this method.

Figure 6-2. You will get a white background if the image fails to load

Hit the X button again to bring the month back up, and hit the X button a third time to confirm without changing the date. If the picture is properly formatted, it should load now, since it no longer has to compete with another image for that memory space. If it doesn't load, make a note of which image it was so that you can replace it with another image the next time you run PSPersonalize.

Keep switching the date month by month, as shown in Figure 6-3, to make sure all the background images you created or downloaded off the Internet properly load. If they don't load, simply set up some new images and run PSPersonalize again. Keep doing this until you have all of the different months on the PSP loaded with your favorite background pictures. Enjoy!

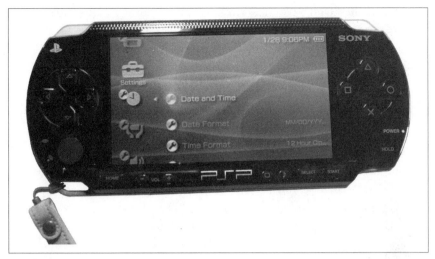

Figure 6-3. Mac OS X's Aqua background on the PSP

Hack the Color of the PSP Activity LEDs

Ever wish that the Memory Stick Duo Activity LED and the WiFi Activity LED on your PSP were pink and chartreuse? Well, these colors might be a bit of a stretch, but this hack will show you how to change the default LEDs to colors of your choice.

There is no doubt that the gaming world has come a long way from producing gaming systems that look very boxlike to a new age of sleek and stylish systems like the PSP. But no matter what, each new system rolls off a production line of unoriginality. As consumers, we love to add our own style. So here is a tutorial that describes the process to replace the original Memory Stick Duo Activity LED and the WiFi Activity LED with different LED colors of your choice. This is pretty simple to do; however, I don't suggest you try this at all (unless you are sure you can do it), since the cost of the PSP and the size of the components you'll be working with both lie at their respective extremes. This will void your warranty and other fun stuff like that.

> Seriously, if you are a novice at such things, *do not try this.* Get your soldering iron guru friend to help out.

Now, with the "Don't try this" warning out of the way, let's move on to making the PSP more personally aesthetically pleasing.

Things You Will Need

- Sony PSP (any firmware version)
- Memory Stick Duo (required for testing)
- Small Phillips head screwdriver
- Soldering iron, 15 watt or less (a fine tip helps)
- Surface Mount LED (type 0603 of your choice of color; find them at *http://www.lsdiodes.com/smd*)
- Multimeter (for testing polarity on the LEDs)
- Miscellaneous utilities (Xacto knife or razor knife, solder braid)
- Soft cloth (optional)

Opening the Case

With all the parts and tools on hand, you're ready to start your journey into case modding **[Hack #8]**. The first thing to do is to remove the seven screws that hold on the faceplate. Two screws are on the back side, four screws are in the battery compartment, and the last screw is on the bottom, just to the right of the bar code.

> I suggest finding a soft cloth to lay your PSP face down on, to prevent scratches to that beautiful screen.

Looking at the back side of the PSP, remove the battery cover and the battery. You will see two labels under the battery: one has info about your system, such as the serial number, and the other is a warning that says that removing the label will void your warranty. Pull back both of these labels. You have reached the point of no return.

Under the labels, you will find four screws, as shown in Figure 6-4, that you need to remove in addition to the two screws on the back and the last screw on the bottom (see Figure 6-5), next to the serial number under the PSP logo.

Once you remove all seven screws, turn the unit over onto its back side and slowly pull up the faceplate from the system. There are no clips or wires attached to the faceplate, so remove it and set it aside somewhere safe, where it won't be disturbed. Remember to be careful and take your time, since fingerprints inside the case are not fun to remove.

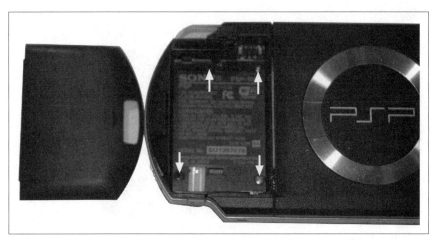

Figure 6-4. Battery compartment screws

Figure 6-5. Backside screws

The Mod

For this mod, you will be focusing on the area displayed in Figure 6-6.

A comparison really puts into perspective how small these LEDs are. In Figure 6-7, you can clearly see a common 5mm LED, which is used in many LED mods. However, the LEDs you are working with are the size of the dot the arrow is pointing to. This is truly the size of a common Surface Mount LED (SMD). Originally used in cell phones, the SMD LED is now more widely used in applications such as the PS2 Power/Eject Switch, and in the GameCube WaveBird Controllers.

Figure 6-8 displays the locations of the Memory Stick Duo Activity LED and the WiFi Activity LED.

Figure 6-6. Focus part

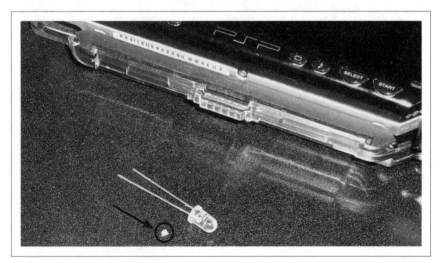

Figure 6-7. LED versus SMD

As with all LEDs, the polarity must be correct for them to work correctly; I find a multimeter on the continuity setting is very handy for checking LED polarity, as it offers just enough current to power an LED. Check the original LEDs before you remove them, and make a note of the polarity so that when you replace them with your new surface mount LEDs, the polarity will be the same.

The first step is to desolder the original SMD LEDs. For this, I find an Xacto knife (razor knife) to be handy. Apply the soldering iron to one side of the SMD and gently use the razor blade to raise that side. Be careful not to force the LED up, since you may damage the traces on the printed circuit board

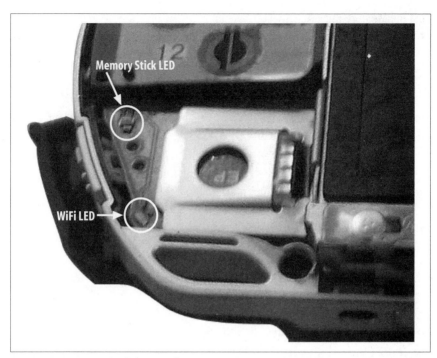

Figure 6-8. Memory Stick LED and WiFi LED

(PCB). Repeat this step to the other side, and the LED should be removed. Then, if you have solder braid, you can use that to clean up the solder points and prepare to solder your new, more colorful SMDs into place.

Be careful. There really are no tricks to this, but again, using a razor knife or small screwdriver to hold the SMD in place may help. Also, do not hold the soldering iron to the LED for too long, as this will physically melt the LED and destroy it.

After you install the LED, use the multimeter to check that the LED still works.

Testing Your Work

Once you get the LEDs attached, you can test them without putting the system back together, but this is a little difficult. The easier option is to put the faceplate back on and put the battery back in, while leaving all the screws out. Once you have the PSP reassembled, sans the screws, you can start testing your work.

Test the Memory Stick Activity LED. Basically, turn on the PSP and just browse around the memory card. I find processing pictures to provide the most response. If you see the new color flashing, you've done a good job. If not, turn off the PSP, take everything apart again, and double-check the LED and its polarity.

Test the WiFi Activity LED. In the PSP menu, go to Games, then select Game Sharing. This will make your PSP activate the WiFi as it searches for other PSP Systems.

Again, if you see the new color flashing, you've done a good job. If not, it's time to recheck the LED and its polarity.

What If It Still Doesn't Work

If it's not working, try checking a few things:

- Make sure that you're testing it correctly (battery in, system on, etc.).
- Test the LED to make sure that you didn't melt it with the soldering iron.
- Check to make sure that your LED has a good connection.
- If the LED is still good, check the polarity to make sure that you have it configured properly.

Reassembly

If you are fully satisfied with your lights, then you may begin the assembly of your PSP by putting the faceplate back on (check for those pesky fingerprints first) and reinstalling the seven screws.

Good luck, and take your time.

Hacking the Hack

This was a pretty basic mod, almost like changing tiny light bulbs. Check the other hacks in this book and at my site, Duey2k (*www.duey2k.com*), for more mods for your PSP and other systems.

—*Dan Mastin*

Hack the Color of the PSP's Hold Indicator

#50 Don't like the color of the hold indicator? Change it.

This hack is something to think about doing while you're messing with the activity LEDs [Hack #49], since it also requires you to open up your PSP [Hack #8] and void your warranty. If this sounds a bit beyond your normal hacking skills, find a guru friend to help out.

Things You Will Need

- Sony PSP (any firmware version)
- Silver Sharpie marker (or any color paint marker)
- Small Phillips head screwdriver
- Soft cloth (optional)

Opening the Case

If you've already changed the color of the activity LEDs [Hack #49], then this step is going to be a nice slice of déjà vu. If you haven't read it, take a look at the "Opening the Case" section from that hack for instructions on opening your PSP.

The Mod

To change the color, you just need to paint the yellow parts of the hold switch piece inside the PSP.

Keep in mind that brighter colors will probably show up better in the hold switch than darker ones, as the only lighting involved with the hold switch is the natural light of the room.

If you really want a hold switch that stands out, consider using some sort of glow paint.

Make sure that the marker or paint is dry. Once that's done, you may begin the reassembly of your PSP by putting the faceplate back on (check for those pesky fingerprints first) and reinstalling the seven screws.

See how simple that was?

—Dan Mastin

Index

We'd like to hear your suggestions for improving our indexes. Send email to *index@oreilly.com*.

Colophon

The image on the cover of *PSP Hacks* is a PlayStation Portable (PSP). The successor to Sony's powerful and popular PS2, the PSP was unveiled in May 2004. While it is mainly a gaming system, the PSP combines the portability of the Game Boy that Nintendo first introduced in 1989 with the multimedia power of the PS2, and it can be used as a portable entertainment device, giving its users the ability to listen to MP3s or to watch UMD movies while on the go. Certain versions of the firmware allow the PSP to run homebrewed software, letting users not only make their own games, but create and enjoy emulators to play games of yore.

The cover image is an original photograph by Frank Deras. The cover font is Adobe ITC Garamond. The text font is Linotype Birka; the heading font is Adobe Helvetica Neue Condensed; and the code font is LucasFont's TheSans Mono Condensed.

Better than e-books

Buy *PSP Hacks* and access the digital edition FREE on Safari for 45 days.

Go to www.oreilly.com/go/safarienabled
and type in coupon code 42GU-FK1F-DJ58-JGFQ-QWLI

Search
thousands of
top tech books

Download
whole chapters

Cut and Paste
code examples

Find
answers fast

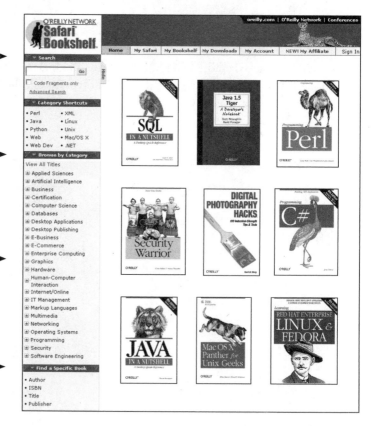

Search Safari! The premier electronic reference
library for programmers and IT professionals.